'Isn't All This Bloody?'

SCOTTISH WRITING FROM
THE FIRST WORLD WAR

Dear Jock

xo Sandra

Christmas 2017

ISN'T ALL THIS BLOODY?

SCOTTISH WRITING FROM THE FIRST WORLD WAR

Edited by

TREVOR ROYLE

EDINBURGH

First published in 2014 by
Birlinn Limited
West Newington House
10 Newington Road
Edinburgh
EH9 1QS

www.birlinn.co.uk

Introductory material copyright © Trevor Royle 2014

See p. ix for copyright information

ISBN: 978 1 78027 224 5

British Library Cataloguing-in-Publication Data
A catalogue record for this book is available
from the British Library

Designed by Mark Blackadder

Printed and bound by Grafica Veneta
www.graficaveneta.com

Contents

Acknowledgements

For permission to use copyright material I am grateful to the following copyright holders:

The Agency (London) Ltd for the extract from James Bridie, *One Way of Living*, Constable, 1939

Michael Russell Ltd for the extract from *In Good Company: The First World War Diaries of The Hon. William Fraser, Gordon Highlanders*, edited by David Fraser, 1990

Peters, Fraser and Dunlop Ltd for the extract from Eric Linklater, *The Man on my Back*, Macmillan, 1941

Carcanet Press Ltd for the extracts from Hugh MacDiarmid, 'Casualties' and Ogilvie Letters

The Society of Authors for the extract from Compton Mackenzie, *Gallipoli Memories*, Cassell, 1929

Lois Godfrey for the extract from Naomi Mitchison, *All Change Here: Girlhood and Marriage*, The Bodley Head, 1975

Peters, Fraser and Dunlop for Rebecca West, 'The Cordite Makers', 1916

Some of the pieces appeared previously in Trevor Royle, ed., *In Flanders Fields: Scottish Poetry and Prose of the First World War*, Mainstream, 1990 and in Trevor Royle, ed. *Scottish War Stories*, Polygon, 1999. The Introduction is an adaptation of Trevor Royle, 'Literature and World War One', in Ian Brown and Alan Riach, *The Edinburgh Companion to Twentieth Century Scottish Literature*, Edinburgh University Press, 2009.

Every attempt has been made to contact copyright holders and I apologise for accidental omissions. Due acknowledgement will be made in later editions if the information is forthcoming.

Introduction

THE FIRST WORLD WAR CHANGED SCOTLAND
in many profound ways. In May 1914, a Home Rule Bill passed
its second reading in the House of Commons, mainly as a result
of the promptings of the Scottish Home Rule Association and
the Young Scots Society, a radical-minded grouping within the
ruling Liberal Party who were in favour of free trade, social
reform and what they called 'the unquenchable and indefinable
spirit of nationalism'. The outbreak of war three months later
meant that the Bill was never enacted, and the devolution debate
would not be reopened until towards the end of the century. But
there were other significant changes. War came as a boost to the
country's heavy industries, especially those situated in the west;
it encouraged the employment of women – by 1918, the
munitions industries in Scotland were employing 31,500 female
workers; and in the early months of the war the proportion of
men enlisting voluntarily in the 18–41 age group was higher than
in any other part of the United Kingdom. To expand Britain's
small Regular Army, Lord Kitchener, the Secretary for War, had
called for the creation of a huge 'New Army' manned by volunteers, and the response in Scotland, as in other parts of the
country, was enthusiastic.

Despite initial doubts, the volunteer principle worked: by the
end of 1915, the British total was 2,466,719 men, more than
would be achieved after the introduction of conscription in May
1916 and just under half the wartime total of 5.7 million men
who served in the army during the war years. Of their number,
320,589, or 13 per cent of the total, were Scots. By the end of
the war, the number of Scots in the armed forces amounted to

688,416, consisting of 71,707 in the Royal Navy, 584,098 in the army (Regular, New and Territorial) and 32,611 in the Royal Flying Corps and Royal Air Force. Culture, too, was affected: although it would take time for the effects to be felt, literature in Scotland was transformed by the experience of the First World War.

At the time of the outbreak of hostilities, Scottish literature was in the doldrums. Robert Louis Stevenson (1850–94), Scotland's greatest writer of the late nineteenth century, had died by 1894, and much of the poetry that was being published was either sentimental, historical verse or the mystical vapours of the Celtic Twilight. Fiction had been left behind in the Kailyard, the catch-all phrase used by the critic J.H. Millar (1864–1929) in the April 1895 issue of the *New Review* to describe the novels of J.M. Barrie (1860–1937), S.R. Crockett (1859–1914) and Ian Maclaren, the pen name of John Watson (1850–1907). Here was a well-defined arcadia of village life, a school of rural sentimentality that ignored the ills of turn of the century Scotland, its faltering industrial development, poverty and high mortality rate. Of Scottish drama there was nothing to be said until the 1930s, when James Bridie came on the scene. Critics like Millar regarded Scottish writing in an overall British context and doubted if Scots as a literary language was capable of survival in the twentieth century.

The signs of hope were few and far between. In 1901, George Douglas Brown (1869–1902) had exposed the limitations of the Kailyard School in his novel *The House with the Green Shutters*. Having borrowed many of the features and characteristics of the Kailyard – the rural setting, the raised expectations and a familiar cast of characters – he had then destroyed them by showing the impact caused by external social change. John MacDougall Hay (1879–1919) had employed a similar structure in *Gillespie* (1914), which includes many of the themes explored by Brown. Although neither writer lived long enough to enjoy their literary success, both *The House with the Green Shutters* and *Gillespie* pointed to one direction that would be taken by Scottish fiction.

The first reaction to the declaration of war in Scotland, as in other parts of Britain, was one of excitement and relief. Contemporary evidence shows that thousands of Scottish people were prepared to voice their support for war and found themselves taking part in demonstrations of national pride and patriotism that often bordered on hysteria. Even realists who normally had their feet on the ground were caught up in the excitement. Shortly after war had been declared, the novelist and journalist Neil Munro travelled by train to Glasgow and later shamefacedly admitted: 'What silly patriotic and romantic elations were stirred in me when I found that already there were armed guards on every railway viaduct, on reservoirs, and the Loch Long torpedo testing station.' By that time, Munro was fifty and a successful novelist – *The New Road* (1914), an adventure in the tradition of Stevenson, had just been published – but even he was caught up in the excitement of the hour and wanted to do something. That sense of enthusiastic conviction was shared by many others and gave the early days of the war an unreal quality, creating a feeling that war was a great adventure, and that man had been transformed and liberated from the doldrums of a humdrum existence. Chivalry, self-sacrifice and heroism were the catchwords of those early days of the war and there were very few people who did not respond to their call.

Artless verses, patriotic articles and short stories flooded by the thousand into local publications, speaking of the noble necessity of doing one's duty; everywhere tub-thumping patri-otism was rife, and the elation even found its way into mainstream literature. Two years later, in 1916, long after the initial enthusiasm had waned, Neil Munro produced a series of poems under the collective title 'Bagpipe Ballads', which were published in *Blackwood's Magazine*. By then, his son Hugh had been killed in action at the Battle of Loos while serving with 8th Argyll and Sutherland Highlanders, and he himself had visited the Western Front as a correspondent, but, as he told George Blackwood, the poems were a compensation of sorts, having been 'suggested by the names of bagpipe airs, so that some of them take on that spirit of braggadocio which comes so natural to youth: and to races like the Gaels, who loiter so much in their past that they are always the youngest and most ardent when it comes to sentiment – the first and last excuse for poetry'.

Even when the volunteers started to move across to France and the initial battles brought the first heavy casualties, the mood in the country remained strangely optimistic. Following the deployment of the Regular Army in the third week of August 1914, the first Territorial Force battalions arrived in the late summer and early autumn and these were followed by the volunteer battalions of the New Army. John Hay Beith, an officer serving in 10th Argyll and Sutherland Highlanders, celebrated the move in a poem 'K (1)', which he believed summed up his men's feelings as they set off for France and war:

> And now to-day has come along,
> With rifle, haversack and pack,
> We're off, a Hundred Thousand strong,
> And – some of us will not come back.

> But all we ask, if that befall,
> Is this. Within our hearts be writ,
> This single-line memorial:
> *He did his duty – and his bit!*

Beith was a schoolmaster and author-turned-soldier who usually wrote under the pseudonym 'Ian Hay' and had attracted an enthusiastic following for a succession of whimsical light novels written in the pre-war period. At the outbreak of hostilities, he volunteered and was commissioned in a New Army battalion of the Argyll and Sutherland Highlanders, and the experience led him to write a number of monthly sketches for *Blackwood's Magazine* under the pseudonym 'Junior Sub' in order to preserve his identity as a serving officer. The first of these appeared in November 1914, with an account of the tribulations of learning close-order drill. Throughout the autumn and winter, The Junior Sub's musings took the reader through the training of the fictional battalion referred to as the 'Bruce and Wallace Highlanders' until it was ready to cross over to France to go into action. Brilliantly conceived and narrated in the first person and present tense, it was akin to a homely correspondence and the sketches became an immediate bestseller when they were published in book form in December 1915 under the title *The First Hundred Thousand*.

Hay's book is also an intensely Scottish account seen from the perspective of a man who, though born in England, was deeply proud of his northern heritage, telling his readers early on 'we are Scotsmen, with all the Scotsman's curious reserve and contempt for social airs and graces'. Beyond that, the novel also provided a keen insight into the military mind, so much so that many brigade and divisional commanders recommended it as reading matter for their newly joined officers. For readers at home, it was an accurate portrayal of the enthusiasm and optimism of those early days before the New Armies went into action at Loos. The reviewer in *The Spectator* praised Hay's ability to capture the mood of the New Armies, while the *Saturday Review* claimed that finally the British soldier had found a voice by making his experience appear 'irrepressibly brave, comical, devoted, prosaic, glorious or dull'. A similar comment could well have been made about two other Scottish novels that were equally popular and seemed to catch the mood of the moment: J.J. Bell's *Wee MacGreegor Enlists* and R.W.

Campbell's *Private Spud Tamson*, although in the latter novel the roguish hero is transformed by the war, being promoted to sergeant, saving his Colonel's life and winning the Victoria Cross.

However, it was not all patriotism and braggadocio. Two Scottish writers spoke out against the glory of war and condemned the gadarene rush to 'hate the Hun', and they are arguably the finest English-speaking Scots poets of the First World War: Charles Hamilton Sorley (1895–1915) and Ewart Alan Mackintosh (1893–1917). Both poets were similar in that they were born into Scottish families but were brought up and educated in England and stand, therefore, somewhat outside the contemporary Scottish literary tradition, with its emphasis on verse written in the vernacular. Both, though, were intensely aware of their heritage – Mackintosh was a Gaelic speaker, and in his correspondence Sorley admitted that he felt no sense of patriotism towards England. Both, too, were destined to die during the fighting – Sorley during the Battle of Loos in October 1915 and Mackintosh at Cambrai in November 1917; the poetry of both men was published posthumously.

Sorley was attending the University of Jena when war broke out. With a friend, he managed to get back to Britain, travelling by train and on a specially commandeered ferry from Antwerp. Having spent seven enjoyable months in Germany, he was disposed to be understanding about the country he had just visited, telling an old schoolmaster, Wynne Willson, in a letter: 'They are a splendid lot, and I wish the silly papers would realise that they are fighting for a principle just as much as we are.' But what took him aback was the hysteria and unthinking patriotism. A letter to another friend, Alan Hutchinson, reflected his exasperation with the mood he found on his return:

> But isn't all this bloody? I am full of mute and burning rage and annoyance and sulkiness about it. I could wager that out of twelve million eventual combatants

there aren't twelve who really want it. And 'serving one's country' is so unpicturesque and unheroic when it comes to the point. Spending a year in a beastly Territorial camp guarding telegraph wires has nothing poetical about it: nor very useful as far as I can see.

Even so, despite his cynicism about patriotic impulses, like thousands of others of his class, Sorley soon joined up as a volunteer and was gazetted a second lieutenant in the 7th Suffolk Regiment, a New Army battalion composed of volunteers. Clearly, he realised that he had to serve his country, that joining up in the armed forces was expected of him, but he refused to take the sentimental approach of the jingoist: there is a delicate sense of irony in the final refrain of one of his earliest war poems, 'All the Hills and Vales Along', which he wrote shortly after enlisting. At first reading, it appears to be a traditional soldier's poem, the rhythms reflecting the sound of marching men, but the final lines reveal a subtle understanding of the brutalisation of military life and the fate that lay ahead for many fighting soldiers:

On, marching men, on
To the gates of death with song.
Sow your gladness for earth's reaping,
So you may be glad, though sleeping,
Strew your gladness on earth's bed,
So be merry, so be dead.

In common with every infantryman of the First World War, Sorley had an intimate relationship with sudden and violent death; it is not surprising that the theme finds its way into his early war poems. There is also a good deal of moral indignation in the focus of Sorley's poetry, much of which was written while he was in the trenches. In one of his last letters to his friend

Arthur Watts, he admitted that the constant casualties and the sight of mutilated men had gnawed at his humanity, leaving an empty shell: 'One is hardened by now: purged of all false pity: perhaps more selfish than before. The spiritual and the animal get so much more sharply divided in hours of encounter, taking possession of the body by swift turns.' In that sense there is a strong feeling in Sorley's work of the writer as witness. Like many other war poets, he believed that he had to come to terms with the experience of battle and then record it so that others could understand that there was no glory in violent death and no victory in the demise of the individual.

Other writers were more strident in their approach and made little secret of the fact that they detested what was happening. John Maclean, a teacher by training and Marxist by evolution, was totally against the war: following his first arrest in October 1915 on the charge of 'making statements likely to prejudice recruiting', he made no secret of his opposition to the war, claiming in court that he had 'enlisted in the Socialist army fifteen years ago, the only army worth fighting for'. His anti-war publication, *The Vanguard*, was closed down under the Defence of the Realm Act, the catch-all legislation for preserving the nation's security, as was Tom Johnston's *Forward* in 1915 during the Glasgow rent strikes and industrial action in the Clyde shipyards. Other similar sentiments could be found in the writings of many of the women connected with Dr Elsie Inglis's Scottish Women's Hospitals. Nor were mental issues ignored. A.F. Whyte's 'Sunk' describes a naval officer clearly suffering from some form of post-traumatic stress disorder; albeit writing after the war, the novelist Lewis Grassic Gibbon was unsparing in his description of a man facing the firing squad, having suffered a different kind of mental anguish.

As happens in most conflicts, the private writings of frontline soldiers provide an immediate response to the conflict and Scottish writers were no exception – from Douglas Haig and

James Jack wrestling with the problems of command to Willie Fraser and John Jackson giving a fighting soldier's view of battle. The same can be said of the correspondence produced by Sorley, Hugh MacDiarmid and Naomi Mitchison. Their letters and diaries have the right to be counted as literary offerings, not least because they betray a great deal of the character and personality of the authors, all of whom were involved in one way or another in the war effort. Even official papers can reveal the character of the author. Throughout the war Haig's private papers expose a man who believed that in no small measure he was an instrument of God's will, a belief that was clearly fashioned by his faith and his Presbyterian background. In no other piece of writing can this be better demonstrated than in his famous 'backs to the wall' Special Order written on 11 April 1918, when it seemed quite possible that the great German Spring offensive might succeed in its objective of rupturing the Allied line. Haig's message was not just an order to the army but a personal plea to every soldier as well:

> There is no other course open to us but to fight it out. Every position must be held to the last man: there must be no retirement. With our backs to the wall and believing in the justice of our cause each one of us must fight on to the end. The safety of our homes and the Freedom of mankind alike depend upon the conduct of each one of us at this critical moment.

On a different level, James Bridie, Eric Linklater and Compton Mackenzie continued to be fascinated by the war long after it was over. It would have been surprising if this were not the case, for all had different experiences of combat. Linklater and Bridie were under fire in front-line positions and Mackenzie experienced the ill-starred campaign in Gallipoli. Naturally in each case there is a strong sense of the writer distancing himself from past events and, in the case of Bridie and Linklater, of making light of the difficulties, but they still manage to convey the horror, futility and boredom of war. It is also instructive to compare Mackenzie's and Sir Ian Hamilton's accounts of the Gallipoli operation.

War, the great bringer of change, also transformed the course of Scottish writing and the country's literary scene. Twenty years after the end of the First World War the poet Hugh MacDiarmid (Christopher Murray Grieve) addressed Scotland in his poem 'Towards a New Scotland', and asked:

Was it for little Belgium's sake
Sae mony thoosand Scotsman dee'd?
And never ane for Scotland fegs
Wi' twenty thoosand times mair need!

In a sense MacDiarmid had already answered the question himself. He had served on the Salonika front as a sergeant in the Royal Army Medical Corps and on demobilisation he had been transfigured, literally and metaphysically. During the war he had written little of any value for publication, but in the 1920s he began writing poetry in Scots and from those efforts he evolved the idea of a renaissance movement whose aim was to dissociate Scottish writing from the sentimentality of the vernacular-based poetry of the pre-war years and to bring it into line with contemporary European thinking. His first serious publication was *Northern Numbers* (1920), an anthology based on the example of Edward Marsh's *Georgian Poetry*. It was followed by two further editions, in 1921 and 1922, and the contributors included many writers who had written poetry or fiction during the recent war – John Buchan, Violet Jacob, Roderick Watson Kerr, Joseph Lee, Neil Munro, Charles Murray and Mary Symon. He founded a magazine, the *Scottish Chapbook*, and began to challenge established literary assumptions in a series of

articles for the *Scottish Educational Journal* under the title
'Contemporary Scottish Studies'. His campaign also had a
political aspect: he was one of the founders of the Scottish
committee of International PEN and in 1928 he joined the
National Party of Scotland. As described by Catherine Kerrigan,
Grieve had used his time in the military to good effect to develop
his literary and political ideas:

> With an almost military precision he began putting his
> plan to transform the Scottish cultural scene into action
> and within a few years Quartermaster-Sergeant Grieve
> had metamorphosed into Hugh MacDiarmid, the
> modern Scottish vernacular poet and leader of what he
> was optimistically to call the 'Scottish Renaissance'.

Like other poets of the immediate post-war period – Yeats, Eliot
and Pound – MacDiarmid was aware of the exhaustion of
English culture in the 1920s and of the need to explore new
means of national self-expression. He was also aware that the
war had changed the cohesion of European civilisation in
general. In those circumstances it would be the duty of countries
like Scotland to redeem those cultural values and like many of
his contemporaries he realised that in no small measure the
global conflict had been fought to protect the rights of small
nations. In that respect the First World War hastened the development of Scottish literature, and the soldier-writers of that
period can be seen as harbingers of that change.

J.J. Bell
The Alarm

To the astonishment of his family and his best friend Willie Thomson, Wee Macgreegor has enlisted in the 9th Highland Light Infantry, the Glasgow Highlanders. Partly he has done this out of a sense of patriotism but it is also to impress his girlfriend Christina. The Glasgow Highlanders, a Territorial Battalion, mobilised at Greendyke Street in Glasgow in August 1914 and crossed over to France on 5 November that same year, which makes a deployment to Gallipoli (Dardanelles) impossible.

───────────

It came, as Christina would have expressed it in her early days, like a 'blot from the blue'. On a certain fine morning, while battalion drill was in progress, a mounted officer dashed upon the scene and was forthwith engaged in earnest conversation with the colonel. The news was evidently urgent, and it was received with an obvious gravity. A thrill ran through the ranks; you would have fancied you heard breaths of anticipation.

A minute later the companies were making for camp at the double. Arrived there they were instructed to repair to billets and, with all speed, pack up. And presently ammunition was being served out, a hundred rounds to each man; and, later, 'iron' rations.

'We're awa' noo,' gasped Macgregor, recovering forcibly from Willie's greedy clutch a pair of socks knitted by Christina.

'Ay, we're awa'; an' I'll bet ye we're for Flanders,' said Willie, no less excited.

'Dardanelles!' shouted Macgregor, above the din that filled the billet.

'Flanders!' yelled Willie, wildly, and started to dance – unfortunately upon a thin piece of soap.

'Dardanelles!' Macgregor repeated, as he gave his friend a hand up.

'Oh!' groaned Willie, rubbing the back of his head. 'But what'll ye bet?'

'What ha'e ye got?'

'I'll bet ye thruppence – the thruppence ye lent me the day afore yesterday.'

'Done! If ye win, we'll be quits; if ye loss—'

'Na, na! If I win, ye'll ha'e to pay me—'

'Ach, I've nae time to listen to ye. I've twa letters to write.'

'Letters! What aboot the bet?'

'Awa' an' chase yersel'! Are ye no gaun to drap a line to yer aunt?'

'No dashed likely! She's never sent the postal order I asked her for. If I had got it, I wud ha'e payed what I'm owin' ye, Macgreegor. By heavens, I wud! I'll tak' ma oath I—'

'Aweel, never heed aboot that,' Macgregor said, soothingly. 'Send her a post caird an' let me get peace for three meenutes.'

'Ye canna get peace in this,' said Willie, with a glance round the tumultuous billet.

'I can – if ye haud yer silly tongue.' Macgregor thereupon got his pad and envelopes (a gift from Miss Tod), squatted on his bed and proceeded to gnaw his pencil. The voice of the sergeant was heard ordering the men to hurry up.

'I'll tell ye what I'll dae,' said Willie, sitting down at his friend's elbow. 'I'll bet ye a' I owe ye to a bob it's Flanders. Ye see, I'll maybe get shot, an' I dinna want to dee in debt. An' I'll send the auld cat a caird wi' something nice on it, to please ye ... Eh?'

'Aw, onything ye like, but for ony sake clay up! Shift!' cried the distracted Macgregor.

'Weel, gi'e's a fag ... an' a match,' said Willie.

He received them in his face, but merely grinned as he languidly removed himself.

The two scrawls so hastily and under such difficulties produced by Macgregor are sacred. He would never write anything more boyish and loving, nor yet more manly and brave, than those 'few lines' to his mother and sweetheart. There was no time left for posting them when the order came to fall in, but he anticipated an opportunity at one of the stations on the journey south.

Out in the sunshine stood the hundreds of lads whose training had been so brief that some carried ammunition for the first time. There were few grave faces, though possibly some of the many grins were more reflected than original. Yet there was a fine general air of eagerness, and at the word 'attention' the varied expressions gave place to one of determination.

'Boom! boom! boom! . . . Boom! boom! boom! Dirl and skirl; skirl and dirl!' So to the heart-lifting, hell-raising music of pipes and drums they marched down to the railway.

At the station it seemed as though they had been expected to break all records in military entraining. There was terrific haste and occasional confusion, the latter at the loading of the vans. The enthusiasm was equalled only by the perspiration. But at last everything and nearly everybody was aboard, and the rumour went along that they had actually broken such and such a battalion's record.

Private William Thomson, however, had already started his inevitable grumbling. There were eight in the compartment and he had stupidly omitted to secure a corner seat.

'I'll bet ye I'm a corp[oral] afore we get to Dover,' he bleated.

'That's as near as ever ye'll be to bein' a corporal,' remarked the cheerful Jake. 'But hoo d'ye ken it'll be Dover?'

'I'll bet ye – Na! I'll no tak' on ony mair wagers. I've a tremenjous bet on wi' this yin' – indicating Macgregor – 'every dashed penny I possess – that we're boun' for Flanders. He says the Dardanelles.'

All excepting Macgregor fell to debating the question. He had just remembered something he had forgotten to say to Christina; also, he was going away without the ring she was to have given him. He was not sorry he was going, but he felt sad . . .

The debate waxed furious.

'I tell ye,' bawled Willie, 'we're for Flanders! The Ninth's been there since the—'

A sudden silence! What the – was that? Surely not – ay, it was! – an order to detrain!

And soon the whisper went round that they were not bound for anywhere – unless the – old camp. The morning's alarm and all that followed had been merely by way of practice.

At such a time different men have different feelings, or, at least, different ways of expressing them. Jake laughed philosophically and appeared to dismiss the whole affair. Willie swore with a curious and seemingly unnecessary bitterness, at frequent intervals, for the next hour or so. Macgregor remained in a semi-stunned condition of mind until the opportunity came for making a little private bonfire of the two letters; after which melancholy operation he straightaway recovered his usual good spirits.

'Never heed, Wullie,' he said, later; 'we'll get oor chance yet.'

Willie exploded. 'What for did ye get me to mak' sic a – cod o' masel'?'

'Cod o' yersel'? Me?'

'Ay, you! – gettin' me to send a caird to ma – aunt! What for did ye dae it?'

Macgregor stared. 'But ye didna post it,' he began.

'Ay, but I did. I gi'ed it to a man at the station.'

'Oh! . . . Weel, ye'll just ha'e to send her anither.'

'That'll no mak' me less o' a cod.'

'What way? What did ye write on the caird?'

Willie hesitated, muttered a few curses and said slowly yet savagely:

'"Off to Flanders, wi' – wi' kind love" – *oh, dammit!*'

James Bridie
The Three Musketeers

In common with much of his drama, James Bridie's autobiog-
raphy One Way of Living *is evasive, amusing and suffused with*
extravagant exuberance. Written in ten chapters, or 'fives', the
narrative follows the course of the author's life from childhood
in Glasgow, through university and his military service, to his
fiftieth year. In the opening pages Bridie declared that he reserved
'the right to break the narrative with any reflections that seem
pertinent to my purpose' and that helped to set the tone for the
book. However, not everyone approved or understood. Review-
ing it in The Spectator, *Evelyn Waugh found that 'The bulk of*
the book is discursive and, I think, humorous in intent, rich in
anecdotes which perhaps need to be told aloud by one Lowland
Scot to another Lowland Scot for their full point to be clear.
Pawky is the word.'

Following a brief description of his wartime experiences on
the Western Front as a medical officer, Bridie launches into a
typical reverie involving his superior officer and fellow doctor
Douglas Reid King. Marlowe is probably the shade of Christo-
pher Marlowe and the inclusion of the three musketeers is
apposite, as it was in Arras that D'Artagnan encountered the
mysterious stranger 'whom I have always met with when
threatened by some misfortune'.

'I find your War petty and frivolous,' said Marlowe.

'I cannot help that, you bombastic old blatherskite,' I replied.
'I wish you had seen all the guns of Ypres opening fire on the
morning when the Bosche first put over blazing treacle when I

was wandering about Sanctuary Wood. That would have given you something to bang your big drum about. For me, I play the penny whistle and, at times, the oboe. King and I were once talking about that – I mean about how impossible it was to describe this War in rousing words. We were very comfortable. We were sitting by the fireside in an Arras music master's house. The front windows of our room opened on the pleasant Quai de Caserne, the back on a tangled garden and a glass-roofed porch. We were having our bedtime toddy and the Germans were shelling a 75 battery along the street. All of a sudden a shell hit our house and down came the glass porch. King crouched under the windowsill and I sat down in an arched doorway, while the air became full of flashes and bangs and clatterings. We then bethought ourselves of our faithful batmen who slept upstairs and were rushing to their aid when they knocked us backward downstairs. They were wrapped in blankets. We adjourned to the cellar, but it was full of water and the shelling soon stopped.

My room on the first floor was full of moonlight and I walked on two inches of finely powdered dust. The blanket window screen had been blown in and the nosecap had gone through my bed at the point where my umbilicus would have been if I hadn't persuaded King to have one more toddy. But that wasn't War . . . I remember . . .

Aramis, Porthos and Athos dined in the house of Athos twenty years after. Because they did not know each other very well, Mrs Athos, Mrs Porthos and Mrs Aramis went to the drawing room after the fearless old fashion instead of staying to drink port wine and smoke cigarettes with their husbands.

Aramis, Athos and Porthos were silent for a little, began to talk all at once and then begged one another's pardon.

'You were saying?' said Athos.

'No, no, you go on,' said Aramis.

'It was nothing,' said Porthos.

'Please, Aramis,' said Athos.

'No, Porthos was speaking,' said Aramis.

'Go on, Porthos,' said Athos.

'I was just thinking,' said Porthos, 'that twenty years ago today I was sitting in the Hotel de Paris at St Pol eating truffles and drinking Louis Roederer 1906 at eight francs the bottle. I should have got it for less if I hadn't been on the Staff. That was an inn, Aramis, where they could roast a chicken. I had come from the blasted Salient – Cassel, you know. Talk about hardship! My groom was my cook. I found he could do macaroni and cheese. Very well, I said. You cook. So he cooked macaroni and cheese, day in day out, week in week out . . . My God! And bully rissoles. And do you remember that vang rouge? Though you could make salad dressing with vang rouge and melted butter, you know.

'It was after a month of such horror, as I dare not describe to you fellows, that St Catherine of Sienna, or some such blessed saint, materialised. The local padre told me of her. She was living in sin with some gendarme in the neighbourhood. The padre said she could cook. Cook! . . . Oh, luncheon! Little bits of this and that like a fairy dance for hors d'oeuvres. Fat olives, most benignant. The soup looked like Primavera's dress and dreamt its way down as yachts do in a light wind. Then there were artichokes, green and melting and sentimental. Then a round of beef. Damned Canterbury, gentlemen, moulded and transformed by some ultra-sculptural cantrip, and swimming in dark mahogany sauce . . . I beg your pardon, Athos, you gave us a very nice dinner tonight, but your cook is only a woman. And some Barsac, all golden. The drink you cannot take across the water. And I only paid her fifteen francs a week. And then the General came. Well, Porthos, how are you? Sir, will you wait for dinner? I have a cook.

'Ah! Forgive me, friends, there was an Ercildoune dreaming on me, and I knew not what I did. The General stole her. More, he sent me, like the Hittite in the Bible, to the thickest of the fight. To St Pol . . . Ah well! They could roast a chicken there!'

'The first cocktail I invented during the war,' said Athos, his fine face deeply lined with thought, 'was in the Chateau Barly, on the Western Front. It was called a Tangerine Sling. It was a cocktail rather of necessity than of choice. The only two drinks left to us in the mess after the Christmas dinner were St Julien and rum. There were also some tangerine oranges and raisins. Into one glass I put a tablespoonful of rum, into another two tablespoonfuls of claret. I put two crushed raisins into the rum and squeezed the juice of a single lith of the orange into the claret. With a spoon I then squeezed and buffeted the peel of the orange in the claret glass. I then threw the peel and the two raisins into the fire, mixed and shook the two beverages, placed a second tangerine lith in the mixture, and put it on a frosty windowsill to cool. After ten minutes I shook it again and finally drank it. It imparted a pleasant and enlivening sensation to the fingers and toes, and made me wish to join the Flying Corps. The last cocktail I invented was after the armistice in Tiflis. Long drinks were the vogue, as at that time the weather was warm. The drink was called the Pink Devil. It contained gin, orange bitters, Angostura bitters, lime juice, liqueur whisky, cherry brandy, cognac, burgundy, sherry and vodka. I would tell you the proportions and how to mix it, but I really think we ought to join the ladies.'

'When I was in Amiens, I took the French General's mistress to dinner one night,' said Aramis. 'The French General complained to GHQ in the following terms . . .'

'Another time, perhaps, old boy,' said Athos. 'But the ladies will be impatient.'

John Buchan
The King of Ypres

In May 1915, John Buchan visited the Western Front as a special correspondent of The Times. *His role was to report on the Second Battle of Ypres and the subsequent articles were notable for his grasp of detail and ability to evoke the war-torn landscape. There were also romantic touches, such as the story of a British private who had been left behind by his battalion and who restored a modicum of order. This found its way into a short story, which was published in 1918 in the collection* The Watcher by the Threshold.

Private Peter Galbraith, of the 3rd Lennox Highlanders, awoke with a splitting headache and the consciousness of an intolerable din. At first he thought it was the whistle from the forge, which a year ago had pulled him from his bed when he was a puddler in Motherwell. He scrambled to his feet, and nearly cracked his skull against a low roof. That, and a sound which suggested that the heavens were made of canvas which a giant hand was rending, cleared his wits and recalled him to the disagreeable present. He lit the dottle in his pipe, and began to piece out his whereabouts.

Late the night before, the remnants of his battalion had been brought in from the Gheluvelt trenches to billets in Ypres. That last week he had gone clean off his sleep. He had not been dry for a fortnight, his puttees had rotted away, his greatcoat had disappeared in a mud-hole, and he had had no stomach for what food could be got. He had seen half his battalion die before his eyes, and day and night the shells had burst round him till the place looked like the ironworks at Motherwell on a foggy night. The worst of it was that he had never come to grips with the Boches, which he had long decided was the one pleasure left to him in life. He had got far beyond cursing, though he had once had a talent that way. His mind was as sodden as his body, and his thoughts had been focused on the penetrating power of a bayonet when directed against a plump Teutonic chest. There had been a German barber in Motherwell called Schultz, and he imagined the enemy as a million Schultzes – large, round men who talked with the back of their throat.

In billets he had scraped off the worst part of the mud, and drunk half a bottle of wine which a woman had given him. It tasted like red ink, but anything liquid was better than food. Sleep was what he longed for, but he could not get it. The Boches were shelling the town, and the room he shared with six others seemed as noisy as the Gallowgate on a Saturday night. He wanted to get deep down into the earth where there was no sound; so, while the others snored, he started out to look for a cellar. In the black darkness, while the house rocked to the shell reverberations, he had groped his way down the stairs, found a door which led to another flight, and, slipping and stumbling, had come to a narrow, stuffy chamber which smelt of potatoes. There he had lain down on some sacks and fallen into a frowsty slumber.

His head was spinning, but the hours of sleep had done him good. He felt a slight appetite for breakfast, as well as an intolerable thirst. He groped his way up the stairs, and came out in a dilapidated hall lit by a dim November morning.

There was no sign of the packs which had been stacked there the night before. He looked for a Boche's helmet, which he had brought in as a souvenir, but that was gone. Then he found the room where he had been billeted. It was empty, and only the stale smell of tobacco told of its occupants.

Lonely, disconsolate, and oppressed with thoughts of future

punishment, he moved towards the street door. Suddenly the door of a side room opened and a man came out, a furtive figure with a large, pasty face. His pockets bulged, and in one hand was a silver candlestick. At the sight of Galbraith he jumped back and held up a pistol.

'Pit it down, man, and tell's what's come ower this place?' said the soldier. For answer, a bullet sang past his ear and shivered a plaster Venus.

Galbraith gave his enemy the butt of his rifle and laid him out. From his pockets he shook out a mixed collection of loot. He took possession of his pistol, and kicked him with some vehemence into a cupboard.

'That yin's a thief,' was his spoken reflection.

'There's something michty wrong wi' Wipers the day.'

His head was clearing, and he was getting very wroth. His battalion had gone off and left him in a cellar, and miscreants were abroad. It was time for a respectable man to be up and doing. Besides, he wanted his breakfast. He fixed his bayonet, put the pistol in his pocket, and emerged into the November drizzle.

The streets suddenly were curiously still. The occasional shell-fire came to his ears as if through layers of cotton wool. He put this down to dizziness from lack of food, and made his way to what looked like an estaminet. The place was full of riotous people who were helping themselves to drinks, while a distracted landlord wrung his hands. He flew to Galbraith, the tears running down his cheeks, and implored him in broken words.

'Vere ze Engleesh?' he cried. 'Ze mechants rob me. Zere is une émeute. Vere ze officers?'

'That's what I'm wantin' to ken mysel',' said Galbraith.

'Zey are gone,' wailed the innkeeper. 'Zere is no gendarme or anyzing, and I am rob.'

'Where's the polis? Get the Provost, man. D'ye tell me there's no polis left?'

'I am rob,' the wail continued. 'Ze méchants rob ze magasins and ve vill be assassinés.'

Light was dawning upon Private Galbraith. The British troops had left Ypres for some reason which he could not fathom, and there was no law or order in the little city. At other times he had hated the law as much as any man, and his relations with the police had often been strained. Now he realised that he had done them an injustice. Disorder suddenly seemed to him the one thing intolerable. Here had he been undergoing a stiff discipline for weeks, and if that was his fate no civilian should be allowed on the loose. He was a British soldier marooned here by no fault of his own and it was his business to keep up the end of the British Army and impose the King's peace upon the unruly. His temper was getting hot, but he was curiously happy. He marched into the *estaminet*. 'Oot o' here, ye scum!' he bellowed. 'Sortez, ye cochons!'

The revellers were silent before the apparition. Then one, drunker than the rest, flung a bottle, which grazed his right ear. That put the finishing touch to his temper. Roaring like a bull, he was among them, prodding their hinder parts with his bayonet, and now and then reversing his rifle to crack a head. He had not played centre-forward in the old days at Celtic Park for nothing. The place emptied in a twinkling all but one man whose legs could not support him. Him Private Galbraith seized by the scruff and the slack of his trousers, and tossed into the street.

'Now I'll hae my breakfast,' he said to the trembling land-lord.

Private Galbraith, much the better for his exercise, made a hearty meal of bread and cold ham, and quenched his thirst with two bottles of Hazebrouck beer. He had also a little brandy, and pocketed the flask, for which the landlord refused all payment. Then, feeling a giant refreshed, he sallied into the street

'I'm off to look for your Provost,' he said.

'If ye have ony mair trouble, ye'll find me at the Toun Hall.'

A shell had plumped into the middle of the causeway, and the place was empty. Private Galbraith, despising shells, swaggered up the open, his disreputable kilt swinging about his putteeless legs, the remnant of a bonnet set well on the side of his shaggy red head, and the light of battle in his eyes. For once he was arrayed on the side of the angels, and the thought encouraged him mightily. The brandy had fired his imagination.

Adventure faced him at the next corner. A woman was struggling with two men, a slim pale girl with dark hair. No sound came from her lips, but her eyes were bright with terror. Galbraith started to run, shouting sound British oaths. The men let the woman go, and turned to face him. One had a pistol, and for the second time that day a bullet just missed its mark. An instant later a clean bayonet thrust had ended the mortal career of the marksman, and the other had taken to his heels.

'I'll learn thae lads to be sae free wi' their popguns,' said the irate soldier. 'Haud up, Mem. It's a' by wi' noo. Losh! The wumman's fentit!'

Private Galbraith was as shy of women as of his Commanding Officer, and he had not bargained for this duty. She was clearly a lady from her dress and appearance, and this did not make it easier. He supported her manfully, addressing to her the kind of encouragements which a groom gives to a horse. 'Canny now, Mem. Haud up! Ye've no cause to be feared.'

Then he remembered the brandy in his pocket, and with much awkwardness managed to force some drops between her lips. To his vast relief she began to come to. Her eyes opened and stared uncomprehendingly at her preserver. Then she found her voice.

'Thank God, the British have come back!' she said in excellent English.

'No, Mem; not yet. It's just me, Private Galbraith, C Company, 3rd Battalion, Lennox Highlanders. Ye keep some bad lots in this toun.'

'Alas! What can we do? The place is full of spies, and they will stir up the dregs of the people and make Ypres a hell. Oh, why did the British go? Our good men are all with the army, and there are only old folk and wastrels left.'

'Rely upon me, Mem,' said Galbraith stoutly. 'I was just settin' off to find your Provost.'

She puzzled at the word, and then understood.

'He has gone!' she cried. 'The Maire went to Dunkirk a week ago, and there is no authority in Ypres.'

'Then we'll make yin. Here's the minister. We'll speir at him.'

An old priest, with a lean, grave face, had come up.

'Ah, Mam'selle Omèrine,' he cried, 'the devil in our city is unchained. Who is this soldier?'

The two talked in French, while Galbraith whistled and looked at the sky. A shrapnel shell was bursting behind the cathedral, making a splash of colour in the November fog. Then the priest spoke in careful and constrained English.

'There is yet a chance for a strong man. But he must be very strong. Mam'selle will summon her father, Monsieur le Procureur, and we will meet at the Mairie. I will guide you there, *mon brave.*'

The Grande Place was deserted, and in the middle there was a new gaping shell-hole. At the door of a great building, which Galbraith assumed to be the Town Hall, a feeble old porter was struggling with a man. Galbraith scragged the latter and pitched him into the shell-hole. There was a riot going on in a cafe on the far side, which he itched to have a hand in, but he postponed that pleasure to a more convenient season.

Twenty minutes later, in a noble room with frescoed and tapestried walls, here was a strange conference. The priest was there, and Galbraith, and Mam'selle Omèrine, and her father, M. St Marais. There was a doctor too, and three elderly citizens, and an old warrior who had left an arm on the Yser. Galbraith took charge, with Mam'selle as his interpreter, and in half an hour had constituted a Committee of Public Safety. He had nervous folk to deal with.

'The Germans may enter at any moment, and then we will all be hanged,' said one.

'Nae doot,' said Galbraith; 'but ye needna get your throats cut afore they come.'

'The city is full of the ill-disposed,' said another. 'The Boches have their spies in every alley. We who are so few cannot control them.'

'If it's spies,' said Galbraith firmly, 'I'll take on the job my lone. D'ye think a terrier dowg's feared of a wheen rottens [rats]?'

In the end he had his way, with Mam'selle's help, and had put some confidence into civic breasts. It took him the best part of the afternoon to collect his posse. He got every wounded Belgian that had the use of his legs, some well-grown boys, one or two ancients, and several dozen robust women. There was no lack of weapons, and he armed the lot with a strange collection of French and English rifles, giving pistols to the section leaders. With the help of the Procureur, he divided the city into beats and gave his followers instructions. They were drastic orders, for the situation craved for violence.

He spent the evening of his life. So far as he remembered afterwards, he was in seventeen different scraps. Strayed revellers were leniently dealt with – the canal was a cooling experience. Looters were rounded up and, if they showed fight, summarily disposed of. One band of bullies made a stout resistance, killed two of his guards, and lost half a dozen dead. He got a black eye, a pistol-bullet through his sleeve, a wipe on the cheek from a carving-knife, and he lost the remnants of his bonnet. Fifty-two prisoners spent the night in the cellars of the Mairie.

About midnight he found himself in the tapestried chamber. 'We'll hae to get a Proclamation,' he had announced; 'a gude

strong yin, for we maun conduct this job according to the rules.'
So the Procureur had a document drawn up, bidding all inhabi-
tants of Ypres keep indoors except between the hours of 10 a.m.
and noon, and 3 and 5 p.m.; forbidding the sale of alcohol in all
forms; and making theft and violence and the carrying of arms
punishable by death. There was a host of other provisions which
Galbraith imperfectly understood, but when the thing was translated to him he approved its spirit. He signed the document in
his large sprawling hand 'Peter Galbraith, 1473, Pte, 3rd Lennox
Highlanders, Acting Provost of Wipers'.

'Get that prentit,' he said, 'and pit up copies at every street
corner and on a' the public-hooses. And see that the doors o' the
publics are boardit up. That'll do for the day. I'm feelin' verra
like my bed.'

Mam'selle Omèrine watched him with a smile. She caught
his eye and dropped him a curtsey.

'Monsieur le Roi d'Ypres,' she said.

He blushed hotly.

For the next few days Private Galbraith worked harder than
ever before in his existence. For the first time he knew responsibility, and that toil which brings honour with it. He tasted the
sweets of office; and he, whose aim in life had been to scrape
through with the minimum of exertion, now found himself the
inspirer of the maximum in others.

At first he scorned advice, being shy and nervous. Gradually,
as he felt his feet, he became glad of other people's wisdom.
Especially he leaned on two, Mam'selle Omèrine and her father.
Likewise the priest, whom he called the minister.

By the second day the order in Ypres was remarkable. By the
third day it was phenomenal; and by the fourth a tyranny. The
little city for the first time for seven hundred years fell under the
sway of a despot. A citizen had to be on his best behaviour, for
the Acting Provost's eye was on him. Never was seen so sober a
place. Three permits for alcohol and no more were issued, and

then only on the plea of medical necessity. Peter handed over to the doctor the flask of brandy he had carried off from the *estaminet*. Provosts must set an example.

The Draconian code promulgated the first night was not adhered to. Looters and violent fellows went to gaol instead of the gallows. But three spies were taken and shot after a full trial. That trial was the master effort of Private Galbraith – based on his own regimental experience and memories of a Sheriff Court in Lanarkshire, where he had twice appeared for poaching. He was extraordinarily punctilious about forms, and the three criminals – their guilt was clear, and they were the scum of creation – had something more than justice. The Acting Provost pronounced sentence, which the priest translated, and a file of *mutilés* in the yard did the rest.

'If the Boches get in here, we'll pay for this day's work,' said the judge cheerfully; 'but I'll gang easier to the grave for havin' got rid o' thae swine.'

On the fourth day he had a sudden sense of dignity. He examined his apparel, and found it very bad. He needed a new bonnet, a new kilt, and puttees, and he would be the better of a new shirt. Being aware that commandeering for personal use ill-suited with his office, he put the case before the Procureur, and a *Commission de Ravitaillement* was appointed. Shirts and puttees were easily got, but the kilt and bonnet were difficulties. But next morning Mam'selle Omérine brought a gift. It was a bonnet with such a dicing round the rim as no Jock ever wore, and a skirt – it is the truest word – of that pattern which graces the persons of small girls in France. It was not the Lennox tartan, it was not any kind of tartan, but Private Galbraith did not laugh. He accepted the garments with a stammer of thanks – 'They're awfu' braw, and I'm much obliged, Mem' – and, what is more, he put them on. The Ypriotes saw his splendour with approval. It was a proof of his new frame of mind that he did not even trouble to reflect what his comrades would think of his costume, and that he kissed the bonnet affectionately before he went to bed.

That night he had evil dreams. He suddenly saw the upshot of it all himself degraded and shot as a deserter, and his brief glory pricked like a bubble. Grim forebodings of court-martials assailed him. What would Mam'selle think of him when he was led away in disgrace, he who for a little had been a king? He walked about the floor in a frenzy of disquiet, and stood long at the window peering over the Place, lit by a sudden blink of moonlight. It could never be, he decided. Something desperate would happen first. The crash of a shell a quarter of a mile off reminded him that he was in the midst of war – war with all its chances of cutting knots.

Next morning no Procureur appeared. Then came the priest with a sad face and a sadder tale. Mam'selle had been out late the night before on an errand of mercy, and a shell, crashing through a gable, had sent an avalanche of masonry into the street. She was dead, without pain, said the priest, and in the sure hope of Heaven.

The others wept, but Private Galbraith strode from the room, and in a very little time was at the house of the Procureur. He saw his little colleague laid out for death after the fashion of her Church, and his head suddenly grew very clear and his heart hotter than fire.

'I maun resign this job,' he told the Committee of Public Safety. 'I've been forgettin' that I'm a sodger and no a Provost. It's my duty to get a nick at thae Boches.'

They tried to dissuade him, but he was adamant. His rule was over, and he was going back to serve.

But he was not allowed to resign. For that afternoon, after a week's absence, the British troops came again into Ypres.

They found a decorous little city, and many people who spoke of 'le Roi' – which they assumed to signify the good King Albert. Also, in a corner of the cathedral yard, sitting disconsolately on the edge of a fallen monument, Company Sergeant-Major Macvittie of the 3rd Lennox Highlanders found Private Peter Galbraith.

'Ma God, Galbraith, ye've done it this time! *You'll* catch it in the neck! Absent for a week wi'out leave, and getting' yoursel' up to look like Harry Lauder! You come along wi' me!'

'I'll come quiet,' said Galbraith with strange meekness. He was wondering how to spell Omèrine St Marais in case he wanted to write it in his Bible.

The events of the next week were confusing to a plain man. Galbraith was very silent, and made no reply to the chaff with which at first he was greeted. Soon his fellows forbore to chaff him, regarding him as a doomed man who had come well within the pale of the ultimate penalties.

He was examined by his Commanding Officer, and interviewed by still more exalted personages. The story he told was so bare as to be unintelligible. He asked for no mercy, and gave no explanations. But there were other witnesses besides him – the priest, for example, and Monsieur St Marais, in a sober suit of black and very dark under the eyes.

By-and-by the court gave its verdict. Private Peter Galbraith was found guilty of riding roughshod over the King's Regulations; he had absented himself from his battalion without permission; he had neglected his own duties and usurped without authority a number of superior functions; he had been the cause of the death or maltreatment of various persons who, whatever their moral deficiencies, must be regarded for the purposes of the case as civilian Allies. The Court, however, taking into consideration the exceptional circumstances in which Private Galbraith had been placed, inflicted no penalty and summarily discharged the prisoner.

Privately, his Commanding Officer and the still more exalted personages shook hands with him, and told him that he was a devilish good fellow and a credit to the British Army.

But Peter Galbraith cared for none of these things. As he sat again in the trenches at St Eloi in six inches of water and a foot of mud, he asked his neighbour how many Germans were opposite them.

'I was hearin' that there was maybe fifty thoosand,' was the answer.

Private Galbraith was content. He thought that the whole fifty thousand would scarcely atone for the death of one slim, dark-eyed girl.

John Buchan
From *Mr Standfast*

John Buchan's Mr Standfast *is one of the better British novels from the First World War. It was written between the summers of 1917 and 1918, while he was working for the Ministry of Information, and it is remarkable for the accuracy of the details concerning the war. The central character is Richard Hannay, who is based partially on the real life Field Marshal Lord Edmund Ironside, while many other characters from previous Buchan novels, such as Walter Bullivant, John Blenkiron and Peter Pienaar, make a reappearance. They join Hannay, now working at the War Office, to frustrate the work of a group of German spies known as the 'Wild Birds' and the action takes them from London to Glasgow, Skye, Switzerland and the Western Front. The novel is noteworthy for Buchan's sympathetic treatment of a conscientious objector in the shape of the pacifist Launcelot Wake and for his understanding of the background to the Red Clydeside agitation in Glasgow.*

Having commanded a brigade at Arras in 1917, Hannay arrives in Glasgow disguised as a South African pacifist called Brand. He is in pursuit of Abel Gresson, an American who is part of the Wild Birds spy-ring run by Moxom Ivery. The anti-war meeting has been called to found a British Council of Workers and Soldiers.

A Pacifists' Meeting in Glasgow

I followed [the earlier speakers] with extreme nervousness, and to my surprise got a fair hearing. I felt as mean as a mangy dog

on a cold morning, for I hated to talk rot before soldiers –
especially before a couple of Royal Scots Fusiliers, who, for all I
knew, might have been in my own brigade. My line was the
plain, practical, patriotic man, just come from the colonies, who
looked at things with fresh eyes, and called for a new deal. I was
very moderate, but to justify my appearance there I had to put
in a wild patch or two, and I got these by impassioned attacks
on the Ministry of Munitions. I mixed up a little mild praise of
the Germans, whom I said I had known all over the world for
decent fellows. I received little applause, but no marked dissent,
and sat down with deep thankfulness.

The next speaker put the lid on it. I believe he was a noted
agitator, who had already been deported. Towards him there was
no lukewarmness, for one half of the audience cheered wildly when
he rose, and the other half hissed and groaned. He began with
whirlwind abuse of the idle rich, then of the middle-classes (he
called them the 'rich man's flunkeys'), and finally of the
Government. All that was fairly well received, for it is the fashion
of the Briton to run down every Government and yet to be very
averse to parting from it. Then he started on the soldiers and
slanged the officers ('gentry pups' was his name for them), and the
generals, whom he accused of idleness, of cowardice, and of
habitual intoxication. He told us that our own kith and kin were
sacrificed in every battle by leaders who had not the guts to share
their risks. The Scots Fusiliers looked perturbed, as if they were in
doubt of his meaning. Then he put it more plainly. 'Will any soldier
deny that the men are the barrage to keep the officers' skins whole?'

'That's a bloody lee,' said one of the Fusilier Jocks.

The man took no notice of the interruption, being carried
away by the torrent of his own rhetoric, but he had not allowed
for the persistence of the interrupter. The Jock got slowly to his
feet, and announced that he wanted satisfaction. 'If ye open your
dirty gab to blagyird honest men, I'll come up on the platform
and wring your neck.'

At that there was a fine old row, some crying out 'Order', some 'Fair play', and some applauding. A Canadian at the back of the hall started a song, and there was an ugly press forward. The hall seemed to be moving up from the back, and already men were standing in all the passages and right to the edge of the platform. I did not like the look in the eyes of these newcomers, and among the crowd I saw several who were obviously plain-clothes policemen.

The chairman whispered a word to the speaker, who continued when the noise had temporarily died down. He kept off the army and returned to the Government, and for a little sluiced out pure anarchism. But he got his foot in it again, for he pointed to the Sinn Feiners as examples of manly independence. At that, pandemonium broke loose, and he never had another look in. There were several fights going on in the hall between the public and courageous supporters of the orator.

Then Gresson advanced to the edge of the platform in a vain endeavour to retrieve the day. I must say he did it uncommonly well. He was clearly a practised speaker, and for a moment his appeal 'Now, boys, let's cool down a bit and talk sense,' had an effect. But the mischief had been done, and the crowd was surging round the lonely redoubt where we sat. Besides, I could see that for all his clever talk the meeting did not like the look of him. He was as mild as a turtle dove, but they wouldn't stand for it. A missile hurtled past my nose, and I saw a rotten cabbage envelop the baldish head of the ex-deportee. Someone reached out a long arm and grabbed a chair, and with it took the legs from Gresson. Then the lights suddenly went out, and we retreated in good order by the platform door with a yelling crowd at our heels.

It was here that the plain-clothes men came in handy. They held the door while the ex-deportee was smuggled out by some side entrance. That class of lad would soon cease to exist but for the protection of the law which he would abolish. The rest of us, having less to fear, were suffered to leak into Newmilns Street. I found myself next to Gresson, and took his arm. There was something hard in his coat pocket.

Unfortunately there was a big lamp at the point where we emerged, and there for our confusion were the Fusilier Jocks. Both were strung to fighting pitch, and were determined to have someone's blood. Of me they took no notice, but Gresson had spoken after their ire had been roused, and was marked out as a victim. With a howl of joy they rushed for him.

I felt his hand steal to his side-pocket. 'Let that alone, you fool,' I growled in his ear.

'Sure, mister,' he said, and the next second we were in the thick of it.

It was like so many street fights I have seen – an immense crowd which surged up around us, and yet left a clear ring. Gresson and I got against the wall on the sidewalk, and faced the furious soldiery. My intention was to do as little as possible, but the first minute convinced me that my companion had no idea how to use his fists, and I was mortally afraid that he would get busy with the gun in his pocket. It was that fear that brought me into the scrap. The Jocks were sportsmen every bit of them, and only one advanced to the combat. He hit Gresson a clip on the jaw with his left, and but for the wall would have laid him out. I saw in the lamplight the vicious gleam in the American's eye and the twitch of his hand to his pocket. That decided me to interfere and I got in front of him.

This brought the second Jock into the fray. He was a broad, thickset fellow, of the adorable bandy-legged stocky type that I had seen go through the Railway Triangle at Arras as though it were blotting-paper. He had some notion of fighting, too, and gave me a rough time, for I had to keep edging the other fellow off Gresson.

'Go home, you fool,' I shouted. 'Let this gentleman alone. I don't want to hurt you.'

The only answer was a hook-hit which I just managed to guard, followed by a mighty drive with his right which I dodged so that he barked his knuckles on the wall. I heard a yell of rage, and observed that Gresson seemed to have kicked his assailant on the shin. I began to long for the police.

Then there was that swaying of the crowd which betokens the approach of the forces of law and order. But they were too late to prevent trouble. In self-defence I had to take my Jock seriously, and got in my blow when he had overreached himself and lost his balance. I never hit anyone so unwillingly in my life. He went over like a poled ox, and measured his length on the causeway.

I found myself explaining things politely to the constables. 'These men objected to this gentleman's speech at the meeting, and I had to interfere to protect him. No, no! I don't want to charge anybody. It was all a misunderstanding.' I helped the stricken Jock to rise and offered him ten bob for consolation.

He looked at me sullenly and spat on the ground. 'Keep your dirty money,' he said 'I'll be even with ye yet, my man – you and that red-headed scab. I'll mind the looks of ye the next time I see ye.'

Gresson was wiping the blood from his cheek with a silk handkerchief. 'I guess I'm in your debt, Mr Brand,' he said. 'You may bet I won't forget it.'

After a series of adventures in which he has fallen in love with a Secret Service agent, Mary Lamington, Hannay returns to London, this time in the disguise of a British private soldier and is immediately caught up in a German air raid.

The Advantages of an Air Raid

The train was abominably late. It was due at eight-twenty-seven, but it was nearly ten when we reached St Pancras. I had resolved to go straight to my rooms in Westminster, buying on the way a cap and waterproof to conceal my uniform should anyone be near my door on my arrival. Then I would ring up Blenkiron and tell him all my adventures. I breakfasted at a coffee-stall, left my pack and rifle in the cloak-room, and walked out into the clear sunny morning.

I was feeling very pleased with myself. Looking back on my madcap journey, I seemed to have had an amazing run of luck and to be entitled to a little credit too. I told myself that persistence always pays and that nobody is beaten till he is dead. All Blenkiron's instructions had been faithfully carried out. I had found Ivery's post office. I had laid the lines of our own special communications with the enemy, and so far as I could see I had left no clue behind me. Ivery and Gresson took me for a well-meaning nincompoop. It was true that I had aroused profound suspicion in the breasts of the Scottish police. But that mattered nothing, for Cornelius Brand, the suspect, would presently disappear, and there was nothing against that rising soldier, Brigadier-General Richard Hannay, who would soon be on his way to France. After all this piece of service had not been so very unpleasant. I laughed when I remembered my grim forebodings in Gloucestershire. Bullivant had said it would be damnably risky in the long run, but here was the end and I had never been in danger of anything worse than making a fool of myself.

I remember that, as I made my way through Bloomsbury, I was not thinking so much of my triumphant report to Blenkiron as of my speedy return to the Front. Soon I would be with my beloved brigade again. I had missed Messines and the first part of Third Ypres, but the battle was still going on, and I had yet a chance. I might get a division, for there had been talk of that before I left. I knew the Army Commander thought a lot of me. But on the whole I hoped I would be left with the brigade. After all I was an amateur soldier, and I wasn't certain of my powers with a bigger command.

In Charing Cross Road I thought of Mary, and the brigade seemed suddenly less attractive. I hoped the war wouldn't last much longer, though with Russia heading straight for the devil I didn't know how it was going to stop very soon. I was determined to see Mary before I left, and I had a good excuse, for I had taken my orders from her. The prospect entranced me, and I was mooning along in a happy dream, when I collided violently with in agitated citizen.

Then I realised that something very odd was happening.

There was a dull sound like the popping of the corks of flat soda-water bottles. There was a humming, too, from very far up in the skies. People in the street were either staring at the heavens or running wildly for shelter. A motor-bus in front of me emptied its contents in a twinkling; a taxi pulled up with a jar and the driver and fare dived into a second-hand bookshop. It took me a moment or two to realise the meaning of it all, and I had scarcely done this when I got a very practical proof. A hundred yards away a bomb fell on a street island, shivering every window-pane in a wide radius, and sending splinters of stone flying about my head. I did what I had done a hundred times before at the Front, and dropped flat on my face.

The man who says he doesn't mind being bombed or shelled is either a liar or a maniac. This London air raid seemed to me a singularly unpleasant business. I think it was the sight of the decent civilised life around one and the orderly streets, for what was perfectly natural in a rubble-heap like Ypres or Arras seemed an outrage here. I remember once being in billets in a Flanders village where I had the Maire's house and sat in a room uphol-stered in cut velvet, with wax flowers on the mantelpiece and oil paintings of three generations on the walls. The Boche took it into his head to shell the place with a long-range naval gun, and I simply loathed it. It was horrible to have dust and splinters blown into that snug, homely room, whereas if I had been in a ruined barn I wouldn't have given the thing two thoughts. In the same way bombs dropping in central London seemed a grotesque indecency. I hated to see plump citizens with wild eyes, and nursemaids with scared children, and miserable women scuttling like rabbits in a warren.

The drone grew louder, and, looking up, I could see the enemy planes flying in a beautiful formation, very leisurely, as it seemed, with all London at their mercy. Another bomb fell to the right, and presently bits of our own shrapnel were clattering viciously around me. I thought it about time to take cover, and ran shamelessly for the best place I could see, which was a Tube station. Five minutes before the street had been crowded; now I left behind me a desert dotted with one bus and three empty taxicabs.

I found the Tube entrance filled with excited humanity. One stout lady had fainted, and a nurse had become hysterical, but on the whole people were behaving well. Oddly enough they did not seem inclined to go down the stairs to the complete security of underground; but preferred rather to collect where they could still get a glimpse of the upper world, as if they were torn between fear of their lives and interest in the spectacle. That crowd gave me a good deal of respect for my countrymen.

Towards the end of the novel, Hannay returns to the army to
serve on the Western Front in time for the great German offensive
of spring 1918 – Operation Michael – which was aimed at
pushing the British back towards the Channel and opening the
way to Paris. Although the Germans forced a gap in the Allied
lines between Arras and St Quentin, the offensive was blocked
and by the middle of the summer counter-attacks on the Amiens
front had introduced the possibility of an Allied victory. The
reviewer in The Times *praised Buchan for his 'grasp of the*
military history of the war and his personal knowledge of opera-
tions on the Western Front'.

The German Offensive of March 1918

This is not the place to write the story of the week that followed.
I could not write it even if I wanted to, for I don't know it. There
was a plan somewhere, which you will find in the history books,
but with me it was blank chaos. Orders came, but long before they
arrived the situation had changed, and I could no more obey them
than fly to the moon. Often I had lost touch with the divisions on
both flanks. Intelligence arrived erratically out of the void, and for
the most part we worried along without it. I heard we were under
the French – first it was said to be Foch, and then Fayolle, whom
I had met in Paris. But the higher command seemed a million miles
away, and we were left to use our mother wits. My problem was
to give ground as slowly as possible and at the same time not to
delay too long, for retreat we must, with the Boche sending in
brand-new divisions each morning. It was a kind of war worlds
distant from the old trench battles, and since I had been taught no
other I had to invent rules as I went along. Looking back, it seems
a miracle that any of us came out of it. Only the grace of God and
the uncommon toughness of the British soldier bluffed the Hun
and prevented him pouring through the breach to Abbeville and

the sea. We were no better than a mosquito curtain stuck in a
doorway to stop the advance of an angry bull.

The Army Commander was right; we were hanging on with
our eyelashes. We must have been easily the weakest part of the
whole front, for we were holding a line which was never less
than two miles and was often, as I judged, nearer five, and there
was nothing in reserve to us except some oddments of cavalry
who chased about the whole battle-field under vague orders.
Mercifully for us, the Boche blundered. Perhaps he did not know
our condition, for our airmen were magnificent and you never
saw a Boche plane over our line by day, though they bombed us
merrily by night. If he had called our bluff, we should have been
done, but he put his main strength to the north and the south of
us. North he pressed hard on the Third Army, but he got well
hammered by the Guards north of Bapaume and he could make
no headway at Arras. South he drove at the Paris railway and
down the Oise valley, but there Petain's reserves had arrived, and
the French made a noble stand.

Not that he didn't fight hard in the centre where we were,
but he hadn't his best troops, and after we got west of the bend
of the Somme he was outrunning his heavy guns. Still, it was a
desperate enough business, for our flanks were all the time falling
back, and we had to conform to movements we could only guess
at. After all, we were on the direct route to Amiens, and it was
up to us to yield slowly so as to give Haig and Petain time to get
up supports. I was a miser about every yard of ground, for every
yard and every minute were precious. We alone stood between
the enemy and the city, and in the city was Mary.

If you ask me about our plans, I can't tell you. I had a new
one every hour. I got instructions from the Corps, but, as I have
said, they were usually out of date before they arrived, and most
of my tactics I had to invent myself. I had a plain task, and to
fulfil it I had to use what methods the Almighty allowed me. I
hardly slept, I ate little, I was on the move day and night, but I

never felt so strong in my life. It seemed as if I couldn't tire, and, oddly enough, I was happy. If a man's whole being is focused on one aim, he has no time to worry . . . I remember we were all very gentle and soft-spoken those days. Lefroy, whose tongue was famous for its edge, now cooed like a dove. The troops were on their uppers, but as steady as rocks. We were against the end of the world, and that stiffens a man . . .

Day after day saw the same performance. I held my wavering front with an outpost line which delayed each new attack till I could take its bearings. I had special companies for counter-attack at selected points, when I wanted time to retire the rest of the division. I think we must have fought more than a dozen of such little battles. We lost men all the time, but the enemy made no big scoop, though he was always on the edge of one. Looking back, it seems like a succession of miracles. Often I was in one end of a village when the Boche was in the other. Our batteries were always on the move, and the work of the gunners was past praising. Sometimes we faced east, sometimes north, and once at a most critical moment due south, for our front waved and blew like a flag at a masthead . . . Thank God, the enemy was getting away from his big engine, and his ordinary troops were fagged and poor in quality. It was when his fresh shock battalions came on that I held my breath . . . He had a heathenish amount of machine-guns and he used them beautifully. Oh, I take my hat off to the Boche performance. He was doing what we had tried to do at the Somme and the Aisne and Arras and Ypres, and he was more or less succeeding. And the reason was that he was going bald-headed for victory.

The men, as I have said, were wonderfully steady and patient under the fiercest trial that soldiers can endure. I had all kinds in the division – old army, new army, Territorials – and you couldn't pick and choose between them. They fought like Trojans, and, dirty, weary, and hungry, found still some salt of humour in their sufferings. It was a proof of the rock-bottom sanity of human nature.

John Buchan
War in the Air

Buchan's History of the First World War *was written in twenty-four volumes and was the only history to be written while the war was being fought. It was also enlivened by his own experience as a war correspondent and as Director of Information, two roles that provided him with insights denied to other writers. He was also astute about the potential of air power and recognised the role played by his friend Major-General Sir David Henderson who, as Director-General of Military Aeronautics, was one of the founders of the Royal Air Force. Years later, Buchan wrote of him: 'To David Henderson this service owes more than to any single man, and his name must for ever be linked with it.'*

Spring and summer brought easier conditions for the air services of the belligerent Powers; but the comparative stagnation in the Western theatre, where the service had been most highly developed, prevented any conspicuous action by this arm. The work of the winter in reconnaissance and destruction went on, and the story was rather of individual feats than of any great concerted activity. The importance of the air had revealed itself, and all the combatants were busied with new construction. In Britain, we turned out a great number of new machines. We experimented with larger types, and we perfected the different varieties of aerial bomb. The Advisory Committee on Aeronautics, containing some of the chief scientists of the day, solved various difficult problems, and saw to it that theory kept pace with practice. We added largely to the number of our airmen. At the beginning of the war, we had only the Central Flying School, capable of training at one time twenty pupils; by midsummer, we had eleven such schools, able to train upwards of two hundred. The enemy airplanes began to improve in speed and handiness, but where Germany advanced an inch we advanced an ell. Admirable as was the air work of all the Allies, the British service, under its Director-General, Sir David Henderson, had reached by midsummer a height of efficiency which was not exceeded by any other branch of the Army or Navy.

To a student of military affairs, it seemed amazing that a department only a few years old, and with less than one year's experience of actual war, should have attained so soon to so complete an efficiency and so splendid a tradition. Perhaps it was the continuous demand upon nerve and intelligence. Young men gathered from all quarters and all professions became in a little while of one type. They had the same quiet voices, the same gravity, the same dulled eyes, with that strange look in them that a man gets from peering into infinite space. The air, like the deep sea, seemed to create its own gentility, and no service had ever a more perfect breeding. Its tradition, less than a year old, was as high and stiff as that of any historic regiment. Self-advertising at this stage did not exist. In the military wing, at any rate, no names were mentioned; any achievement went to the credit of the corps, not of the aviator, unless the aviator were killed. Its members spoke of their profession with a curious mixture of technical wisdom and boyish adventure. The flying men made one family, and their *esprit de corps* was as great as that of a battleship. To spend some time at their headquarters at the front was an experience which no one could forget, so complete were the unity and loyalty and keenness of every man and officer. To be with them of an evening when they waited for the return of their friends, identifying from far off the thresh of the different propellers, was to realise the warm camaraderie born of a constant facing of danger.

In the air service neither body nor mind dared for one second to be stagnant, and character responded to this noble stimulus. The summer was punctuated with Zeppelin raids, which vied with the submarine exploits in their fascination for the German public. With its curious grandiosity of mind, that public chose to see in the sudden descent of the mighty engine of destruction out of the heavens a sign of the supernatural prowess of their race. A great mystery was made of the business in the hope of exciting among the civilian population of the Allies a dread commensurate with German confidence. In this, Germany was disappointed. The French and British peoples took the danger with calmness. It was a war risk, unpleasant in its character, but very clearly limited in its scope. There was a moment in Britain when the peril was over-estimated; there were also moments when it was unduly minimised; but for the most part the thing was regarded with calm good sense. There were four types of German airship in use – the Zeppelin, the Schütte-Lanz, the Parseval, and the military ship known as the 'M' type – but the term Zeppelin was used popularly to cover them all. During the war, Germany went on building at the rate of about one a month, a rate which more than made up for losses. Her chief difficulty was the supply of trained crews, for her reserves at the beginning of the campaign were speedily absorbed. The eastern and south-eastern coasts, and the capital itself were in England the main objects of the German raids. During the first year of war seventy-one civilian adults and eighteen children were killed; and one hundred and eighty-nine civilian adults and thirty-one children injured. No soldier or sailor was killed, and only on one occasion was any damage inflicted which could be described as of the smallest military importance. The principal French centres assailed were Calais and Paris, and there, too, the victims were few. No military or naval depot was damaged. Little shops and the cottages of the working classes alone bore the brunt of the enemy's fury. It was very different with the Allied air work. The yellow smoke of burning chemical factories and the glare of blazing Zeppelin sheds attested the fruitfulness of their enterprises. The truth was that the boasted Zeppelin proved an unhandy instrument of war. Its blows were directed blindly and at random. This was not to say that it might not achieve a surprising result, but that achievement would be more by accident than design.

It had been foreseen that the true weapon against such raids was the airplane itself. A fight between a Zeppelin and an airplane had been long looked forward to as, sooner or later, inevitable, and the Allied aircraft had instructions to engage a German airship whenever it appeared. It was not till the morning of 7 June that such a duel took place. About 3 a.m. Flight-Sub-Lieutenant R.A.J. Warneford, an officer of the British Naval Air Service, discovered a Zeppelin between Ghent and Brussels. He was flying in a very light monoplane, and managed to rise above the airship, which was moving at a height of about 6,000 feet. Descending to a distance of about 50 feet, he dropped six bombs, the last of which burst the envelope and caused the whole ship to explode in a mass of flame. The force of the explosion turned the monoplane upside down, but the skill and presence of mind of the airman enabled him to right it. He was compelled to descend in the enemy's country, but was able to re-start his engine and return safely to his base. The Zeppelin fell in a blazing mass to the ground and was destroyed with all its crew. The hero of this brilliant exploit had only received his flying certificate a few months before. It would be hard to overpraise the courage and devotion which inspired such an attack, or the nerve and fortitude which enabled him to return safely. Flight-Sub-Lieutenant Warneford's name became at once a household word in France and Britain, and he was most deservedly awarded the Victoria Cross and the Cross of the Legion of Honour. His career was destined to be as short as it had been splendid, for on 17 June he was accidentally killed while flying in the aerodrome at Versailles.

D.W. Cameron of Lochiel
The Cameron Highlanders at
the Battle at Loos, Hill 70, Fosse 8
and the Quarries

Press reporting of the war was constrained by the Defence of the Realm Act, which created a system of strict censorship of stories from the battlefront. For example, it was not until May 1915 that the Glasgow Herald *shared reporting facilities on the Western Front with the* Daily Chronicle, *but even then the war correspondents were kept well clear of the actual fighting and had to submit their stories to military censors before they were filed, a routine which meant that all despatches were sanitised before publication. Officially the system was supposed to prevent confidential information reaching the enemy, but the reality was that only good news was published and disasters were camouflaged or ignored. That did not stop news from the front being published, albeit with the names of places and military formations omitted. During the initial part of the war, local papers continued to publish soldiers' letters from the front and these provided romanticised and frequently fanciful descriptions of the fighting from soldiers. Loos was no exception. Readers of the* Inverness Courier, *for example, might have been spared the exact details of what actually happened, but in an interview with Lieutenant-Colonel D.W. Cameron of Lochiel, conducted while he was on leave at his estate at Achnacarry, they were left in no doubt that the men of their local regiment, the Camerons, had just experienced a heroic though no doubt bloody and terrifying battle.*

Colonel D.W. Cameron of Lochiel, Commanding the 5th Battalion Cameron Highlanders, has been good enough, during his short furlough at Achnacarry, to give details to our Fort William reporter of the part played by the 5th Camerons in the recent advance.

'Our objective was Fosse No. 8 and with the Seaforths on our right we started our advance at 6.40 on the 25th September, the two local Inverness-shire companies lying in the front line. We had to cross a long open ridge which was subject to a heavy enfilading rifle fire and machine-gun fire from the left, and when headquarters came up it was found that line after line of our men was simply mown down. The men faced the ordeal bravely, and when the remnants had been gathered together we succeeded in reaching our objective, where we found a few of our lot who had come up on the left of the Seaforths. The place we were ordered to hold was about 1,300 yards in front of our lines. Unfortunately the troops on our left never came up at all, with the result that our left was "in the air" the whole day, and the only thing which prevented the Germans getting in behind us was the action of our machine-gun sergeants who most heroically defended our left flank from our position in the rear. A Battalion of the Black Watch came on splendidly in our support, but they, too, unhappily, were considerably thinned. These were moments which can never be forgotten, and undoubtedly will tend to bind closer the very friendly ties which have always existed between the Camerons and the Seaforths. Defending what we had taken, we remained here until we were relieved by another brigade early in the following morning.

A Splendid Charge

'We remained in our trenches all day on 26th, and on the afternoon of 27th the battalion was ordered again to charge to reinforce the brigade in front of us, who were being hard-pressed by the Germans. This last charge was probably the finest thing a battalion had ever done, because the ranks, enormously attenuated in the action of 25th had on this occasion to go forward with practically no officers to lead them. As it was, they went forward out of their trenches as though nothing had happened in absolutely perfect alignment, as if on parade. The charge having had the desired effect, the battalion was withdrawn into billets early the next morning, and a more pathetic spectacle I never witnessed than the march back of all that remained of my battalion. The remnant was addressed by Sir John French, who thanked us for what we had done; but what pleased the men most was the words used by the Brigadier when he said that from Sir John French downwards amongst those who had been out during the whole war, nothing finer had been seen than the advance of the Camerons through that bullet-swept zone on the morning of the 25th. To me it was the saddest and proudest day of my life. I do not suppose any commanding officer, ever in the annals of the British Army, had better or braver men to serve under him and Inverness-shire may rest absolutely contented that the Highlanders of the 5th Battalion proved themselves in every way worthy of their gallant forefathers. In saying this, I do not underrate the part played in the advance by the Highland Brigade as a whole, and when the story comes to be written the country will doubtless learn how valiantly each unit fought.

Gallant Deeds

'Instances of personal bravery in my battalion are far too numerous to recount, but two might be cited as examples. A lance-corporal, finding the telephone connection between the Brigadier and myself cut, climbed to the top of a slag heap to get into visual communication. Here he went on waving his flags amidst the perfect tornado of shell fire, until a shell burst over him, and all that was found afterwards was a piece of his kilt and a notebook.

Another corporal did yeoman service as a bomb-thrower. The German bombers were coming along a trench, and owing to the presence of snipers it was courting death for our men to get out of the trenches. The corporal in question, however, volunteered to go, and taking up a bag of bombs, he got on to the parapet of the enemy trench and continued to throw the bombs down on the Germans. While so occupied he was exposed to fire from all directions, but he succeeded in driving back the other bombers until he was himself wounded.'

The casualties in 5th Camerons have been very heavy, and out of those of the battalion who took part in the operation, 25–27th September, only Lochiel and the Adjutant were left amongst the officers.

R.W. Campbell
Trench Fighting on the
Western Front

In a prefatory note to the novel Private Spud Tamson, *R.W. Campbell insisted that 'THE GLESCA MILEESHY is no regiment in particular. The story is simply a composite study of the types who fill the ranks of our Militia Regiments, now known as The Special Reserve.' Having finished its training, the fictional battalion crossed over to France under its commanding officer, Colonel Corkleg, and after a brief delay went into the line. The other officers mentioned in the narrative of the first battle are all different types whose names give some idea of their character or general characteristics: Major Tartan, Captain Hardup, Captain Coronet, Lieutenant Longlegs and Lieutenant 'Giddy' Greens.*

This was war. And they were plunged into the midst of all in less than a day. It was their job to relieve a regiment of regulars who had been fighting since Mons. This corps was stuck in trenches a hundred yards from the enemy's lines. Snipers had thinned the officers' ranks; repeated assaults had killed and worn out the NCOs and men. To relieve them was a problem, for the area behind their trenches was a shell-swept zone. But it had to be done. The safest time was at night, so when dusk had come they cautiously went forward. Sometimes they ran, at other points they had to creep and crawl. For a while all seemed well, but aerial scouts had told their tale. Just as the regiment reached the trenches, all were startled with the lurid flashing of great star-shells in the sky. This lit up the whole area and showed the lines of men advancing into the trenches.

Crack! went a Mauser rifle. This was a signal for hundreds more. More star-shells went up, and then the Maxim guns of the enemy opened a deadly fire.

'Double to the trenches!' roared a staff officer, who was the guide. In a few minutes the whole were jumping into the long, water-logged fortresses. Many were left behind wounded and dying, but the danger ahead was too great to study these casualties. Volley after volley came across the narrow zone. The hits were now few, for sighting was impossible. To the crouching men, who had just been baptised, the affair was somewhat awe-inspiring. Many a man shivered, just as nearly all brave men shiver in their first fight. The moans of the wounded men who lay behind did not help matters. Worse, however, was yet to come.

The Germans, somehow, feared a night attack. Determined to check this, they sallied out on a counter-assault. Across the hundred-yard zone they ran, cursed, yelled, and stumbled. It was an anxious moment, for the star-shells only lit the ground in a dim way. Colonel Corkleg, however, was equal to the hour.

'Out men and at them!' he roared from a point somewhere in the darkened region. There was a loud clatter as his gallants leapt out of their trenches. A second to fix their bayonets, then passing through the little avenues in the barbed wire they quickly formed and charged.

'Give them Hell, lads!' roared Coronet.

And then there was a crash of bodies and of steel. The sickening plug of bayonets into flesh was heard all along the line. Still, these Bavarian men were game. They took their punishment and nobly tried to wrest the laurels of this night affair. But they were up against the toughest lot of men in the whole line. The impact was terrific, the onslaught fierce and frightful. They felt the backward push of those determined Militiamen. Their counter-assault was useless, so, with a yell, they turned and fled. The victors pursued them, routed them out of their own trenches, captured two Maxim guns and smashed them, and after denuding the knapsacks of their fleeing enemy, returned across the darkened zone into their own lines.

'Well done, colonel,' whispered the staff officer to Corkleg. 'Your men are the right stuff,' he concluded, as he disappeared into the night en route for headquarters of the Brigade.

Next morning the regiment counted the cost and the gains. In front of their own lines lay a hundred Germans dead; side by side lay fifty of their own; while in the rear of the trenches more dead were found.

'Not bad for a first night,' said Greens, peeping out.

'Hardly a comedy,' replied Coronet, bandaging up a wounded hand. 'No, melodrama, with full effects. Corkleg's a sound actor manager. But, I say, how can we get those dead men buried? They'll soon smell like polecats.'

'Not during the day. It isn't safe,' remarked the captain, putting his cap up out of the trench on top of a stick. *Crack!* went a bullet

'A bull!' shouted the owner, drawing it down and surveying a battered cap badge.

'Sniper, eh?'

'Yes, Greens, a top-hole one at that. We'll need to be careful.'

The men, however, enjoyed the sport. Spud Tamson and his friends delighted in putting up empty jam-tins on the end of sticks. In a second there was the usual crack, and down came the tin with a bullet-hole through it. When an unfortunate sentry popped his head up too far, he generally met the same fate, and was immediately struck off the strength of the regiment. In some cases the men signalled such hits by putting up a white piece of cardboard, meaning a bull's-eye to the sniper. These German snipers were also sportsmen. Each time a Tommy inoculated the square head of a Teuton with a dose of lead, they also signalled a hit. In this way the troops managed to keep a musketry record. Of course, all sorts of tricks were employed. One section placed a row of turnips with Balaclava hats and Glengarrys on them at the edge of the trench. At once there was a terrible fusillade, and for half an hour each sniper had a go. Indeed, the refusal of these turnips to become casualties so annoyed the opposing Germans that they all commenced to pop at them. While their whole attention was thus concentrated, a small body of marksmen under Lieutenant Greens suddenly popped out of a sap-head. They placed steel plates for protection in front of them. All then took a deliberate aim at the enemy. In three minutes they shot twelve men through the head, and would have got more but for the sudden attack of a Maxim gun. This was rather unpleasant, so Greens and his merry men flopped down into their burrow again.

There were three kinds of trenches in which the men were placed. The first line nearest the enemy was long and as deep as the holes in a graveyard. No head-cover was allowed, and luxuries were barred. For forty-eight hours all danced, cursed, snored, or shivered according to the thermometer and the fullness (or emptiness) of the stomach.

When one grew tired of being a mole and absorbing the germs of rheumatism, pneumonia, and enteric, he simply put up his head and got a free discharge from an obliging sniper.

A communicating trench led to the supporting trenches. There was also a telephone to inform the Brigadier when the first line had been sent to heaven and more living targets required. Trunk calls to Oxford Street and Piccadilly, of course, were barred, an annoying restriction. In these supporting trenches, however, a man could manage to scrape a hole in the earth and there lie down. This was not exactly a comfortable experience, especially for those who slept with mouths open. Worms, snails, and other messy slugs would persist in dropping right into the gullets of the sleeping innocents. Only Frenchmen who had eaten frogs could enjoy such delicacies.

From the supporting trenches another communicating line led to the reserve trenches. These trenches were the last word in cunning, comfort, and luxury. They were literally dug-outs or caves, where officers and men improvised everything, from biscuit tins to toilet paper, in the making of underground homes to while away the weary days. Bridge and nap was played not for money, but full tins of jam, which a beneficent commissariat showers upon all British soldiers to keep off scurvy and other Whitechapel diseases. Nights were made merry by liberal issues of rum, and hope was inspired by the regular arrival of love epistles through the FPO [Field Post Office]. Replies to these communications had to be vague and somewhat guarded, for the colonel censored all officers' letters, while the officers acted similarly with the correspondence of the rank and file. Parcels of tucker cheered the somewhat plain fare, and bundles of New Testaments from anxious maiden ladies taught many that their former deeds would eventually make them stokers down under.

When things became too monotonous, the German artillery plunked a few Jack Johnsons* over. This employed all hands on burial services and writing letters of sympathy to the widows and orphans.

The most wonderful person in this system was the transport officer, Lieutenant Grain. He had an army of enlisted ostlers, carters, and jockeys to bring up the rations from the rear. This had to be done over quagmires and along serpent-like roads which were packed with Hammersmith omnibuses, field guns, motor-cars, and hare-brained motor cyclists. Worse, his job had to be done at night. It was enough to try the will and nerves of Hannibal. But Grain did it every time. It was his boast that the regiment had fresh bread, fresh meat, cigarettes and tobacco every night – a great accomplishment.

---

* British nickname for a 15-cm shell, after world heavyweight boxing champion Jack Johnson

Fancy delivering cans of hot tea and dixeys of good stew to the front trenches at midnight!

This had never been done in any previous campaign. No wonder some men wrote home saying that they were 'still well, but overfed'.

This life in the trenches levelled all distinctions, and revealed all that was good and bad. The skunk came forth in all his shady colours; the loyal and patient soul quickly won the affection of all. Discipline was difficult, especially when rain and frost gripped the flesh and bones. Cold feet in the first line of trenches is more demoralising than a thousand shells. Men object to being killed on a frosty morning. It is very uncomfortable, and certainly unromantic.

They feel it better to die on the greensward with the sun lighting up the scene and the birds twittering out a grand amen. But war is never waged to suit the convenience of all.

It is a battle for the fittest. The strong must survive and the weakest die. And war in the trenches is the most awful strain on officers and men. Perhaps it is worst for an officer. He suffers just the same hardships; worse, he has the anxiety of responsibility. Men seldom understand this. While they may sleep, the officer has to be awake, ever watchful for the assault and ever jealous of the honour of his regiment and his name.

Only men who have been thoroughly disciplined can stand such a strain. The amateur at this game is usually a nuisance, and better at home.

The disadvantage of trench-fighting is that it robs even the best soldiers of their dash and initiative. Men who have been stuck in trenches for months get out of condition and, at times, fail to seize opportunities to strengthen and consolidate their lines. Perhaps that was the reason for the deliberate progression of the Allied Army.

Each week a certain forward movement had to be done, even if this only amounted to a few yards. Saps were made underneath the enemy's barbed wire, explosions levelled these obstructions low, then with a rush our men would have a go to capture another of the German trenches. This work provided scope for all. Variety was frequently afforded in village fighting, the toughest job in war. The most interesting was a fight for a little house which commanded a short bridge and road over a Belgian canal. It was important to gain this point. Half a battalion of the Glesca Mileeshy, under Major Tartan, was ordered out to the job. The house itself was loopholed and sandbagged. There were two machine guns inside, as well as fifty snipers. Outside there was a circular redoubt, manned by three hundred more. The whole place was thoroughly protected by barbed wire and other tricky lures.

'It will cost us a lot of men, major,' said Colonel Corkleg; 'but the Brigadier says it must be done.'

'Yes, and we'll do it, sir,' replied Tartan, with a decision in his words which was inspiring:

'Very well, Tartan, I leave it to you – you know your job.'

Tartan's attack was preceded by a terrific bombardment by our artillery. But these shells did not dislodge the enemy. They stuck gamely to their job, and opened a fierce fusillade on the three skirmishing lines, which moved forward after the bombardment.

Captain Hardup had the first line. He took his men forward inch by inch. Trees, walls, holes, fence-posts, all sorts of cover were used by the men. Now and again a groan and curse was heard as men fell back wounded or dead.

'Come on, lads!' roared Lieutenant Longlegs, who was Hardup's subaltern. They gallantly replied and pushed forward to within one hundred yards of the barbed-wire entanglements. Matters were serious here, and casualties heavy. Ten men were knocked out in twenty minutes.

'Sergeant Brown, have a go with your cutters.'

'Right, sir,' said the sturdy little fellow, crawling forward. He wriggled like a snake right up to the wires. *Click!* went his cutters through one strand, *click!* through another, and up went his arm to get a strand higher up. All the while he was under a terrible fire. Just as he cut the third strand a bullet struck his arm. It fell limp and shattered. With wonderful fortitude he adjusted his body and cut the fourth strand with his other hand. *Zip!* sang a bullet again. It went right through his head. He rolled over dead.

Lieutenant Longlegs saw it all, and looked round for another man. But he had no need to shout. A young lance-corporal jumped over a wall and crawled up to the wires. Seizing the dead man's cutters, he coolly commenced to cut right and left. Bullets whizzed around, they even passed through his cap and clothes, but still he went on, making a great gap in the strands of wires.

He was succeeding splendidly when a bullet struck the wire-cutters, smashed them, and pierced his right hand. At once he lay low, tore out his field dressing, bandaged his hand, then commenced to crawl back to his lines. He got half-way when a bullet struck him in the spine. A weird yell told all of his fate.

'By God,' muttered Longlegs, 'that's too brave a lad to leave out there.' He jumped over the wall, and, heedless of the fire, ran forward, picked up his man and brought him into the shelter of his line. A great cheer went up as he returned. Longlegs had asserted his pluck.

This success at cutting the wires inspired many more to go forward. In three hours, five good gaps had been made and the way paved for a final assault. Meantime Major Tartan had arrived in the firing line with the reserves. He opened a fierce fusillade and accounted for almost a hundred of the enemy. Having done all that was possible at that point, he passed the word along.

'Prepare to charge!' Bayonets were fixed, and every eye centred on the tough figure of the old Highland Chief. Like a deer he rose, and, raising his arm, shouted, 'Up, lads, and at them.' What a din! Four hundred gallants running, yelling, cursing, and panting. Through the gaps in the wire they rushed, leaving many on the way.

Things were going well till a bullet struck the old major in a vital part. He fell mortally wounded. The sight checked the whole advance. His eyes saw the pause.

'Go on, men – give them it – never mind—' and he rolled back dead. Hardup and Longlegs now called them on. With a mighty rush, they scaled the great redoubt and leapt down into the ranks of the Germans. Some of the Teutons fought gamely; others cowered back, listless and powerless, an awful fear and awe in their eyes. The sight chilled the men, but a bloodthirsty old sergeant shouted, 'Remember the Belgian atrocities, boys.' That was enough. They bayoneted every man on the spot. During this bloody combat, the machine-guns and snipers in the house were pumping out volleys of death.

'Take the house now, men,' roared Hardup.

'By God, we'll soon do that,' answered Muldoon, the worst character in the regiment. Running forward to the walls, this powerful man got near the mouth of a Maxim gun projecting through the wall. With a terrible swipe, he smashed the end of the tube, breaking his butt at the job. Another man did the same for the other gun, while the remainder of the men made for the doors. A check happened here. The doors were barred and the enemy firing furiously from within.

'Smash it in,' ordered Hardup, standing near Longlegs. Three men sprang forward. First they smashed the protruding rifle barrels and then they tackled the doors. In ten minutes great holes were made. Captain Hardup was the first man through. Longlegs followed at his heels. The captain pinned a great big German with his bayonet, but another of the enemy stuck the gallant officer right through the chest. Longlegs had just got in when he saw his captain fall. Jumping forward he clubbed the man's brains out. The remaining Germans cleared up a stair to the next floor. This gave a breathing space and time to get more

men through. When enough had been collected, Longlegs led the
way. Another barred door was found. Willing hands quickly
ended this, and into a room Longlegs and his men dashed. The
enemy stood at the end of the room with bayonets fixed.

'Come on, lads, wipe them out.' Forward they went. There
was a terrific tussle for five minutes. Longlegs had the muscle of
his arm torn away with a bayonet, while three of his men were
killed on the spot; but every German was bayoneted to death.
Longlegs had his arm hastily bandaged.

'Come on,' he shouted again, and up to the top flat they
rushed to end their job. There they found a German officer and
a host of men inside a loft. The door of the place was also barred.
But this was easily smashed, and into the den the gallants rushed.
As they went an old sergeant pushed Longlegs back out of
danger.

'What's wrong?' he enquired angrily.

'I'm in charge o' this lot, sir. You're owre braw a fechter tae
get kill't.'

'Nonsense, sergeant.'

'Nae nonsense aboot it, sir. Staund there,' kindly insisted the
old non-com*, who saw that Longlegs would soon faint from
loss of blood. Meantime the din inside the room was deafening.
Squeals, groans, and curses rent the air. It was a battle to the
death. The officer fought like a Trojan for his life, but, in the
end, he was bayoneted to death. Half of the enemy were killed,
the other half surrendered or jumped through the windows,
smashing their legs on the hard stones below.

'We've won, sir,' reported the sergeant, rushing out of the
shambles to where the pale-faced officer was standing at the top
of the stair.

'Good!' said the subaltern, tumbling in a heap from loss of
blood. At that moment a thundering cheer was heard outside the

* non-commissioned officer

house. It was the colonel and the other half of the battalion, who had been sent up in support. The job, however, had been well done. Old Corkleg was met at the door by the faithful sergeant.

'We've done it, sir,' said he, saluting.

'Yes,' said the colonel gravely, as he looked at his dead and wounded men. Then, looking up, he remarked, 'Where is Major Tartan?'

'Killed, sir.'

'And Captain Hardup?'

'Inside, sir, badly wounded.'

'What about Mr Longlegs?'

'He's lying upstairs, wounded too.'

'Any other casualties?'

'Two other officers wounded, sir, and I think we've lost over a hundred men.'

'Sad, very sad, and some of the best,' said the old colonel, turning away to hide the moisture in his eyes.

'Well done, Corkleg,' said the Brigadier, walking up to the scene.

'Yes. Our men have done well, but our casualties have been awful.'

'Still, Corkleg, your men have captured the key to the whole German lines here. They will have to retire for almost a mile now. Good business! Good business! Terrible scamps, these men of yours, but heroes every time. Let me have any recommendations.'

Hardup and Longlegs got the DSO [Distinguished Service Order], the old sergeant and wire-cutting corporal received the Distinguished Conduct Medal, while every paper in Britain wrote columns about the gallantry of the Glesca Mileeshy.

'Useful men! Useful men!' said Corkleg, on reading the appreciation in *The Times* a few days later.

'Yes, sir,' replied the adjutant.

J. Storer Clouston
The Narrative of Lieutenant von Belke of the German Navy

Set in 1917, at a time when the war was in deadlock, the story follows the fortunes of Lieutenant von Belke of the German Navy, who is landed on a Scottish island by Captain Wiedermann to make contact with a traitor who will help German submarines to launch an attack on the British fleet. Due to the needs of wartime censorship, the place is called the Windy Isles, but the backdrop is, in fact, Orkney, with the fleet lying at anchor in Scapa Flow.

The Landing

If any one had been watching the bay that August night (which, fortunately for us, there was not), they would have seen up till an hour after midnight as lonely and peaceful a scene as if it had been some inlet in Greenland. The war might have been waging on another planet. The segment of a waning moon was just rising, but the sky was covered with clouds, except right overhead where a bevy of stars twinkled, and it was a dim though not a dark night. The sea was as flat and calm as you can ever get on an Atlantic coast – a glassy surface, but always a gentle regular bursting of foam upon the beach. In a semicircle the shore rose black, towering at either horn (and especially on the south) into high dark cliffs.

I suppose a bird or two may have been crying then as they were a little later, but there was not a light nor a sign of anything human being within a hundred miles. If one of the Vikings who used to live in those islands had revisited that particular glimpse of the moon, he could never have guessed that his old haunts had altered a little. But if he had waited a while he would have rubbed his eyes and wondered. Right between the headlands he would have seen it dimly: – a great thing that was not a fish rising out of the calm water, and then very stealthily creeping in, and in towards the southern shore.

When we were fairly on the surface, I came on deck and gazed over the dark waters to the darker shore, with – I don't mind confessing it now – a rather curious sensation. To tell the truth, I was a little nervous, but I think I showed no sign of it to Wiedermann.

'You have thought of everything you can possibly need?' he asked in a low voice.

'Everything, sir, I think,' I answered confidently.

'No need to give you tips!' he said with a laugh.

I felt flattered – but still my heart was beating just a little faster than usual!

In we crept closer and closer, with the gentlest pulsation of our engines that could not have been heard above the lapping of the waves on the pebbles. An invisible gull or two wheeled and cried above us, but otherwise there was an almost too perfect stillness. I could not help an uncomfortable suspicion that someone was watching. Someone would soon be giving the alarm, someone would presently be playing the devil with my schemes. It was sheer nonsense, but then I had never played the spy before – at least, not in war-time.

Along the middle of the bay ran a beach of sand and pebbles, with dunes and grass links above, but at the southern end the water was deep close inshore, and there were several convenient ledges of rock between the end of this beach and the beginning of the cliffs. The submarine came in as close as she dared, and then, without an instant's delay, the boat was launched.

Wiedermann, myself, two sailors, and the motor-bicycle just managed to squeeze in, and we cautiously pulled for the ledges.

The tide was just right (we had thought of everything, I must say that), and after a minute or two's groping along the rocks, we found a capital landing. Wiedermann and I jumped ashore as easily as if it had been a quay, and my bicycle should have been landed without a hitch. How it happened I know not, but just as the sailors were lifting it out, the boat swayed a little and one of the clumsy fellows let his end of it slip. A splash of spray broke over it; a mere nothing, it seemed at the time, and then I had hold of it and we lifted it on to the ledge.

Wiedermann spoke sharply to the man, but I assured him no harm had been done, and between us we wheeled the thing over the flat rocks, and pulled it up to the top of the grass bank beyond.

'I can manage all right by myself now,' I said. 'Good bye, sir!'

He gave my hand a hard clasp.

'This is Thursday night,' he said. 'We shall be back on Sunday, Monday, and Tuesday nights, remember.'

'The British Navy and the weather permitting!' I laughed.

'Do not fear!' said he 'I shall be here, and we shall get you aboard somehow. Come any one of those nights that suits him.'

'That suits him?' I laughed. 'Say rather that suits Providence!'

'Well,' he repeated, 'I'll be here anyhow. Good luck!'

We saluted, and I started on my way, wheeling my bicycle over the grass. I confess, however, that I had not gone many yards before I stopped and looked back. Wiedermann had disappeared from the top of the bank, and in a moment I heard the faint sounds of the boat rowing back. Very dimly against the grey sea I could just pick out the conning tower and low side of the submarine. The gulls were still crying, but in a more sombre key, I fancied.

So here was I, Conrad von Belke, lieutenant in the German Navy, treading British turf underfoot, cut off from any hope of escape for three full days at least! And it was not ordinary British turf either. I was on the holy of holies, actually landed on those sacred, jealously-guarded islands (which, I presume, I must not even name here), where the Grand Fleet had its lair. As to the mere act of landing, well, you have just seen that there was no insuperable difficulty in stepping ashore from a submarine at certain places, if the conditions were favourable and the moment cunningly chosen; but I proposed to penetrate to the innermost sanctuary, and spend at least three days there – a very different proposition!

I had been chosen for this service for three reasons: because I was supposed to be a cool hand in what the English call a 'tight place'; because I could talk English not merely fluently, but with the real accent and intonation – like a native, in fact; and I believe because they thought me not quite a fool. As you shall hear, there was to be one much wiser than I to guide me. He was indeed the brain of this desperate enterprise, and I but his messenger and assistant. Still, one wants a messenger with certain qualities, and as it is the chief object of this narrative to clear my honour in the eyes of those who sent me, I wish to point out that they deliberately chose me for this job – I did not select myself – and that I did my best.

It was my own idea to take a motor-bicycle, but it was an idea cordially approved by those above me. There were several obvious advantages. A motor-cyclist is not an uncommon object on the roads even of those out-of-the-way islands, so that my mere appearance would attract no suspicion; and besides, they would scarcely expect a visitor of my sort to come ashore equipped with such an article. Also, I would cover the ground quickly, and, if it came to the worst, might have a chance of evading pursuit. But there was one reason which particularly appealed to me: I could wear my naval uniform underneath a suit of cyclist's overalls, and so if I were caught might make a strong plea to escape the fate of a spy; in fact, I told myself I was not a spy – simply a venturesome scout. Whether the British would take the same view of me was another question! Still, the motor-cycle did give me a chance.

My first task was to cover the better part of twenty miles before daybreak and join forces with 'him' in the very innermost shrine of this sanctuary – or rather, on the shore of it. This seemed a simple enough job; I had plenty of time, the roads, I knew, were good, nobody would be stirring (or anyhow, ought to be) at that hour, and the arrangements for my safe reception were, as you shall hear, remarkably ingenious. If I once struck the hard main road, I really saw nothing that could stop me.

The first thing was to strike this road. Of course I knew the map by heart, and had a copy in my pocket as a precaution that was almost superfluous, but working by map memory in the dark is not so easy when one is going across country.

The grassy bank fell gently before me as the land sloped down from the cliffs to the beach, and I knew that within a couple of hundred yards I should find a rough road which followed the shore for a short way, and then when it reached the links above the beach, turned at right angles across them to join the highroad. Accordingly I bumped my motor-cycle patiently over the rough grass, keeping close to the edge of the bank so as to guide myself, and every now and then making a detour of a few yards inland to see whether the road had begun. The minutes passed, the ground kept falling till I was but a little above the level of the glimmering sea, the road ought to have begun to keep me company long ago, but never a sign of it could I find. Twice in my detours I stumbled into what seemed sand-holes, and turned back out of them sharply. And then at last I realised that I had ceased to descend for the last hundred yards or more, and in fact must be on the broad stretch of undulating sea links that fringed the head of the bay. But where was my road?

I stopped, bade myself keep quite cool and composed, and peered round me into the night. The moon was farther up and it had become a little lighter, but the clouds still obscured most of the sky and it was not light enough to see much. Overhead were the stars; on one hand the pale sea merged into the dark horizon; all around me were low black hummocks that seem to fade into an infinity of shadows. The gulls still cried mournfully, and a strong pungent odour of seaweed filled the night air. I remember that pause very vividly.

I should have been reckless enough to light a cigarette had I not feared that our submarine might still be on the surface, and Wiedermann might see the flash and dub me an idiot. I certainly needed a smoke very badly and took some credit to myself for refraining (though perhaps I ought really have given it to Wiedermann). And then I decided to turn back, slanting, however, a little away from the sea so as to try and cut across the road. A minute or two later I tumbled into a small chasm and came down with the bicycle on top of me. I had found my road.

The fact was that the thing, though marked on the large-scale map as a road of the third, fourth, or tenth quality (I forget which), was actually nothing more or less than three parallel crevasses in the turf filled with loose sand. It was into these crevasses that I had twice stumbled already. Now with my back to the sea and keeping a yard or two away from this wretched track, but with its white sand to guide me, I pushed my motorcycle laboriously over the rough turf for what seemed the better part of half an hour. In reality I suppose it was under ten minutes, but with the night passing and that long ride before me, I never want a more patience-testing job. And then suddenly the white sand ceased. I stepped across to see what was the matter, and found myself on a hard highroad. It was a branch of the main road that led towards the shore, and for the moment I had quite forgotten its existence. I could have shouted for joy.

'Now,' I said to myself, 'I'm off!'

And off I went, phut-phut-phutting through the cool night air, with a heart extraordinarily lightened. That little bit of trouble at the start had made the rest of the whole wild enterprise seem quite simple now that it was safely over.

I reached the end of this branch, swung round to the right into the highroad proper and buzzed along like a tornado. The sea by this time had vanished, but I saw the glimmer of a loch on my left, and close at hand low walls and dim vistas of culti-vated fields. A dark low building whizzed by, and then a gaunt eerie-looking standing stone, and then came a dip and beyond it a little rise in the ground. As I took this rise there suddenly came upon me a terrible sinking of the heart. Phut-phut! went my cycle, loudly and emphatically, and then came a horrible pause. Phut! once more; then two or three feeble explosions, and then silence. My way stopped; I threw over my leg and landed on the road.

'What the devil!' I muttered.

I had cleaned the thing, oiled it, seen that everything was in order; what in heaven's name could be the matter? And then with a dreadful sensation I remembered that wave of salt water.

V.C.C. Collum
Torpedoed

On 24 March 1916, the cross-Channel ferry SS Sussex *was on a regular run from Folkestone to Dieppe when she was torpedoed by the German submarine UB-29. The ship was severely damaged, with the entire bow forward of the bridge blown off. Some of the lifeboats were launched, but at least two of them capsized and passengers were drowned: of the fifty-three crew and 325 passengers, fifty were killed. The ferry remained afloat and was towed stern-first into Boulogne, where she was eventually salvaged. Amongst the passengers was V.C.C. Collum, who was returning to her post at the Scottish Women's Hospital at Royaumont; her injuries were severe enough to keep her out of action for three months. Due to wartime censorship, the names of ships and ports were not given.*

Never was the sea in the Channel more blue than on the afternoon of March 24th when the *Sussex* left Folkestone harbour for Dieppe. I felt in high spirits. My month's leave had been just long enough to clear away all the feeling of staleness that had crept over me after twelve months' work at the Hospital, and to give me an appetite for more. A year is a long time in War. In a year the members of a corps, a ship's company, or the staff of a hospital, get to know one another very intimately, especially if, as in our case, the unit is somewhat isolated. In a year our Hospital had become a living thing, and our Head Surgeon a Chief who commanded that something that is more than loyalty and respect, yet which an Englishman hesitates to describe as devotion. So I was right glad to be going back to a life I loved, to a Chief I delighted to work with, to comrades proven in long months of alternating stress and monotony, and to a little group of friends. Then there was also the prospect of bearing a share in the terrific work of the expected spring offensive. The sea was blue and calm, the sun shone brightly: the English coast and the shipping in the harbour grew less and less distinct. Overhead a gallant little British dirigible performed aerial evolutions, as though to suggest to us that Britain was on the watch in the skies as well as on the seas. We steamed out punctually at 1.30 to the rousing cheers of British troops soon to follow us to France. In less than an hour we had a reminder that the enemy also keeps his watch by sea. We passed thousands of floating bags of jettisoned cargo wool or forage. One that floated apart, quite close to us, bore the name 'Essex' in black letters. A little group of passengers stood by the rail that divided the forecastle deck from the first-class promenade deck and discussed the matter. 'A sinister reminder of possibilities,' I said to my neighbour, a stout elderly man. A British officer who had braved worse dangers at Mudros [Gallipoli, 1915] laughed, and said they had probably been thrown overboard – this was not submarine weather. The Germans were afraid to show themselves in calm seas: they preferred to work when the crests of the waves were cut off and there was a lather of foam to hide their periscopes. Presently they strolled aft. I was left nearly alone, watching a Belgian officer who had fetched his dog from the forecastle companion and was exercising it on the deck. Then he too disappeared. I turned to the sea again, and watched for a periscope. It grew cold, and I was beginning to think of going back to my sheltered chair to roll myself up in my rug, when in a moment the whole earth and heaven seemed to explode in one head-splitting roar. In the thousandth part of a second my mind told me 'Torpedo forward on my right' and then the sensation of falling, with my limbs spread-eagled, through blind space.

When I came to myself again, I was groping amid a tangle
of broken wires, with an agonising pain in my back and the
fiercest headache I have ever known. My hair was down and
plastered to my chin with blood that seemed to be coming from
my mouth. There was more blood on my coat sleeve. I was
conscious that I was bleeding freely internally with every
movement. My first definite thought was, 'If only it is all a
ghastly nightmare!' But I remembered. My next thought was a
passionately strong desire not to die by drowning then. I crawled
free of the wires that were coiled all about me and stood up. In
one unsteady glance I took in a number of things. Near me a
horrible piece of something, and a dead woman. (Afterwards I
wondered why I was so sure she was dead and never stopped to
make sure.) Below me, on the quarter-deck and second-class
promenade deck, numbers of people moving to and fro, many
with lifebelts on. I never heard a sound from them, but it did not
strike me as odd then. Now I know I was deafened. So I had
been blown up on to the top deck, to the other end of the ship.
I swayed to and fro, and looked for a stairway, but could find
none, and began to be aware that I had only a few moments of
consciousness left me. Something must be done if I was not to
drown. I forced my will to concentrate on it, and came to the
side, where I found three men looking down on a lowered boat.
I also saw a lifebelt on the ground. I picked it up, and not having
the strength to put it on, I tried to ask the men to tie it for me.
Then I found I could not speak. So I held it up, and one, an
American, understood, and hastily tied it. Then I saw one of
them catch hold of a loose davit rope and swarm down it to the
boat. There was my one chance, I decided. My arms were all
right, but would my legs work? I took hold, and made a mighty
effort to cross my knees round the rope: I succeeded. Then I slid
down till I was just above the water. I waited till the roll of the
ship brought me near enough to the boat to catch, with my right
hand, another rope that I saw hanging plumb above it, while I

hung on with my left. It came within reach: I caught it, let go with my left, and lowered myself into the boat. Then I wanted to sink down in her bottom and forget everything, but I dared not, for men were pouring into her. I saw a man's knee hooked over the side of the boat where I sat. I could not see his body, but it was in the water, between us and the side of the *Sussex*. As in a dream I held on to his knee with my left hand with all the grip I had left, and with my right held on to the seat on which I sat. I could do nothing to help him in, but on the other hand, so long as I remained conscious, his knee-hold should not be allowed to slip. No one took any notice of either of us. Gradually I began to hear again. The men in the boat were shouting that there was no more room, that the boat was full. One last man tumbled in and then the people in the boat pushed away, and men on the *Sussex* helped. Others continually threw gratings and planks overboard.

Our boat was dangerously overcrowded. Already she was half swamped. I wondered when she would upset. A man on either side seized gratings and towed them alongside. One made a herculean effort and pulled the man whose knee I had been holding into our boat, and nearly upset her. No one said a word. He was an elderly man, and his fat face was white and piteous. His hands never ceased trembling. He had had a terrible fright. Someone suggested getting out the oars, and others said it was impossible, as they were underneath us all. However, it was managed, and several men stood up and changed places. Again we nearly upset. I joined with the others in commanding these wild folk to sit still. Three oars were produced. One was given to a young and sickly-looking Frenchman opposite to me. He did not know how to use it. Every one shouted to get away from the steamer. The water had now reached my knees, and I began to notice how cold it was. I saw three other women in the boat. They sat together, white and silent, in the stern, nor ever moved. They were French women. Someone noticed that the water was increasing, and there was a wild hullabaloo of alarm. A Belgian, the man who had pulled into the boat the man whose knee I held, called for hats with which to bale, setting the example with his own. But we were so tightly packed that no one could get at the water, whereupon the Belgian climbed overboard on to one of the gratings I have already mentioned, and a young Belgian soldier followed his example on the other side. They held on to our gunwale with their fingers.

Sometimes the people in the boat baled furiously, sometimes they stopped and stared stupidly about them. Some shouted to '*Ramez! Ramez!*' Others equally excited yelled '*Mais non! Videz l'eau! Videz l'eau!*' I apologised to my immediate neighbours for that I had no hat to lend, and for that I was too hurt to stoop, but I put my hands on the erring oar the young Frenchman was feebly moving across my knees, and did my best to guide his efforts. As often as not he put it flat on the water, and sometimes he merely desisted altogether, and gazed vacantly in front of him. The Belgian asked for a handkerhief, and groping in the water at the bottom of the boat, found a hole and caulked it as best he could. Thereafter the balers kept the water from increasing, but did little to reduce it. Looking around I saw our steamer riding quite happily on the water with her bows clean gone. Afterwards I learned that the torpedo had cut off her forepart, to within an inch or two of where I had been standing, and that it had sunk. I saw another full boat being rowed away from the ship, and an overturned one with two people sitting on her keel. I saw a man seated on a grating. All were convinced that help would be forthcoming speedily. And still the *Sussex* floated. Four times I remarked by way of a *ballon d'essai* that it seemed as if she were not going to sink, and always there was an outcry to row, and get away from her. The Belgian and the Belgian soldier evidently thought as I did. They proposed that we should return before we were swamped ourselves. Once again a hysterical outburst. One man jumped to his feet and shrieked, and asked us if it were to hell that we intended returning? I began to be afraid that he and those who thought as he did would to row us others into the sea, but common-sense told me that to remain all night in that overcrowded half-swamped boat would be to court death.

We saw at last that the other boat was returning. This was our chance. Example is a wonderful thing in dealing with mob hysteria. Tentatively the two Belgians and I proposed that we should go as close to the steamer as prudence permitted, and ask the Captain if she were going to sink. If his answer were favourable, those who desired should go on board, and any who liked could go off again in the boat. If his answer were unfavourable, we would stand off again. The maniac still shrieked his protests, but the rest of the boat was with us. But no one seemed to know how to turn the boat. As soon as we told one to backwater, the other two did likewise. It seemed hopeless. Finally, we let the other two oars pull, and I myself tried to induce my vis-à-vis to '*ramez au sens contraire*', which was the nearest approach I could get to 'backwater' in French! He was too dazed to understand, so I simply set my teeth and pulled against him, and in about fifteen minutes the boat gradually came round in a wide circle. How I longed to be whole again so that I could take his oar right away and cox that mad boat! With my injured back and inside, I could only just compass what I did. The pain kept me from collapsing, and the exertion from freezing. Even now a mutinous mood came over the boat every few moments, and they wavered and prepared to flee the ship again. It was like a political meeting. The boat followed the wishes of those who shouted loudest. So we who wished to return shouted monotonously, '*Retournez au bateau.*' When the oars ceased dipping, I called out as encouragingly as I could, sub-consciously following, I believe, the example of newspaper sergeants I had read of in French accounts of battles: '*Courage, mes amis! Ramez! Ramez! Courage, mes enfants!*' No one thought it odd. The dazed ears heard, and the nerveless arms

worked again. Finally, the Belgian dragged me aside that
someone might have another tussle with the rising water. It
looked as though we were to be swamped, after all, within ten
yards of the *Sussex*'s gaping bows, for our crew, in their
excitement, had forgotten to bale for some minutes. As we
floated in under her sides I made a final appeal, which a young
Belgian put into more forcible French, for everybody to keep
calm and not upset the boat at the last.

The women now spoke for the first time and it was to appeal
to the excited boat's load to let me be taken off first, since I was
injured. I found I could not stand, so sat in the middle of the seat
trying to trim the boat while the men scrambled out. I was left
alone at last; and the water that came over the gunwale poured
over my legs to my waist, some of it soaking through my thick
great coat and chilling me to the bone. The boat was floating
away. Someone shouted to me to get up. I got on to my hands
and knees on the seat and tried to crawl along the side, but the
change of position nearly caused me to faint with pain. Then the
Belgian managed to get hold of the boat and hold her, and some
sailors leaned out of the hatchway in the *Sussex*'s side and
grasped me by the arms and pulled me up and in as though I had
been a sack. There were many far worse hurt than I, and they
left me propped against a wall. The Belgian again came to the
rescue, and half dragged me to the top of the second saloon
stairway. I got down by levering myself on my hands on the rails,
while he supported me under the arms. Once in the saloon, he
and the young Belgian soldier took off my loosely fixed lifebelt
and laid me on a couch. One forced a glass of whisky down my
throat, which burned and gave me back renewed consciousness,
while the other ran for brandy. I was terribly cold, and the good
Belgian took off my boots and puttees and stockings and chafed
my feet till one was warm. The other had no sensation for over
twelve hours, and five days later, when it was radio-graphed,
proved to be sprained and fractured. He placed a pillow over

them then, and proceeded to chafe my hands, first taking off my draggled fur gloves, which I still wore. He sat and held my hands for at least a quarter of an hour till they were warm. Then he disappeared to help 'the other women'. Meanwhile the young Belgian soldier came and gave me a glass of brandy, giving me no choice, but insisting on my drinking it, and spilling a good deal on my bloody chin and coat collar in his zeal. Soon I felt quite warm again.

Presently the electric lights were turned up, to my great astonishment. The Belgian surprised me still further by taking away my boots and stockings 'to dry before the kitchen fire.' I did not yet realise what we owed to the strong watertight bulkheads of that well-constructed little vessel (built, I learn, by a man who has done more than almost any other for our Hospital, even to the willing sacrifice of his daughter. Her health was ruined by the hardships and exposure in those first few weeks of December 1914, when our pioneers found a long uninhabited building and were faced with the unexpected task of lighting, heating, and draining it, in addition to cleaning and fitting it up).

After that, long hours of waiting. A woman shrieked incessantly up on deck. A man with a wounded head came and sat patiently in a corner. A girl, complaining of a pain in her chest, came down the stairs and lay down on a corner couch. She never moved nor spoke again. By midnight she was dead. None of us guessed, none of us knew. She died bravely and silently, quite alone. Another woman showed signs of approaching hysteria. A young Belgian officer, who had been attending her, suddenly ceased his gallantry, and, standing sternly before her, said brusquely, 'After all, if the very worst comes, you can only die. What is it to die?' The words acted on her like a douche of cold water. She became herself again and never murmured. We others, perhaps, benefited too. It is nerve-wracking work lying helpless in a damaged vessel, wondering whether the rescue ship or

another enemy submarine will appear first on the scene. And no
ship came. At intervals the Belgian boy soldiers came down to
reassure us: 'The wireless had been repaired. Forty vessels were
searching for us. There was a light to starboard. We were drifting
towards Boulogne. The Phares [lighthouse] of the coast were in
sight.' But no ship came. The light to starboard faded. Another
appeared, and faded too. Then we heard the regular boom of a
cannon or a rocket. We all knew that something must have
blocked our wireless, but no one said so. The Belgian came down
to sleep, fixing his lifebelt first. With him came a good French-
woman, who was very kind to me and washed the blood from
my face and rinsed out my bleeding mouth. She was very hungry,
and all I could do to help her was to hold her jewels while she
went on deck to search for her hand baggage, and, later, to give
her some soaked food out of my pocket. There was no food left
anywhere. She said some brave words, too, about death coming
to all, only coming once, and being soon over. How much one
person's courage can help others at such a time! Then she tied
on a lifebelt and went to sleep beside me. The ship was rolling
now, and the seas slapped noisily against her somewhere, jarring
her all through her frame. But the Captain had said she would
not sink for eighteen hours, and we all believed his word
implicitly. Still, it was an ugly noise, and seemed to betoken her
helplessness.

And then at last the news of rescue! A French fishing-boat
was coming! 'Women and children first,' the young Belgians
cried. My Belgian succourer roused himself and fetched my
stockings and boots. My right boot would not go on. My putties
he could not manage, and so he tied them round me. He was
always cool and practical and matter-of-fact. 'I have been in the
Belgian Congo,' he explained, 'and in shipwrecks before. I know
what to do, and I am not alarmed. You can trust entirely to me.'
And I did. There was a great bump as the fishing-boat came
along-side, and a rush upstairs. Once more I was left alone, for

my Belgian friend had gone up to see about getting me helped
on board. He came back to say that the crush was so great that
he would wait till it was over and then take me. It seemed a long
time, but he came back at last, only to find he could not lift me.
Then he went away calling for an *'homme de bonne volonté'* to
help. A young Chinese responded, and together they staggered
up the heaving stairway with me. When they reached the ship's
rail, it was to hear that the boat had gone! A British torpedo-
boat was coming, we were told, and so the fisherman had gone
off with as many as she could safely carry to Boulogne. With her
went my hope of reaching my own hospital in France. I was sure
the destroyer would take her load to England.

Once more I was on the point of collapse, and very seasick
to boot. The Belgian supported me as if I had been a little child,
and I tried to convince myself that I was not in dreadful pain.
Perhaps half an hour passed, and then the destroyer came. This
time one of the French sailors helped him to carry me, and I was
placed on my back, across the ship's rail, and when the roll
brought her near enough to the destroyer, British sailors grasped
my arms and pulled me over. For one sickening second my legs
dangled between the two ships, but the sailors hauled me in just
before the impact came. They carried me to the charthouse and
laid me on the couch, and before long the Belgian joined me,
and, utterly exhausted, lay down on the floor. From that moment
I felt entirely safe. We English are brought up to feel complete
confidence in the British Navy, much as they teach us to trust in
Providence. And the Navy deserves our confidence.

It took a long time to transfer all the remaining passengers
of the *Sussex* to HMS ——, for the sea was becoming restless, and
the two ships hammered and thumped at each other's sides to
such purpose that the rescuing destroyer had to go into dock for
repairs when her labours were over and she had landed us all
safely. The injured were at once attended to, and I had not been
more than half an hour onboard before the surgeon came to visit

me. Having sent the Belgian below, he did all he could for me, and then, assured that I was by no means *in extremis*, he hurried back to attend to three others who were. The mate of the destroyer came and made me comfortable, and sent me tea, and a young gunner to keep me from falling off the couch when we should move, and reappeared at intervals to see how I was getting on. He gave me chocolate, which I ate quite greedily, having had nothing for over twelve hours. Unfortunately, as soon as the destroyer began its homeward race, I was very seasick. How these little ships of ours can move! Had I guessed then, as report now has it, that a submarine fired two torpedoes at us on our way back to England, I should have felt more kindly towards the prodigious speed of our rescuer. As it was, I took pride in, but got little comfort out of it.

Somewhere near 4 a.m. the kind mate came to tell me we were coming in to ——. The young sailor had already gone to his station. Thoughtful always, the mate wrote out a telegram to send to my home, which should reassure my people before ever they read the morning's news. (But War is War, and that telegram, so censored that it appeared to come from me in France, did not reach my home till late that evening!)

I was carried by sailors out onto the deck and placed on a stretcher, and then a RAMC surgeon with orderlies took charge of me and carried me aboard the hospital ship, a sister boat to the *Sussex*, where, with one other Italian woman, whose legs were broken and her skull fractured, and eleven men, I was put to bed in an empty ward. Several surgeons, the matron, and three military nursing sisters attended to us, and by 6 a.m. we had had our wounds and hurts dressed and been made as comfortable as our condition would allow. The dying woman and a dying man had been taken almost at once to the little civil hospital in the town, where they died later.

The tenderness and goodness of those Army Sisters was wonderful. I have worked for a year in a hospital and I have learned to know nurses for human beings cheerful, hard-working, conscientious, unselfish to the last degree where their patients are concerned; but here I actually fell in with that ideal of an Army Nurse which many a chivalrous man has built up in his mind round stories of Florence Nightingale and imaginations of his own. I really met her; I was not dreaming. I was in very great pain, and suffering physically more than I have ever suffered in my life, but my memory of those long hours between dark and daylight is one not of personal misery, but of the beautiful tenderness of those Nursing Sisters. This may bring comfort to many whose menfolk travel homewards in hospital ships.

At midday we were moved – the men to a Military Hospital, and I to the small overworked civil hospital. Followed days and nights of great pain and misery, till on the fourth day I was fetched away in a motor ambulance and brought to one of London's great hospitals in an ambulance train. Here again I met a kind Nursing Sister, and was touched deeply by the gentleness of the RAMC orderlies, as I had been on the hospital ship. I had felt so alone since the sailors and my good Belgian succourer had come to say good-bye to me on the Saturday morning, and later the surgeons of the destroyer and the hospital ship, and those kind Nursing Sisters so that it felt like being back among 'ours' again, when the Ambulance Train Sister and her military orderlies took charge of me. At the station I was unloaded by men of the City of London Transport Column Volunteer Red Cross, men from the city, and placed in an ambulance whose owner-driver had been doing this work since the war began. It was a long, long drive, and never have I been in an ambulance more carefully driven. A good Red Cross lady accompanied me and took charge of my bundles and my coat, and did not lose sight of me till I was in charge of the nurses at the —— Hospital, where I am now. There is little more to tell. I was overhauled that same afternoon by a surgeon, and radio-graphed and hurt though I was, I was already professional enough to take a keen interest in the beautiful apparatus in the X-ray room, but amateur enough to realise with a thrill of pride that our radiographs, though our installation is small and comparatively cheap, are as good as any I saw on the show frames that day. One up for the old Hospital in France! The Huns had smashed my foot, broken one of the lumbar processes of my spine, strained back and thigh muscles, and bruised me internally. Worse they had placed me *hors de combat* for nearly three months!

William Fraser
Armistice – The Last Eleven Days

*Written while he was in command of 1st Gordon Highlanders,
Fraser's diary entries and a letter to his father describe the last
days of the fighting on the Western Front, where his battalion
was part of 3rd Division's advance towards the Hindenburg
Line.*

October 31st 1918 – Carnières

We moved off soon after 11 a.m. marching as a battalion. Traffic
was not too bad on the road and we got to Carnières by 2 p.m.
This is a good village – it has not been knocked about and there
are no civilians in it at all. So the men are all in houses, and very
comfortable. A fortnight here would do us a lot of good.

We got a draft of 200 this afternoon, mostly 7th battalion
men, but the physique by no means as good as the last one we
had. The battalion is now very considerably over-strength.

November 1st 1918 – Carnières

Started training and two companies had baths. In the afternoon
I rode over to Corps HQ to see the AB and find out how long
we were to be out of the line. The AB was out, but I found out
the other thing and I find our promised fortnight is not likely to
materialise and that we move forward again the day after
tomorrow. Which is sad.

The news is good, though – Austria really appears to be right
out of it, and the Armistice terms with Turkey seem to be satis-

factory enough. Our terms to Germany are nothing short of unconditional surrender – so rumour has it – and it's not likely that she will accept that at present, so I suppose we may look forward to another winter's campaign.

November 6th 1918 – Letter home

Dear Father,
Many thanks for your letter. I should have answered it earlier, but sudden moves have been the order of the day lately, and one never knows where one will be in 24 hours.

We are in reserve at the moment, but not for very much longer I should think. The battle seems to be going not too badly, but we think the Boche has got a strong position on the Mons-Maubeuge line and that we shall have a stiff battle there. The general impression seems to be that we shall go on fighting until the Boche sends over a white flag and asks for an armistice. So it may go on for some months yet. But I really think the time can be measured in months, and not in years now. He has got quite a lot to pay for, the old Boche, hasn't he? The people in the occupied territories of France wouldn't have much mercy on him if they had their way. It would be a good scheme to collect a few of them to go over and speak at some of these labour meetings where they sing the Red Flag and advocate letting the Boche down lightly. In this village they have got hold of an old story which they think is new and delight hugely in: 'In the beginning God made man. The devil being jealous decided to make one too, and he made a German. He saw there was something wrong. "Lor," says he, after scratching his head for a minute, "I've gone and made him with two stomachs and no heart."'

The weather is perfectly awful, and of course rain is the last thing we want just now. However it will take more than rain to stop us hammering at the Boche just now. Only it makes things slower. I don't think anyone is for a return to trench warfare if it can be avoided. And the only way to avoid it is to beat him now.

Au revoir and love to Mother.
Your affectionate son,
Willie

November 8th 1918 – Gommegnies

Orders had come yesterday to move forward and we marched off at 10 a.m. A wet morning and much mud on the roads, also a vast number of motor lorries and cars. So the march was not altogether a pleasant one. Our destination was to be Fasnoy but there was no room when we got there so we came on to Gommegnies. We are in quite good billets here but as things stand at present we have got to move out at 9 a.m. tomorrow to make room for Corps HQ, which is coming in here. I saw Uncle Harper on the way – he was in very good form and looking very well.

The news today – the Americans are at Sedan and the French at Mezières, and the Boche plenipotentiaries are being interviewed today by Foch at Paris with a view to an armistice. A mutiny in the Boche fleet is also reported. It looks as if the end were very near. Pray God it is.

November 9th 1918 – Le Grand Sart

Marched here early in the morning, as we had to turn out of the other place to make room for Corps HQ. Got in about 10.30 a.m. The billets are much better than the other place; bn HQ* the best I've ever had. Did a little training and got billets cleaned up, also found a party for work on road-mending.

The population were enthusiastic in their reception – it was like the early days of the war back again. After the pipes had

* battalion headquarters

played 'Retreat' in the evening there was great clapping of hands and cries of 'Vive l'Angleterre'. When will these people learn to distinguish between England and Scotland! Went for a ride in the Forêt de Mormal in the afternoon, only the Boche has cut down most of it. But some still stands and I found one beautiful bit, all green and gold. It was a glorious autumn day.

Dined with Uncle Harper at Le Quesnoy – he sent a car for me.

News came while we were at dinner that the Kaiser had abdicated and the Crown Prince had renounced his claim to the throne, but it's hardly official yet. The armistice is to be signed by 11.00 a.m. on Monday if at all and everyone said that the Boche was certain to sign it. We played bridge after dinner.

Had expected to be here two or three days but orders came in this evening to move early tomorrow to Longueville. Thought these billets were too good to be true.

The Boche has apparently gone off and the 3rd Div. is to be the advanced guard for the 3rd Army, and the 76th Bde for the 3rd Division. So we may have some long treks ahead of us – if the Boche does not sign the Armistice.

November 10th 1918 – La Longueville*

Left soon after 9 a.m. The mud on the roads was simply awful, and a lot of lorries into the bargain made the march rather an unpleasant one. We got in about 2 p.m. Lots of rumours to effect that revolution has broken out in Germany, especially in Berlin, and that Bavaria has declared itself a republic.

A hitch occurred about the armistice, because when the Boche plenipotentiaries came over under the white flag, the French thought it would be a good opportunity to do a raid, and

---

* About ten miles south of Mons, where the British first met the Germans in 1914; it is here Willie's war ended.

they did and scuppered 350 Huns. Result – when the emissaries tried to return they were fired on from the Boche lines and could not go. Eventually they had to be sent over by aeroplane.

We leave here tomorrow very early and march up to the front. If it's peace, we shan't have much to do; if it's war, we do the advance guard stunt. It's odd sitting here and wondering, 'Is this the last day of the war, or not?' One can still hear guns going. I don't know that one is very excited about it, it's in the day's work either way – but it will be a disappointment if we find the war has got to go on. One expects it to end. Early rise tomorrow and I'm tired.

November 11th 1918 – La Longueville

I suppose this has been a memorable day in the history of the world – though we took it very quietly on the whole. Just as we were about to move off to go and fight the Boche, I got a message from Furnell through Cabane that our move was cancelled, as the armistice would be signed at 11 a.m. So we stood by and I sent down to get official confirmation of the order – which arrived about 8.30 a.m. So the war is ended – rumour has it that the Boche has accepted all our conditions, and ends by begging us to do what we can to feed his starving people.

How does one feel about it all – not very excited certainly; I don't think we realise it at present. It makes no immediate change for us, demobilisation will take months, and we shall probably stand around making roads, etc. Only the danger of life is missing and the excitement, and the 'great end' for which one has been keyed up all these years.

Because the end has come. It's all very strange, but I don't think one could begin again, or go back to yesterday. It's a very difficult time coming in many ways; – the men, or many of them, will be difficult to hold now – the purpose which has held them together is gone, discipline as a power in itself is not a very strong one in our army. But they are good fellows with plenty of common-sense; in that fact and in keeping them occupied the solution lies.

To get back to the events of this day of days – as soon as the news was confirmed the pipes and drums paraded and played national and regimental tunes all round the town, followed by a great concourse of good east country faces in balmorals.

I went down to Brigade HQ, but they had no more news there. They had got theirs from a fellow on the Corps Staff, who was touring the country as fast as his car would go, in pyjamas and an overcoat. We waited about until 11.15, when an official wire came to the effect that hostilities had ceased at 11 a.m. So at 12 noon we had a battalion parade and told the men, adding a few sage words about patience as regards demobilisation. After which the battalion stood at the 'slope' while the Pipes and Drums played the regimental march. Then the companies marched off to the pipes.

After lunch we had a church parade, or rather a voluntary service – but nearly all the men were there. The band played in the square during the afternoon.

No news came in beyond what we had already had, and no information about our immediate movements – we shall be here for a day or two, I should think. All the officers of the battalion dined together in the evening, thirty-four in all, and danced reels after dinner. But they are bad at that. And the doctor recited 'Tam-o'-Shanter', which is almost a 'rite' in the battalion now, and a right good job he made of it. Then Pearson played the 'La Marseillaise' on the piano and Cabane sang it, accompanied by the people of the house – and then to bed at midnight.

And so ended the last day of the great war. One has been feeling one's way through the dark for 4½ years, and now one has come out into the sunlight – and behold!! one is blind, one cannot see the sun. But the blindness will pass in time. But we shall be exiles for a few months yet, I'm afraid.

November 12th 1918 – La Longueville

Most glorious weather – bright days and hard frost. No news of our future moves, no newspapers, as the mail has ceased to arrive with any regularity whatever, and practically the whole battalion on work cleaning up roads. Peace, perfect peace.

Willie's diary continued into 1919, giving a daily account of the great march into Germany of the Allies, including a British army of eleven divisions. The diary records speculations about the phenomenon of Bolshevism, which seemed to threaten not only Germany but all Europe; about how rapidly demobilisation would start: about his own personal future. But it records no doubt about the nature of the triumph he felt.

―――――――――

November 24th 1918 – Lobbes

Well, today I suppose the march to Germany may be said to have begun. Eleven British divisions are going – and surely it is the greatest march in history. The tramp of our marching feet will sound down the ages as the symbol of the progress of the liberty of the World. Was ever a time like this? And we don't realise it, and we must. We have let those materialists pollute us who are so fond of telling us that our country came into the war to save it's own skin – but it's a lie. Politicians may have come into it for that reason, the country came into it to fight for the liberty of the World and *no other reason*. And this march marks the ultimate triumph of our cause

Lewis Grassic Gibbon
Shot at Dawn

In the novel Sunset Song, *Ewan Tavendale enlists in the army and returns to Blawearie a changed man. During his leave, he abuses his wife Chris and goes off to France without resolving the quarrel between them. The memory of his brutal behaviour leads Ewan to desert and encourages Chris to have sex with Long Rob Duncan, a pacifist. Like many such offenders, Ewan is sentenced to death by firing squad, but in the last conversation with his friend, Chae Strachan, his action is seen as a final heroic attempt to return to the old values of the land.*

It had burned up as a fire in a whin-bush, that thing in her life, and it burned out again and was finished. She went about the Blawearie biggings next day singing under breath to herself, quiet and unvexed, tending to hens and kye, seeing to young Ewan's sleep in the day and the setting of old Brigson's supper ere he came at night. She felt shamed not at all, all the vexing fears had gone from her, she made no try to turn from the eyes in the glass that looked out at her, wakened and living again. She was glad she'd gone out with Long Rob, glad and content, they were one and the same now, Ewan and her.

So the telegram boy that came riding to Blawearie found her singing there in the close, mending young Ewan's clothes. She heard the click of the gate and he took the telegram out of his wallet and gave it to her and she stared at him and then at her hands. They were quivering like the leaves of the beech in the forecoming of rain, they quivered in a little mist below her eyes. Then she opened the envelope and read the words and she said

there was no reply, the boy swung on his bicycle again and rode
out, riding and leaning he clicked the gate behind him; and
laughed back at her for the cleverness of that.

She stood up then, she put down her work on the hackstock
and read again the telegram, and began to speak to herself till
that frightened her and she stopped. But she forgot to be
frightened, in a minute she was speaking again, the chirawking
hens in the close stopped and came near and turned up bright
eyes to her loud and toneless whispering, *What do I do – oh,
what do I do?*

She was vexed and startled by that – what was it she did!
Did she go out to France and up to the front line, maybe, into a
room where they'd show her Ewan lying dead, quiet and dead,
white and bloodless, sweat on his hair, killed in action? She went
out to the front door and waved to the harvesters, Brigson,
young Ewan, and a tink they'd hired, they saw her and stared
till she waved again and then John Brigson abandoned the half-
loaded cart and came waddling up the park, so slow he was, *Did
you cry me, Chris?*

Sweat on his hair as sweat on Ewan's. She stared at that and
held out the telegram, he wiped slow hands and took it and read
it, while she clung to the door post and whispered and whispered
What is it I do now, John? Have I to go out to France? And at
last he looked up, his face was grizzled and hot and old, he wiped
the sweat from it slow. *God, mistress, this is sore news, but he's
died like a man out there, your Ewan's died fine.*

But she wouldn't listen to that, wanting to know the thing
she must do; and not till he told her that she did nothing, they
could never take all the widows to France and Ewan must
already be buried, did she stop from that twisting of her hands
and ceaseless whisper. Then anger came, *Why didn't you tell me
before? Oh, damn you, you liked tormenting me!* and she turned
from him into the house and ran up the stairs to the bed, the bed
that was hers and Ewan's, and lay on it, and put her hands over

her ears trying not to hear a cry of agony in a lost French field, not to think that the body that had lain by hers, frank and free and kind and young, was torn and dead and unmoving flesh, blood twisted upon it, not Ewan at all, riven and terrible, still and dead when the harvest stood out in Blawearie's land and the snipe were calling up on the loch and the beech trees whispered and rustled. And *SHE KNEW THAT IT WAS A LIE!*

He wasn't dead, he could never have died or been killed for nothing at all, far away from her over the sea, what matter to him their War and their fighting, their King and their country? Kinraddie was his land, Blawearie his, he was never dead for those things of no concern, he'd the crops to put in and the loch to drain and her to come back to. It had nothing to do with Ewan this telegram. They were only tormenting her, cowards and liars and bloody men, the English generals and their like down there in London. But she wouldn't bear it, she'd have the law on them, cowards and liars as she knew them to be!

It was only then that she knew she was moaning, dreadful to hear; and they heard it outside, John Brigson heard it and nearly went daft, he caught up young Ewan and ran with him into the kitchen and then to the foot of the stairs; and told him to go up to his mother, she wanted him. And young Ewan came, it was his hand tugging at her skirts that brought her out of that moaning coma, and he wasn't crying, fearsome the sounds though she made, his face was white and resolute, *Mother, mother!* She picked him up then and held him close, rocking in an agony of despair because of that look on his face, that lost look and the smouldering eyes he had. *Oh Ewan, your father's dead!* she told him the lie that the world believed. And she wept at last, blindly, freeingly, for a little, old Brigson was to say it was the boy that had saved her from going mad.

But throughout Kinraddie the news went underbreath that mad she'd gone, the death of her man had fair unhinged her. For still she swore it was a lie, that Ewan wasn't dead, he could never have died for nothing. Kirsty Strachan and Mistress Munro came up to see her, they shook their heads and said he'd died fine, for his country and his King he'd died, young Ewan would grow up to be proud of his father. They said that sitting at tea, with long faces on them, and then Chris laughed, they quivered away from her at that laugh.

Country and King? You're havering, havering! What have they to do with my Ewan, what was the King to him, what their damned country? Blawearie's his land it's not his wight that others fight wars!

She went fair daft with rage then, seeing the pity in their faces. And also it was then, and then only, staring through an angry haze at them, that she knew at last she was living a dream in a world gone mad. Ewan was dead, they knew it and she knew it herself; and he'd died for nothing, for nothing, hurt and murdered and crying for her, maybe, killed for nothing: and those bitches sat and spoke of their King and country . . .

They ran out of the house and down the brae, and, panting, she stood and screamed after them. It was fair the speak of Kinraddie next day the way she'd behaved, and nobody else came up to see her. But she'd finished with screaming, she went quiet and cold. Mornings came up, and she saw them come, she minded that morning she'd sent him away, and she might not cry him back. Noons with their sun and rain came over the Howe and she saw the cruelty and pain of life as crimson rainbows that spanned the horizons of the wheeling hours. Nights came soft and grey and quiet across Kinraddie's fields, they brought neither terror nor hope to her now. Behind the walls of a sanity cold and high, locked in from the lie of life, she would live, from the world that had murdered her man for nothing, for a madman's gibberish heard in the night behind the hills.

And then Chae Strachan came home at last on leave, he came home and came swift to Blawearie. She met him out by the kitchen door, a sergeant by then, grown thinner and taller, and he stopped and looked in her frozen face. Then, as her hand dropped down from his, he went past her with swinging kilts, into the kitchen, and sat him down and took off his bonnet. *Chris, I've come to tell you of Ewan.*

She stared at him, waking, a hope like a fluttering bird in her breast. *Ewan? Chae – Chae's he's not living?* And then, as he shook his head, the frozen wall came down on her heart again. *Ewan's dead, don't vex yourself hoping else. They can't hurt him more, even this can't hurt him, though I swore I'd tell you nothing about it. But I know right well you should know it, Chris. Ewan was shot as a coward and deserter out there in France.*

Chae had lain in a camp near by and had heard of the thing by chance, he'd read Ewan's name in some list of papers that was posted up. And he'd gone the night before Ewan was shot, and they'd let him see Ewan, and he'd heard it all, the story he was telling her now – *better always to know what truth's in a thing, for lies come creeping home to roost on unco rees, Chris quean. You're young yet, you've hardly begun to live, and I swore to myself that I'd tell you it all, that you'd never be vexed with some twisted bit in the years to come. Ewan was shot as a deserter, it was fair enough, he'd deserted from the front line trenches.*

He had deserted in a blink of fine weather between the rains that splashed the glutted rat-runs of the front. He had done it quickly and easily, he told to Chae, he had just turned and walked back. And other soldiers that met him had thought him a messenger, or wounded, or maybe on leave, none had questioned him, he'd set out at ten o'clock in the morning and by afternoon, taking to the fields, was ten miles or more from the front. Then the military policemen came on him and took him, he was marched back and court-martialled and found to be guilty.

And Chae said to him, they sat together in the hut where he

waited the coming of the morning, *But why did you do it, Ewan?*
You might well have known you'd never get free. And Ewan
looked at him and shook his head, *It was that wind that came*
with the sun, I minded Blawearie, I seemed to waken up smelling
that smell. And I couldn't believe it was me that stood in the
trench, it was just daft to be there. So I turned and got out of it.

In a flash it had come on him, he had wakened up, he was
daft and a fool to be there; and, like somebody minding things
done in a coarse wild dream there had flashed on him memory
of Chris at Blawearie and his last days there, mad and mad he
had been, he had treated her as a devil might, he had tried to
hurt her and maul her, trying in the nightmare to waken, to make
her waken him up; and now in the blink of sun he saw her face
as last he'd seen it while she quivered away from his taunts. He
knew he had lost her, she'd never be his again, he'd known it in
that moment he clambered back from the trenches; but he knew
that he'd be a coward if he didn't try though all hope was past.

So out he had gone for that, remembering Chris, wanting to
reach her, knowing as he tramped mile on mile that he never
would. But he'd made her that promise that he'd never fail her,
long syne he had made it that night when he'd held her so bonny
and sweet and a quean in his arms, young and desirous and kind.
So mile on mile on the laired French roads: she was lost to him,
but that didn't help, he'd try to win to her side again, to see her
again, to tell her nothing he'd said was his saying, it was the
foulness dripping from the dream that devoured him. And young
Ewan came into his thoughts, he'd so much to tell her of him, so
much he'd to say and do if only he might win to Blawearie . . .

Then the military policemen had taken him and he'd listened
to them and others in the days that followed, listening and not
listening at all, wearied and quiet. *Oh, wearied and wakened at*
last, Chae, and I haven't cared, they can take me out fine and
shoot me tomorrow, I'll be glad for the rest of it, Chris lost to
me through my own coarse daftness. She didn't even come to

give me a kiss at good-bye, Chae, we never said good-bye; but I mind the bonny head of her down-bent there in the close. She'll never know, my dear quean, and that's best – they tell lies about folk they shoot and she'll think I just died like the rest; you're not to tell her.

Then he'd been silent long, and Chae'd had nothing to say, he knew it was useless to make try for reprieve, he was only a sergeant and had no business even in the hut with the prisoner. And then Ewan said, sudden-like, it clean took Chae by surprise, *Mind the smell of dung in the parks on an April morning, Chae? And the peewits over the rigs? Bonny they're flying this night in Kinraddie, and Chris sleeping there, and all the Howe happed in mist.* Chae said that he mustn't mind about that, he was feared that the dawn was close, and Ewan should be thinking of other things now, had he seen a minister? And Ewan said that an old bit billy had come and blethered, an officer creature, but he'd paid no heed, it had nothing to do with him. Even as he spoke there rose a great clamour of guns far up in the front, it was four miles off, not more; and Chae thought of the hurried watches climbing to their posts and the blash and flare of the Verey lights, the machine-gun crackle from pits in the mud, things he himself mightn't hear for long: Ewan'd never hear it at all beyond this night.

And not feared at all he looked, Chae saw, he sat there in his kilt and shirt-sleeves, and he looked no more than a young lad still, his head between his hands, he didn't seem to be thinking at all of the morning so close. For he started to speak of Blawearie then and the parks that he would have drained, though he thought the land would go fair to hell without the woods to shelter it. And Chae said that he thought the same, there were sore changes waiting them when they went back; and then he minded that Ewan would never go back, and could near have bitten his tongue in half, but Ewan hadn't noticed, he'd been speaking of the horses he'd had, Clyde and old Bess, fine beasts, fine beasts – did Chae mind that night of lightning when they found Chris wandering the fields with those two horses? That was the night he had known she liked him well – *nothing more than that, so quick and fierce she was, Chae man, she guarded herself like a queen in a palace, there was nothing between her and me till the night we married. Mind that – and the singing there was, Chae? What was it that Chris sang then?*

And neither could remember that, it had vexed Ewan a while, and then he forgot it, sitting quiet in that hut on the edge of morning. Then at last he'd stood up and gone to the window and said *There's bare a quarter of an hour now, Chae, you'll need to be getting back.*

And they'd shaken hands, the sentry opened the door for Chae, and he tried to say all he could for comfort, the foreshadowing of the morning in Ewan's young eyes was strange and terrible, he couldn't take out his hand from that grip. And all that Ewan said was *Oh man, mind me when next you hear the peewits over Blawearie – look at my lass for me when you see her again, close and close, for that kiss that I'll never give her.* So he'd turned back into the hut, he wasn't feared or crying, he went quiet and calm; and Chae went down through the hut lines grouped about that place, a farm-place it had been, he'd got to the lorry that waited him, he was cursing and weeping then and the driver thought him daft, he hadn't known himself how he'd been. So they'd driven off, the wet morning had come crawling across the laired fields, and Chae had never seen Ewan again, they killed him that morning.

This was the story Chae told to Chris, sitting the two of them in the kitchen of Blawearie. Then he moved and got up and she did the same, and like one coming from a far, dark country, she saw his face now, he'd been all that time but a voice in the dark. And at last she found speech herself *Never vex for me or the telling me this, it was best, it was best!*

She crept up the stairs to their room when he'd gone, she
opened the press where Ewan's clothes were, and kissed them
and held them close, those clothes that had once been his near
as ever he'd come to her now. And she whispered then in the
stillness, with only the beech for a listener, *Oh, Ewan, Ewan,
sleep quiet and sound now, lad, I understand! You did it for me,
and I'm proud and proud, for me and Blawearie, my dear, my
dear – sleep quiet and brave, for I've understood!*

The beech listened and whispered, whispered and listened,
on and on. And a strange impulse and urge came on Chris
Tavendale as she too listened. She ran down the stairs and found
young Ewan and kissed him, *Let's go a jaunt up to the hill.*

Below them, Kinraddie; above, the hill; the loch shimmering
and sleeping in the autumn sun; young Ewan at her feet; the
peewits crying down the Howe.

She gave a long sigh and withdrew her hand from the face
of the Standing Stone. The mist of memories fell away and the
aching urge came back – for what, for what? Sun and sky and
the loneliness of the hills, they had cried her up here – for what?

And then something made her raise her eyes, she stood awful
and rigid, fronting him, coming up the path through the broom.
Laired with glaur was his uniform, his face was white and the
great hole sagged and opened, sagged and opened, red-glazed
and black, at every upwards step he took. Up through the
broom: she saw the grass wave with no press below his feet, her
lad, the light in his eyes that aye she could bring.

The snipe stilled their calling, a cloud came over the sun. He
was close to her now and she held out her hands to him, blind
with tears and bright her eyes, the bright weather in their faces,
her voice shaping a question that she heard him answer in the
rustle of the loch-side rushes as closer his soundless feet carried
him to her lips and hands.

Oh lassie, I've come home! he said, and went into the heart
that was his forever.

Douglas Haig
The Battle of the Somme

The Battle of the Somme, which began on 1 July 1916 and continued over 140 days until the middle of November, was to be remembered not for the expected breakthrough but as the killing ground of the British Army. No other battlefield of the First World War created more casualties per square yard and the opening hours of the battle produced the bloodiest day for the infantry battalions that took part in the initial attack. From the eleven divisions that began the assault, 57,470 men became casualties – 21,392 killed or missing, 35,493 wounded and 585 taken prisoner. In his diary, Haig produced a dispassionate description of the first day of the fighting, but a later entry, written almost a year later, shows his abiding concern for the troops and looks forward to the part he played in founding the Royal British Legion and the Royal British Legion Scotland after the war.

---

1 July 1916

Glass rose slightly during the night. A fine sunny morning with gentle breeze from the west and southwest. At first some mist in the hollows. This very favourable because it concealed the concentration of our troops. The bombardment was carried out as usual, and there was no increase of artillery fire but at 7.30 a.m. (the hour fixed for the infantry to advance) the artillery increased their range and the infantry followed the barrage.

Reports up to 8 a.m. most satisfactory. Our troops had everywhere crossed the Enemy's front trenches.

By 9 a.m. I heard that our troops had in many places reached the 1.20 line (i.e. the line to be breached 1 hour and 20 minutes after the start).

They were held up (29th Division) just south of Hawthorn Ridge but 31st [Division] was moving into Serre village. This was afterwards proved to be incorrect.

The Gommecourt attack was also progressing well. 46th Division by 8 a.m. were in Enemy's third line trench. But eventually right brigade of 46th Division did not press on.

By 9 a.m. it was reported that our troops were held up north of Authuille Wood but on their left were entering Thiepval village. This did not prove to be the case.

St Sauveur station in Lille, which is said to be an important ammunition store, was bombed by us early today. Our machines returned safely, though attacked by 20 Fokkers, 2 of these were destroyed and 2 damaged as the result of the fight.

I wired Admiral Bacon [Sir Reginald, Commander of the Dover Patrol] last night suggesting that he should demonstrate at Ostend coast. By 10 a.m. a young naval officer was at my HQ with the Admiral's proposals for my concurrence. I arranged for French also to co-operate in attacking the Tirpitz Battery from near Nieuport.

Hard fighting continued all day on front of Fourth Army. On a 16-mile front of attack varying fortune must be expected! It is difficult to summarise all that was reported.

After lunch I motored to Querrieu and saw Sir H[enry] Rawlinson. We hold the Mantaubon-Mametz spur and villages of those names. The Enemy are still in Fricourt, but we are round his flank on the north and close to Contalmaison. Ovillers and Thiepval villages have held our troops up, but our men are in the Schwaben redoubt which crowns the ridge of the last-named village. The Enemy counter-attacked here but were driven back. He however got a position with a few men in the river valley.

North of the Ancre, the VIII Division [properly VIII Corps]

(Hunter-Weston) said they began well, but as the day progressed their troops were forced back into the German front line, except 2 battalions which occupied Serre village and were, it is said, cut off. I am inclined to believe from further reports that few of the VIII Corps left their trenches!

The attack on Gommecourt salient started well, especially the 56th Division under General Hull [Major-General Amyat Hull]. The 46th Division (Stuart-Wortley) attacked from the north side but was soon held up. This attack was of the very greatest assistance in helping VIII Corps, because so many of the Enemy's guns and troops were directed on it, and so left the VIII Corps considerably free. In spite of this the VIII Corps achieved very little.

After seeing Sir H. Rawlinson I motored to Villers Bocage (on Amiens-Doullens road) and called at HQ II Corps in Reserve. I left orders for Divisions 38th and 23rd in GHQ Reserve to march in 2 hours (7 p.m.) and close up nearer to the front, as the Fourth Army was getting through is reserves.

Sir William Robertson CIGS [Chief of the Imperial General Staff] arrived from England.

At 7 p.m. as the result of my talk, Sir H. Rawlinson telephones that he is putting the VIII and X Corps under [General Sir Hubert] Gough at 7 a.m. tomorrow. The VIII Corps seems to want looking after!

31 March 1917

No one can visit the Somme battlefield without being impressed with the magnitude of the British Army. For five long months this battle continued. Not one battle, but a series of great battles, were methodically waged by numerous divisions in succession, so that credit for pluck and resolution has been earned by men from every part of the Empire. And credit must be paid too, not only to the private soldier in the ranks, but also to those splendid young officers who commanded platoons, companies and battalions. Although new to this terrible 'game of war' they were able, time and time again, to form up their commands in the darkness of night, and in spite of shell-holes, wire and other obstacles, led them forward in the grey of morning to the attack of these tremendous positions. To many it meant certain death, and all must have known that before they started. Surely it was the knowledge of the great stake at issue, the existence of England as a free nation, that nerved them for such heroic deeds. I have not the time to put down all the thoughts which rush into my mind when I think of these fine fellows, who either have given their lives for their country, or have been maimed in its service. Later on I hope we may have a Prime Minister and a Government who will do them justice.

Cicely Hamilton
Somewhere in France

The Scottish Women's Hospital was the inspired idea of a remarkable woman, Dr Elsie Inglis, who with good reason has been called one of the most inspirational women of her generation. A week after the outbreak of hostilities, she put forward a proposal to the War Office for the establishment of a field hospital consisting of a hundred beds run by women doctors and staffed by trained nurses. The response from the military was not encouraging. In a retort that was to become infamous and widely quoted by the women who worked for the Scottish Women's Hospitals, Elsie Inglis was told 'Go home and sit still.'

Not to be outdone, she then approached the French and Serbian governments, who both accepted the offer in October. It had been one thing to float the idea, but now that it was reality money had to be raised to get the idea off the ground. However, by October the first £1,000 had been raised and plans were put in place to send the first hospital unit to Serbia, where Austrian forces had been repulsed in their attempt to take Belgrade. More money followed and by the end of the year £449,000 had been raised to provide another unit for service in France, where the French Red Cross had provided accommodation at the Cistercian Abbey of Royaumont. Founded by King Louis IX in 1229, this impressive building lay to the north of Paris; but despite its physical beauty and the unspoiled countryside, one of the first members of the hospital later remembered the abbey building as being 'picturesque, impressive and most abominably chilly'.

The Scottish Women's Hospital served in France throughout the war and did not close its doors until the spring of 1919.

*Throughout that period it came under French direction, firstly
under the French Red Cross and latterly under the French Army,
and 23 members of the staff were decorated with the Croix de
Guerre. All told, 10,861 patients were treated in the hospital,
the majority of them wounded soldiers and, being so close to the
battle lines of the Western Front, the medical staff were left in
little doubt about the grim nature of the wounds inflicted in
modern warfare, especially during the Somme and Verdun
battles. Amongst those working there was Cicely Hamilton.*

The building in which our Scottish Women's Hospital ensconced
itself was situated on the edge of the Forest of Chantilly – to the
north of Paris, and some thirty miles or so behind the trenches.
Its foundation, as a Cistercian monastery, dated back to St Louis,
and part of the early building was still in existence; but its abbey
church of the thirteenth century had been laid in ruins by the
zealots of the Revolution. In September '14 the tide of German
invasion had just reached and entered it, but swept back, leaving
it unscathed on the day of the retreat from the Marne. The
building had been offered by its owner to the French Red Cross;
the offer was passed on by the French Red Cross to the
committee of the Scottish Women's Hospitals; and by the
beginning of December 1914 the first contingent was settling
down in its quarters.

The last tenants of the building had been nuns – the
monastery having been transformed into a convent – but with
the passing of the Combes law the nuns had cast the dust of
France from their feet and removed across the border into
Belgium. From that time on, for some eight or nine years, the
Royaumont convent stood derelict, and the task of converting it
into a modern military hospital was neither swift nor easy. The
building was spacious and likewise picturesque, but there its
immediate advantages ceased; water was lacking, and light was

lacking – in all the majestic edifice there was only one stove that could be induced to light, and that under protest, and only one tap that gave results. In my first few days there I learned how easy it is to sink into habits of uncleanliness. The weather was icy, with snow on the ground, and the only facilities for washing were tap and sink situated in a vaulted chamber which had stood unwarmed for the better part of ten years. In these circumstances I confined my washing to hands and face, and washed them as seldom as possible; nor were these uncleanly habits peculiar to myself – no one, I think, was courageous enough to remove their garments in that groined and vaulted gloom for the purpose of scrubbing in an icy flow from the tap. With regard to cleanliness, as well as warmth, the situation in the first few days seemed desperate; all the local plumbers and stove-repairers and glaziers were of military age, and had been swept off into the army. Then things took a turn for the better; a plumber, discharged from his regiment on medical grounds, came back to our neighbourhood, and was welcomed as a treasure should be; and with time and patience we unearthed a glazier to patch up our broken windows. Stoves came pottering out from Paris, and stores came trickling through from England, electric light was installed, water laid on in abundance – and the derelict convent was a hospital.

Our plumber, I think, would allow me to call him a friend; at any rate, when he and I and his wife forgathered at his house, a year or two ago, it was an occasion for rejoicing and the drinking of a *petit verre*. I almost hesitate to write him down a plumber, he was in every way so opposed to our English idea of the trade. Slight, sensitive-looking, intelligent-looking, discharged from the army because *poitrinaire*; well-read and well-spoken, with a Frenchman's sense of the word. I had many conversations with him besides those relating to his professional duties. Once, I remember, he came into my office with the tears not far from his eyes; it was in '17 when the German army retreated unexpectedly from the line of the Somme, and retreating, we were told, had destroyed the orchards in its wake. It was this destruction of fruit trees that had stirred the man's French soul. 'They are ruining our land; it is as if they had wounded our mother. '

I have never forgotten the phrase, and I sat and thought of it long after he had left me, to deal with a refractory sink. It marked for me one of the essential differences between the French and English habit of mind; not only because no Englishman could have used such a phrase, but because the man who used it, like his neighbours in general, had little under-standing of the pleasures we sum up in our phrase 'the country'. The woods – there were leagues on leagues of them around – did not call him as they called to me; he would never have tramped them alone for pleasure, and he thought it rather fine of us that we were content to pass the winter in a hospital building that was situated well away from the village and miles from any town. Yet the tears were in his eyes when he heard of fruit trees destroyed . . . I take it that the Frenchman's love is for the land, not the country; for the soil that is fruitful, the soil that man has tended and subdued. Love of the country, such as can be found in many of us, is at the same time less civilized and more disin-terested; it has nothing to do with the benefits the soil bestows. The difference of outlook shows even in gardens; the Frenchman loves to train his trees, to tidy them and civilize. To be friendly with a Nature that is unsubdued, you must, I think, have something of the North in your blood; and to have tears in your eyes when you hear of the ruin of other men's orchards it may be you must come of French peasant ancestry.

I worked at Royaumont for something like two years and a half, from the winter of '14 to the spring of '17. I kept the accounts of the hospital, wrote most of its letters, French and English; at the outset I was kept fairly busy as interpreter, for though my French was nothing to boast of, it was considerably better than that of most of my associates. Then there were the odd jobs; now and then the getting up of hospital entertainments and, all too often, attendance at funerals. That was a duty that fell to me because, in a time of stress, when the hospital was full, I could be better spared from my office than doctors or nurses from their wards; but it was a duty that I never got hardened to. Travel in those days was difficult and slow, and it was only in the minority of cases that relations would arrive for a funeral; but when they did arrive, I often had to receive them. And that also was a duty I dreaded.

Oddly enough, the side of my work in which I took real interest and pleasure was work entirely new to me, the keeping of the hospital books; I believe my happiest days at Royaumont were those on which I drew up my monthly statement and analysis for the auditor. Once I had grasped the common sense of my figures and begun to think of them not as rows of francs and centimes, but as symbols for food, fuel, medical necessities, furniture – once I had begun to do that, they were a fascinating game. Our auditor was the representative of an English firm which had a branch in Paris, and, as a contribution to war-work, kept an eye on the accounts of some of the voluntary hospitals in France; and I suppose I must have shown a certain aptitude for my figure-game, because when he found I was interested in his explanations and directions he told me that if I could make a stay in Paris, and come in regularly to his office, he would see that I had some real instruction in book-keeping. Nothing came of the offer, since I was not a free agent; and I don't know that in any case I should have considered it wise to start another interest in life; but all the same, the periodical overhaul of my books was one of the bright spots in my life at the Scottish Women's Hospital. To begin with, it involved a visit to Paris, to the Ritz, where my auditor, I think, was chief accountant; and where he always provided me with an excellent tea what time he examined my books. Better still, when accounts were done with, he would tell me the latest Paris war-gossip; and once, I

remember, my visit to the Ritz was a day or so after the arrival
of Gerard, the former American Ambassador to Germany. With
the ex-ambassador came his staff and household – the latter
including (oddly enough) a French maid and an English
chauffeur, who both (thanks to diplomatic immunity) had lived
in Berlin for more than two years, while their countries were at
war with Germany. These two, maid and chauffeur, were
naturally centres of interest to the entire staff of the hotel; which
was mightily encouraged by the chauffeur's astonishment at
being provided with a couple of eggs for his breakfast. It was
not only that no German hotel would have given him two eggs;
from his previous surroundings he had imbibed the belief that
France was on the point of starvation.

To one of the staff, I know I was a source of puzzlement; an
elderly matron, very Scottish by origin, whose life had been
passed in the surroundings of orthodox civilian hospitals. I was
not of the institutional type; in the early days I did all sorts of
odd jobs; I disliked my uniform, and substituted a French
workman's blouse; and altogether she could not fit me in.
Obviously she made inquiry concerning my antecedents, for one
day, when we met on the stairs, she held up a finger and stopped
me. At the moment of our encounter I was returning from an
expedition to the woods, where I had collected a good-sized
faggot for the uses of my bedroom fire; the said faggot was slung
over my shoulder, and I was wearing my usual blouse. More in
sorrow than in anger matron looked me up and down, and then
spoke.

'They tell me, ' she said, 'that you've been an actress. Is that
true? '

'Oh yes, ' I said, 'I've been an actress' – wondering whether
she were puritan-bred and looked upon actresses as daughters
of the Scarlet Woman. That, however, was not the motive of her
query; as I discovered later, she was quite a keen theatre-goer.
But the admission made, she surveyed me thoughtfully, the

faggot on my shoulder, my blouse, my muddy boots, and asked bluntly: 'Then what's brought you to this?'

I cannot remember exactly what I said in answer to this astonishing query; but if she had not been so kindly, so serious, and so Scotch, I should certainly have told her: 'The drink!'

Needless to say, she was at times bewildered by the mentality of our allies; one such occasion was an entertainment given to our patients by four or five French actors and singers who came out from Paris for the purpose. Miss Ivens decided that a speech of thanks must be made to the visitors, and with more confidence in my French than I possessed myself, said I was the person to make it. Accordingly for the greater part of the concert I shut myself up in my room, and in the sweat of my brow and much torment of mind produced the necessary effusion. It was more successful than I had dared to hope; so successful in fact that at one of my remarks the *doyenne* of the party a lady understood to belong to the Comédie Française – rushed onto the platform and clasped me in a vehement embrace. One of the advantages of a stage experience is that it teaches you to disguise your astonishment at the unexpected; thanks to my training I rose to the occasion, and returned the embrace with interest – to the applause of the assembled hospital. Half an hour later, when we had just waved farewell to our departing guests, I felt a tap on my shoulder and turned to see the matron beside me. 'Tell me,' she said, 'that lady who kissed you when you made your speech – had she ever met you before?'

I told her no; we had only met that afternoon.

'H'm!' was her comment. 'It's easy to see she's not Scotch.'

Sir Ian Hamilton
The Straits

The operation to capture the Dardanelles, the straits that led into the Black Sea, was the first part of a campaign intended to capture Constantinople and to knock the Ottoman Empire out of the war. On 18 March 1915 Rear-Admiral John de Robeck, the Allied naval commander, ordered the first phase of the naval attack on the Dardanelles. This involved a fleet of 18 battleships, surrounded by an armada of cruisers and destroyers, sailing through the waters of those straits. Although the force included modern capital ships such as the super-dreadnought HMS Queen Elizabeth, *the attack ended in disaster. The French battleship* Bouvet *was sunk first, followed by the British dreadnoughts* HMS Irresistible *and* HMS Ocean. *The Turkish forces suffered eight shore guns hit and forty men killed. Hamilton watched the operation from the cruiser* HMS Phaeton.

18th March, 1915. HMS *Phaeton*. Cleared Tenedos Harbour at 4 a.m. and reached Lemnos at 6 a.m. I never saw so many ships collected together in my life; no, not even at Hong Kong, Bombay or New York. Filled up with oil fuel and at 7 a.m. [General Albert] d'Amade and Major-General [Archibald] Paris, commanding the Royal Naval Division, came onboard with one or two Staff Officers. After consulting these Officers as well as [Sinclair] McLagan, the Australian Brigadier, cabled Lord K[itchener] to say Alexandria must be our base as 'the Naval Division transports have been loaded up as in peace time and they must be completely discharged and every ship reloaded', in war fashion. At Lemnos, where there are neither wharfs, piers, labour nor water, the thing could not be done. Therefore, 'the closeness of Lemnos to the Dardanelles, as implying the rapid transport of troops, is illusory'.

The moment I got this done, namely at 8.30 a.m., we worked our way out of the long narrow neck of Mudros Harbour and sailed for the Gulf of Saros. Spent the first half of the sixty mile run to the Dardanelles in scribbling. Wrote my first epistle to K, using for the first time the formal 'Dear Lord Kitchener'. My letters to him will have to be formal, and dull also, as he may hand them around. I begin, 'I have just sent you off a cable giving my first impressions of the situation, and am now steaming in company with Generals d'Amade and Paris to inspect the North-western coast of the Gallipoli Peninsula.' I tell him that the real place 'looks a much tougher nut to crack than it did over the map' – I say that his 'impression that the ground between Cape Helles and Krithia was clear of the enemy' was mistaken. 'Not a bit of it.' I say, 'The Admiral tells me that there is a large number of men tucked away in the folds of the ground there, not to speak of several field Batteries.' Therefore, I conclude, 'If it eventually becomes necessary to take the Gallipoli Peninsula by military force, we shall have to proceed bit by bit.' This will vex him no doubt. He likes plans to move as fast as his own wishes and is apt to forget, or to pretend he has forgotten, that swiftness in war comes from slow preparations. It is fairer to tell K this now, when the question has not yet arisen, than hereafter if it does then arise.

Passing the mouth of the Dardanelles, we got a wonderful view of the stage whereon the Great Showman has caused so many of his amusing puppets to strut their tiny hour. For the purpose, it stands matchless. No other panorama can touch it. There, Hero trimmed her little lamp; yonder the amorous breath of Leander changed to soft sea foam. Far away to the Eastwards, painted in dim and lovely hues, lies Mount Ida. Just so, on the far horizon line she lay fair and still, when Hector fell and smoke

from burning Troy blackened the mid-day sun. Against this
enchanted background to deeds done by immortals and mortals
as they struggled for ten long years five thousand years ago –
stands forth formidably the Peninsula. Glowing with bright,
springtime colours it sweeps upwards from the sea like the glacis
of a giant's fortress.

So we sailed on Northwards, giving a wide berth to the
shore. When we got within a mile of the head of the Gulf of
Saros, we turned, steering a South-westerly course, parallel to,
and one to two miles distant from, the coastline. Then my first
fears as to the outworks of the fortress were strengthened. The
head of the Gulf is filled in with a horrible marsh. No landing
there. Did we land far away to the Westward we must still march
round the marsh, or else we must cross it on one single road
whose long and easily destructible bridges we could see spanning
the bog holes some three miles inland. Opposite the fortified lines
we stood in to within easy field gun range, trusting that the Turks
would not wish prematurely to disclose their artillery positions.
So we managed a peep at close quarters, and were startled to see
the ramifications and extent of the spider's web of deep, narrow
trenches along the coast and on either front of the lines of Bulair.
My Staff agree that they must have taken ten thousand men a
month's hard work from dark to dawn. In advance of the
trenches, Williams in the crow's nest reported that with his
strong glasses he could pick out the glitter of wire over a wide
expanse of ground. To the depth of a mile, the whole Aegean
slope of the neck of the Peninsula was scarred with spade work
and it is clear to a tiro that to take these trenches would take
from us a bigger toll of ammunition and life than we can afford:
especially so seeing that we can only see one half of the theatre;
the other half would have to be worked out of sight and support
of our own ships and in view of the Turkish Fleet. Only one small
dent in the rockbound coast offered a chance of landing but that
was also heavily dug in. In a word, if Bulair had been the only

way open to me and I had no alternative but to take it or wash my hands of the whole business, I should have to go right about turn and cable my master he had sent me on a fool's errand.

Between Bulair and Suvla Bay the coastline was precipitous; high cliffs and no sort of creeks or beaches – impracticable. Suvla Bay itself seems a fine harbour but too far North were the aim to combine a landing there together with an attack on the Southern end of the Peninsula. Were we, on the other hand, to try to work the whole force ashore from Suvla Bay, the country is too big; it is the broadest part of the Peninsula; also, we should be too far from its waist and from the Narrows we wish to dominate. Merely to hold our line of Communications we should need a couple of Divisions. All the coast between Suvla Bay and for a little way South of Gaba Tepe seems feasible for landing. I mean we could get ashore on a calm day if there was no enemy. Gaba Tepe itself would be ideal, but, alas, the Turks are not blind; it is a mass of trenches and wire. Further, it must be well under fire of guns from Kilid Bahr plateau, and is entirely commanded by the high ridge to the North of it. To land there would be to enter a defile without first crowning the heights.

Between Gaba Tepe and Cape Helles, the point of the Peninsula, the coastline consists of cliffs from 100 to 300 feet high. But there are, in many places, sandy strips at their base. Opinions differ but I believe myself the cliffs are not unclimbable. I thoroughly believe also in going for at least one spot that seems impracticable.

Sailing Southwards we are becoming more and more conscious of the tremendous bombardment going on in the Straits. Now and then, too, we can see a huge shell hit the top of Achi Baba and turn it into the semblance of a volcano. Everyone excited and trying to look calm.

At 4 p.m., precisely, we rounded Cape Helles. I had promised de Robeck not to take his fastest cruiser, fragile as an egg, into the actual Straits, but the Captain and the Commander

(Cameron and Rosomore), were frightfully keen to see the fight, and I thought it fair to allow one mile as being the mouth of the Straits and not the Straits. Before we had covered that mile we found ourselves on the outskirts of – dream of my life – a naval battle! Nor did the reality pan out short of my hopes. Here it was; we had only to keep on at thirty knots; in one minute we should be in the thick of it; and who would be brave enough to cry halt!

The world had gone mad; common sense was only moonshine after all; the elephant and the whale of Bismarckian parable were at it tooth and nail! Shells of all sizes flew hissing through the skies. Before my very eyes, the graves of those old Gods whom Christ had risen from the dead to destroy were shaking to the shock of Messrs Armstrong's patent thunderbolts!

Ever since the far-away days of Afghanistan and Majuba Hill, friends have been fond of asking me what soldiers feel when death draws close up beside them. Before he charged in at Edgehill, [Sir Jacob] Astley (if my memory serves me) exclaimed, 'O, God, I've been too busy fixing up this battle to think much about you, but, for Heaven's sake, don't you go and forget about me,' or words to that effect.

The Yankee's prayer for fair play just as he joined issue with the grizzly bear gives another glimpse of these secrets between man and his Maker. As for myself, there are two moments; one when I think I would not miss the show for millions; another when I think 'what an ass I am to be here'; and between these two moments there is a border land when the mind runs all about Life's workshop and tries to do one last bit of stock-taking.

But the process can no more be fixed in the memory than the sequence of a dream when the dew is off the grass. All I remember is a sort of wonder: – why these incredible pains to seek out an amphibious battle ground whereon two sets of people who have no cause of quarrel can blow one another to atoms? Why are these Straits the cockpit of the world? What is it all about? What on earth has happened to sanity when the whale and elephant are locked in mortal combat making between them a picture which might be painted by one of HM's Commissioners in Lunacy to decorate an asylum for homicides.

Whizz – flop – bang – what an ass I am to be here. If we keep on another thirty seconds, we are in for a visit to Davy Jones's Locker.

Now above the *Queen Elizabeth*, making slowly backwards and forwards up in the neck of the Narrows, were other men-o'-war spitting tons of hot metal at the Turks. The Forts made no reply – or none that we could make out, either with our ears or with glasses. Perhaps there was an attempt; if so, it must have been very half-hearted. The enemy's fixed defences were silenced but the concealed mobile guns from the Peninsula and from Asia were far too busy and were having it all their own way.

Close to us were steam trawlers and mine-sweepers steaming along with columns of spray spouting up close by them from falling field-gun shells, with here and there a biggish fellow amongst them, probably a five- or six-inch field howitzer. One of them was in the act of catching a great mine as we drew up level with her. Some 250 yards from us was the *Inflexible* slowly coming out of the Straits, her wireless cut away and a number of shrapnel holes through her tops and crow's nest. Suddenly, so quickly did we turn that, going at speed, the decks were at an angle of 45° and several of us (d'Amade, for one) narrowly escaped slipping down the rail-less decks into the sea. The *Inflexible* had signalled us she had struck a mine, and that we must stand by and see her home to Tenedos. We spun round like a top (escaping thereby a salvo of four from a field battery) and followed as close as we dared.

My blood ran cold – for sheer deliberate awfulness, this beat everything. We gazed spellbound: no one knew what moment the great ship might not dive into the depths. The pumps were going hard. We fixed our eyes on marks about the water line to see if the sea was gaining upon them or not. She was very much down by the bows, that was a sure thing. Crew and stokers were in a mass, standing strictly at attention on the main deck. A whole bevy of destroyers crowded round the wounded warrior. In the sight of all those men standing still, silent, orderly in their ranks, facing the imminence of death, I got my answer to the hasty moralisings about war, drawn from me (really) by a regret that I would very soon be drowned. On the deck of that battleship staggering along at a stone's throw was a vindication of war in itself; of war, the state of being, quite apart from war motives or gains. Ten thousand years of peace would fail to produce a spectacle of so great virtue. Where, in peace, passengers have also shown high constancy, it is because war and martial discipline have lent them its standards. Once in a generation a mysterious wish for war passes through the people. Their instinct tells them that there is no other way of progress and of escape from habits that no longer fit them. Whole generations of statesmen will fumble over reforms for a lifetime which are put into full-blooded execution within a week of a declaration of war. There is no other way. Only by intense sufferings can the nations grow, just as the snake once a year must with anguish slough off the once beautiful coat which has now become a strait jacket.

How was it going to end? How touching the devotion of all these small satellites so anxiously forming escort? Onwards, at snail's pace, moved our cortege, which might at any moment be transformed into a funeral affair, but slow as we went we yet went fast enough to give the go-by to the French battleship *Gaulois*, also creeping out towards Tenedos in a lamentable manner attended by another crowd of TBs [torpedo boats] and destroyers eager to stand to and save.

The *Inflexible* managed to crawl into Tenedos under her own steam, but we stood by until we saw the *Gaulois* ground on some rocks called Rabbit Island, when I decided to clear right out so as not to be in the way of the Navy at a time of so much stress. After we had gone ten miles or so, the *Phaeton* intercepted a wireless from the *Queen Elizabeth*, ordering the *Ocean* to take the *Irresistible* in tow, from which it would appear that she (the *Irresistible*) has also met with some misfortune.

Thank God we were in time! That is my dominant feeling. We have seen a spectacle which would be purchased cheap by five years of life and, more vital yet, I have caught a glimpse of the forces of the enemy and of their Forts. What with my hurried scamper down the Aegean coast of the Peninsula and the battle in the Straits, I begin to form some first-hand notion of my problem. More by good luck than good guidance I have got into personal touch with the outer fringes of the thing we are up against and that is so much to the good. But oh, that we had been here earlier! Winston [Churchill] in his hurry to push me out has shown a more soldierly grip than those who said there was no hurry. It is up to me now to revolve to-day's doings in my mind; to digest them and to turn myself into the eyes and ears of the War Office whose own so far have certainly not proved themselves very acute. How much better would I be able to make them see and hear had I been out a week or two; did I know the outside of the Peninsula by heart, had I made friends with the Fleet! And why should I not have been?

Have added a PS to K's letter –

'Between Tenedos and Lemnos. 6 p.m. – This has been a very bad day for us, judging by what has come under my own personal observation. After going right up to Bulair and down again to the South-west point, looking at the network of trenches the Turks have dug, commanding all possible landing places, we turned into the Dardanelles themselves and went up about a mile. The scene was what I believe Naval writers describe as "lively".' (Then follows an account based on my diary jottings). I end:

'I have not had time to reflect over these matters, nor can I yet realise on my present slight information the extent of these losses. Certainly it looks at present as if the Fleet would not be able to carry on at this rate, and, if so, the soldiers will have to do the trick.'

Later.

'The *Irresistible*, the *Ocean* and the *Bouvet* are gone! The *Bouvet*, they say, just slithered down like a saucer slithers down in a bath. The *Inflexible* and the *Gaulois* are badly mauled.'

Ian Hay
And Some Fell by the Wayside

As a preface to the first published edition of The First Hundred
Thousand *in 1915, Ian Hay included the following 'note':*

> The reader is hereby cautioned against regarding this
> narrative as an official history of the Great War.
>
> The following pages are merely a record of some of
> the personal adventures of a typical regiment of Kitch-
> ener's Army.
>
> The chapters were written from day to day, and
> published from month to month. Consequently, pro-
> phecy is occasionally falsified, and opinions moderated,
> in subsequent pages.
>
> The characters are entirely fictitious, but the incid-
> ents described all actually occurred.

I

'Firing parrty, revairse arrms!'

Thus the platoon sergeant – a little anxiously; for we are new
to this feat, and only rehearsed it for a few minutes this morning.

It is a sunny afternoon in late February. The winter of our
discontent is past. (At least, we hope so.) Comfortless months of
training are safely behind us, and lo! we have grown from a
fortuitous concourse of atoms to a cohesive unit of fighting men.
Spring is coming; spring is coming; our blood runs quicker;
active service is within measurable distance; and the future
beckons to us with both hands to step down at last into the

arena, and try our fortune amid the uncertain but illimitable chances of the greatest game in the World.

To all of us, that is, save one.

The road running up the hill from the little mortuary is lined on either side by members of our company, specklessly turned out and standing to attention. At the foot of the slope a gun-carriage is waiting, drawn by two great dray horses and controlled by a private of the Royal Artillery, who looks incongruously perky and cockney amid that silent, kilted assemblage. The firing party form a short lane from the gun-carriage to the door of the mortuary. In response to the sergeant's command, each man turns over his rifle, and setting the muzzle carefully upon his right boot – after all, it argues no extra respect to the dead to get your barrel filled with mud – rests his hands upon the butt-plate and bows his head, as laid down in the King's Regulations.

The bearers move slowly down the path from the mortuary, and place the coffin upon the gun-carriage. Upon the lid lie a very dingy glengarry, a stained leather belt, and a bayonet. They are humble trophies, but we pay them as much reverence as we would to the bâton and cocked hat of a field-marshal, for they are the insignia of a man who has given his life for his country.

On the hill-top above us, where the great military hospital rears its clock-tower foursquare to the sky, a line of convalescents, in natty blue uniforms with white facings and red ties, lean over the railings deeply interested. Some of them are bandaged, others are in slings, and all are more or less maimed. They follow the obsequies below with critical approval. They have been present at enough hurried and promiscuous interments of late – more than one of them has only just escaped being the central figure at one of these functions – that they are capable of appreciating a properly conducted funeral at its true value.

'They're putting away a bloomin' Jock,' remarks a gentleman with an empty sleeve.

'And very nice, too!' responds another on crutches, as the firing party present arms with creditable precision. 'Not 'arf a bad bit of eye-wash at all for a bandy-legged lot of coal-shovellers.'

'That lot's out of K(1),' explains a well-informed invalid with his head in bandages. 'Pretty 'ot stuff they're gettin'. Très moutarde! Now we're off.'

The signal is passed up the road to the band, who are waiting at the head of the procession, and the pipes break into a lament. Corporals step forward and lay four wreaths upon the coffin – one from each company. Not a man in the battalion has failed to contribute his penny to those wreaths; and pennies are not too common with us, especially on a Thursday, which comes just before payday. The British private is commonly reputed to spend all, or most of, his pocket-money upon beer. But I can tell you this, that if you give him his choice between buying himself a pint of beer and subscribing to a wreath, he will most decidedly go thirsty.

The serio-comic charioteer gives his reins a twitch, the horses wake up, and the gun-carriage begins to move slowly along the lane of mourners. As the dead private passes on his way the walls of the lane melt, and his comrades fall into their usual fours behind the gun-carriage.

So we pass up the hill towards the military cemetery, with the pipes wailing their hearts out, and the muffled drums marking the time of our regulation slow step. Each foot seems to hang in the air before the drums bid us put it down.

In the very rear of the procession you may see the company commander and three subalterns. They give no orders, and exact no attention. To employ a colloquialism, this is not their funeral.

Just behind the gun-carriage stalks a solitary figure in civilian clothes – the unmistakable 'blacks' of an Elder of the Kirk. At first sight, you have a feeling that someone has strayed into the procession who has no right there. But no one has a better. The sturdy old man behind the coffin is named Adam Carmichael, and he is here, having travelled south from Dumbarton by the night train, to attend the funeral of his only son.

II

Peter Carmichael was one of the first to enlist in the regiment. There was another Carmichael in the same company, so Peter at roll-call was usually addressed by the sergeant as 'Twenty-seven fufty-fower Carmichael', 2754 being his regimental number. The army does not encourage Christian names. When his attestation paper was filled up, he gave his age as nineteen; his address, vaguely, as Renfrewshire; and his trade, not without an air, as a 'holder-on'. To the mystified Bobby Little, he entered upon a lengthy explanation of the term in a language composed almost entirely of vowels, from which that officer gathered, dimly, that holding-on had something to do with shipbuilding.

Upon the barrack square his platoon commander's attention was again drawn to Peter, owing to the passionate enthusiasm with which he performed the simplest evolutions, such as forming fours and sloping arms – military exercises which do not intrigue the average private to any great extent. Unfortunately, desire frequently outran performance. Peter was undersized, unmuscular, and extraordinarily clumsy. For a long time Bobby Little thought that Peter, like one or two of his comrades, was left-handed, so made allowances. Ultimately he discovered that his indulgence was misplaced: Peter was equally incompetent with either hand. He took longer in learning to fix bayonets or present arms than any other man in the platoon. To be fair, Nature had done little to help him. He was thirty-three inches round the chest, five feet four in height, and weighed possibly nine stone. His complexion was pasty, and, as Captain Wagstaffe remarked, you could hang your hat on any bone in his body. His eyesight was not all that the Regulations require, and on the musketry-range he was 'put back', to his deep distress, 'for further instruction'. Altogether, if you had not known the doctor who passed him, you would have said it was a mystery how he passed the doctor.

But he possessed the one essential attribute of the soldier. He had a big heart. He was keen. He allowed nothing to come between him and his beloved duties. ('He was aye daft for to go sogerin',' his father explained to Captain Blaikie; 'but his mother would never let him away. He was ower wee, and ower young.') His rifle, buttons and boots were always without blemish. Further, he was of the opinion that a merry heart goes all the way. He never sulked when the platoon were kept on parade five minutes after the breakfast bugle had sounded. He made no bones about obeying orders and saluting officers – acts of abasement which grated sorely at times upon his colleagues, who reverenced no one except themselves and their Union. He appeared to revel in muddy route-marches, and invariably provoked and led the choruses. The men called him 'Wee Pe'er' and ultimately adopted him as a sort of company mascot. Whereat Pe'er's heart glowed; for when your associates attach a diminutive to your Christian name, you possess something which millionaires would gladly give half their fortune to purchase.

And certainly he required all the social success he could win, for professionally Peter found life a rigorous affair. Sometimes, as he staggered into barracks after a long day, carrying a rifle made of lead and wearing a pair of boots weighing a hundred-weight apiece, he dropped dead asleep on his bedding before he could eat his dinner. But he always hotly denied the imputation that he was 'sick'.

Time passed. The regiment was shaking down. Seven of Peter's particular cronies were raised to the rank of lance-corporal – but not Peter. He was 'off the square' now – that is to say, he was done with recruit drill forever. He possessed a sound knowledge of advance-guard and outpost work; his conduct-sheet was a blank page. But he was not promoted. He was 'ower wee for a stripe', he told himself. For the present, he must expect to be passed over. His chance would come later, when he had filled out a little and got rid of his cough.

The winter dragged on: the weather was appalling; the grousers gave tongue with no uncertain voice, each streaming field-day. But Wee Pe'er enjoyed it all. He did not care if it snowed ink. He was a 'sojer'.

One day, to his great delight, he was 'warned for guard' – a particularly unpopular branch of a soldier's duties, for it means sitting in the guard-room for twenty-four hours at a stretch, fully dressed and accoutred, with intervals of sentry-go, usually in heavy rain, by way of exercise. When Peter's turn for sentry-go came on, he splashed up and down his muddy beat – the battalion was in billets now, and the usual sentry's verandah was lacking – as proud as a peacock, saluting officers according to their rank, challenging stray civilians with great severity, and turning out the guard on the slightest provocation. He was at his post, soaked right through his greatcoat, when the orderly officer made his night round. Peter summoned his colleagues; the usual inspection of the guard took place; and the sleepy men were then dismissed to their fireside. Peter remained; the officer hesitated. He was supposed to examine the sentry in his knowledge of his duties. It was a profitless task as a rule. The tongue-tied youth merely gaped like a stranded fish, until the sergeant mercifully intervened, in some such words as these –

'This man, sirr, is liable to get over-excited when addressed by an officer.'

Then, soothingly –

'Now, Jimmy, tell the officer what would ye dae in case of fire?'

'Present airrms!' announces the desperate James. Or else, almost tearfully, 'I canna mind. I had it all fine just noo, but it's awa' oot o' ma heid!'

Therefore it was with no great sense of anticipation that the orderly officer said to Private Carmichael –

'Now, sentry, can you repeat any of your duties?'

Peter saluted, took a full breath, closed both eyes, and replied rapidly –

'For tae tak' chairge of all Government property within sicht of this guairdhoose tae turrn out the guaird for all arrmed pairties approaching also the commanding officer once a day tae salute all officers tae challenge all pairsons approaching this post tae—'

His recital was interrupted by a fit of coughing.

'Thank you,' said the officer hastily, 'that will do. Good night!'

Peter, not sure whether it would be correct to say 'good night' too, saluted again, and returned to his cough.

'I say,' said the officer, turning back, 'you have a shocking cold.'

'Och, never heed it, sirr,' gasped Peter politely.

'Call the sergeant,' said the officer.

The fat sergeant came out of the guardhouse again, buttoning his tunic.

'Sirr?'

'Take this man off sentry-duty and roast him at the guard-room fire.'

'I will, sirr,' replied the sergeant; and added paternally, 'This man has no right for to be here at all. He should have reported sick when warned for guard; but he would not. He is very attentive to his duties, sirr.'

'Good boy!' said the officer to Peter. 'I wish we had more like you.'

Wee Pe'er blushed, his teeth momentarily ceased chattering, his heart swelled. Appearances to the contrary, he felt warm all through. The sergeant laid a fatherly hand upon his shoulder.

'Go you your ways intil the guard-room, boy,' he

commanded, 'and send oot Dunshie. He'll no hurt. Get close in ahint the stove, or you'll be for Cambridge!'

(The last phrase carries no academic significance. It simply means that you are likely to become an inmate of the great Cambridge Hospital at Aldershot.)

Peter, feeling thoroughly disgraced, cast an appealing look at the officer.

'In you go!' said that martinet.

Peter silently obeyed. It was the only time in his life that he ever felt mutinous.

A month later Brigade Training set in with customary severity. The life of company officers became a burden. They spent hours in thick woods with their followers, taking cover, ostensibly from the enemy, in reality from brigade-majors and staff officers. A subaltern never tied his platoon in a knot but a general came trotting round the corner. The wet weather had ceased, and a biting east wind reigned in its stead.

On one occasion an elaborate night operation was arranged. Four battalions were to assemble at a given point five miles from camp, and then advance in column across country by the light of the stars to a position indicated on the map, where they were to deploy and dig themselves in! It sounded simple enough in operation orders; but when you try to move four thousand troops – even well-trained troops – across three miles of broken country on a pitch-dark night, there is always a possibility that someone will get mislaid. On this particular occasion a whole battalion lost itself without any delay or difficulty whatsoever. The other three were compelled to wait for two hours and a half, stamping their feet and blowing on their fingers, while over-heated staff officers scoured the country for the truants. They were discovered at last waiting virtuously at the wrong rendez-vous, three-quarters of a mile away. The brazen-hatted strategist who drew up the operation orders had given the point of assembly for the brigade as: ... the field S.W. of WELLINGTON

WOOD and due E. of HANGMAN'S COPSE, immediately below the first O in GHOSTLY BOTTOM' – but omitted to underline the O indicated. The result was that three battalion commanders assembled at the O in 'ghostly', while the fourth, ignoring the adjective in favour of the noun, took up his station at the first O in 'bottom'.

The operations had been somewhat optimistically timed to end at 11 p.m., but by the time that the four battalions had effected a most unloverly tryst, it was close on ten, and beginning to rain. The consequence was that the men got home to bed, soaked to the skin, and asking the Powers Above rhetorical questions, at three o'clock in the morning.

Next day Brigade Orders announced that the movement would be continued at nightfall, by the occupation of the hastily-dug trenches, followed by a night attack upon the hill in front. The captured position would then be retrenched.

When the tidings went round, fourteen of the more quick-witted spirits of 'A' Company hurriedly paraded before the Medical Officer and announced that they were 'sick in the stomach'. Seven more discovered abrasions upon their feet, and proffered their sores for inspection, after the manner of Oriental mendicants. One skrimshanker, despairing of producing any bodily ailment, rather ingeniously assaulted a comrade-in-arms, and was led away, deeply grateful, to the guard-room. Wee Peter, who in the course of last night's operations had stumbled into an old trench half-filled with ice-cold water, and whose temperature to-day, had he known it, was a hundred and two, paraded with his company at the appointed time. The company, he reflected, would get a bad name if too many men reported sick at once.

Next day he was absent from parade. He was 'for Cambridge' at last.

Before he died, he sent for the officer who had befriended him, and supplemented, or rather corrected, some of the information contained in his attestation paper.

He lived in Dumbarton, not Renfrewshire. He was just sixteen. He was not – this confession cost him a great effort – a full-blown 'holder-on' at all; only an apprentice. His father was 'weel kent' in the town of Dumbarton, being a chief engineer, employed by a great firm of shipbuilders to extend new machinery on trial trips.

Needless to say, he made a great fight. But though his heart was big enough, his body was too frail. As they say on the sea, he was over-engined for his beam.

And so, three days later, the simple soul of Twenty-seven fifty-four Carmichael, 'A' Company, was transferred, on promotion, to another company – the great Company of Happy Warriors who walk the Elysian Fields.

III

'Firing parrty, one round blank – load!'

There is a rattle of bolts, and a dozen barrels are pointed heavenwards. The company stands rigid, except the buglers, who are beginning to finger their instruments.

'Fire!'

There is a crackling volley, and the pipes break into a brief, sobbing wail. Wayfarers upon the road below look up curiously. One or two young females with perambulators come hurrying across the grass, exhorting apathetic babies to sit up and admire the pretty funeral.

Twice more the rifles ring out. The pipes cease their wailing, and there is an expectant silence.

The drum-major crooks his little finger, and eight bugles come to the 'ready'. Then 'Last Post', the requiem of every soldier of the King, swells out, sweet and true.

The echoes lose themselves among the dripping pines. The chaplain closes his book, takes off his spectacles, and departs.

Old Carmichael permits himself one brief look into his son's grave, resumes his crape-bound tall hat, and turns heavily away. He finds Captain Blaikie's hand waiting for him. He grips it, and says –

'Weel, the laddie has had a grand sojer's funeral. His mother will be pleased to hear that.'

He passes on, and shakes hands with the platoon sergeant and one or two of Peter's cronies. He declines an invitation to the Sergeants' Mess.

'I hae a trial-trup the morn,' he explains. 'I must be steppin'. God keep ye all, brave lads!'

The old gentleman sets off down the station road. The company falls in, and we march back to barracks, leaving Wee Pe'er – the first name on our Roll of Honour – alone in his glory beneath the Hampshire pines.

James Jack
The Retreat from Le Cateau

James Jack crossed over to France with 1st Cameronians (Scottish Rifles) and had first seen action at the Battle of Mons on 23 August. The battalion, part of II Corps, had been forced to withdraw before halting on 26 August at Le Cateau, where General Sir Horace Smith-Dorrien decided to make a stand in a successful holding action that has been described as 'one of the most remarkable British feats of arms of the whole war'. During the fighting, the British losses were 7,812 officers and men, and thirty-eight guns. Jack takes up the story on 28 August.

After leaving the Argylls at Honnechy in order to seek brigade headquarters, I was too exhausted to remember details clearly till the 28th . . .

At a cross-roads a field battery and the Cameronians were composedly halted as rearguard ready for the Germans, the latter with fixed 'swords', as bayonets are called by Rifle Regiments. Colonel Robertson said he thought Brigade Headquarters were ahead. His battalion had been lightly engaged that day but had had a very wearing time moving about to threatened sectors.

Rain was now falling. I soon joined groups of various regiments and some horse transport stumbling along, the men half-dazed from fatigue, being only kept together, and moving, by the exertions of their few remaining officers . . .

Some time in the night a motor lorry gave me a short lift before stopping to park with others. During this brief pause a little food purchased and devoured at an estaminet made me very sick; I lay down under the lorry to rest till it was ready to proceed with its neighbours. Soon somebody pulled me out saying they were going on; so I rose, numbed by the cold and rain, scarcely caring what happened . . .

About dawn I met, and reported for duty to, Lieut-Colonel C.J. Hickie (H.Q. II Corps). He was accompanied by one or two mounted orderlies and had also lost his headquarters. Both of us were now 'off our maps'. We had, I believe, strayed west of St Quentin. Scarcely any troops were to be seen, but I managed to borrow a spare horse from a single battery and went with the Colonel on a small tour to try and discover our whereabouts. Of soldiery we saw none, but heard heavy gun-fire to the north-west (British and French cavalry rear-guards).

Then we stopped in a village, loosened girths, watered and fed the horses, and bought for ourselves as well as the orderlies beer, raw eggs, rolls and butter. This delicious breakfast was cut short by the approach of mounted men from the north; so thinking they might be Prussians and that we might have wandered behind our rear-guards we girthed up and trotted away. The rain had now ceased, giving way to warm, bright weather.

Directing our way south by the sun, we came upon the main St Quentin—Ham road, straight, white, tree-lined, and running through open cultivated country. On it an endless irregular procession of infantry, batteries, transport and refugees tramped slowly towards Ham . . .

A large number of valises and entrenching tools were absent, having been lost in action or thrown away by order or otherwise; all troops, however, had their arms, besides the residue of their ammunition. The officers were afoot, many of them carrying one or two of their men's rifles. The chargers bore equipment or exhausted soldiers, and towed a man hanging on to the stirrup on either flank. Transport vehicles gave similar assistance.

Frequently someone would fall or sit down for a rest, the first to be picked up by comrades and put on a waggon, and the second urged to his feet again. Here and there in this ghastly queue marched a fairly solid company, platoon or section.

Abandoned equipment littered the roadsides; at intervals waggons had been left for lack of teams . . .

During the morning, things began to improve. Staff officers at road intersections disentangled the medley: '3rd Division on the right of the road, 5th Division on the left, 4th beyond the 3rd.' There the different regiments were sorted out and formed into companies. Ammunition and rations, previously dumped by the transport, were issued.

I heard of one young staff officer being amused – until quelled – at the difference between this Retreat and the Real Professional Retreat performed at Aldershot in perfect order.

In the twinkling of an eye, organisation and food produced a happier air; so when the improvised companies had devoured a meal from the 'cookers' collected at these rendezvous, followed by an hour's sleep or a smoke and chat, they set out again like new men, soldierly and singing although dead-beat . . .

As to the French peasantry: deeply concerned as they were about their own security, and bitterly disappointed at being left to the enemy's hands, their kindness by deed as well as word all the way from Mons can never be exceeded. At no time did I see on their faces, or hear in their remarks, anything but pity for our men. They stood at their doors with pails of water, sometimes wine, long rolls of bread and butter, fruit, just what they had. We must never forget them.

Late in the afternoon I crossed the Somme at Ham on foot, having relinquished my mount earlier – I could *not ride* with that wearied throng *walking* – and was directed to Ollezy, four miles eastwards, where nearly all the brigade was already assembled in bivouacs and barns.

The distance marched from Le Cateau was about forty-four miles, the weather hot, and the men had had practically no proper meal or rest for thirty-six hours or more. Colonel

Robertson estimated that the Cameronians covered fifty-seven miles in that time . . .

In the evening, when visiting the bivouac of my battalion, I fainted – twice, I was told . . .

August 30th: Couloisy

At Ollezy at 4 a.m. on the 28th, the stir of packing up awoke me from a deep sleep; I rose, washed, shaved, breakfasted and resumed duty.

Lieut-Colonel E.E. Ward, 1/Middlesex, the senior battalion commander, has assumed command of the brigade . . .

At 6 a.m. the brigade, covered by cavalry in contact with the enemy, commenced its march of nineteen miles . . . to take up a defensive position at Pontoise about 5 p.m. The country was latterly rather hilly, the weather hot, and the hour's halt on the way for dinners very welcome.

That night I almost collapsed from fatigue and, although it was unnecessary, charming Duval insisted on helping me to remove my accoutrements.

Yesterday we stayed at Pontoise till the evening. The men urgently required rest, proper meals, and a wash. Their feet are terribly raw from seven days' marching and fighting, with no chance to remove their boots. The most exhausted have been carried on army waggons or on farm carts requisitioned locally.

There was, however, no repose at Pontoise for the battalion quartermasters nor for my office, as the tale of deficiencies in stores and equipment is staggering, necessitating the making up of long indents in triplicate for replacements.

After this precious day's rest, which restored the men 'no end', the brigade marched at 8 p.m. to Couloisy . . . down the steep winding road to Attichy, across the Aisne, and up the heights to billet here about noon today . . . the dust very trying and the checks incessant throughout the fifteen-mile march . . .

The Germans have taken Péronne and are before Amiens. Their unbroken successes everywhere are very depressing for us. What is to be the end of it all?

Our rear-guards had a little respite after Le Cateau, but the enemy are again pressing on and there is an attractive sense of security in having these large rivers between us and them at night.

August 31st

. . . On my way back [from Corps HQ] . . . I see a group of British soldiers escorting a Frenchman – none other than Duval – whose face is livid with anger. He has been arrested, stupidly, by a young British departmental officer as a German spy, many of whom are said to be in the Allied lines, and is being marched to Headquarters for identification. At a word from me his freedom is restored and I bid him enter our car; but, still incensed, he demands to know the name of his captor for the purpose of challenging the villain to a duel at the end of the War. My attempt to pass the matter off draws the fierce threat that if I do not get the name he will shoot me instead. Seeing that my friend must have some name, I go over to the now frightened subaltern and return with the bogus information that he is Lieutenant Smith of Stepney. This ends the unfortunate incident.

Poor Duval, a very fine Frenchman, arrested as a German spy, in his own country, by aliens! (His death at Verdun cancelled the risk of this duel.)

John Jackson
Some Fight, Jock!

Loos has been called many things by the soldiers who fought in it and also by historians who have picked over its bones, but most are agreed that the best description is that it was both an unnecessary and an unwanted battle. In strategic terms, it was meaningless. The attacking divisions gained a salient two miles deep and in the early stages of the battle some Scottish battalions had the heady sensation of advancing steadily across no-man's-land – 'the scene resembled nothing so much as a cross-country race with a full field' – but the end result did little to help the French offensive in Artois and Champagne, the main reason why Kitchener insisted that the battle should take place. At the same time, the Germans had learned the lessons of the allied attacks earlier in the year and had created second defensive lines on the reverse slopes to compensate for their lack of reserves, and by occupying the higher ground they enjoyed an open field of fire. Both were used to good effect when the allied offensive opened on 25 September and the high casualty figures tell their own story. By the time the fighting officially came to an end on 16 October, British casualties amounted to 2,466 officers and 59,247 other ranks, killed, wounded or missing.

Loos also deserves to be called a Scottish battlefield: some 30,000 Scots took part in the initial attack, including the men of John Jackson's 6th Queen's Own Cameron Highlanders. Not since the Battle of Culloden in 1746 had so many Scots been involved in such a serious military undertaking. Of the seventy-two infantry battalions that took part in the first phase of the battle, half of them bore Scottish titles.

Saturday, 25th September 1915, stands out very prominently in the history of the glorious 15th division, till then untried in a real battle. On that date the eager, well-trained young men, who enlisted in the early days of the war, gave an account of themselves hardly equalled in any engagement during the whole campaign. For days, previous to the 25th, the whole of the Loos sector had been under a state of continuous bombardment from our artillery, such a bombardment as had never been known before. This continued shelling of the enemy positions was necessary to destroy the enormous barbed-wire defences with which the German lines were protected. It also served the purpose of 'putting the wind up' our 'friends the enemy' across that narrow stretch of wilderness that separated us, and was known as 'No Man's Land'. For some time we had believed there was to be a great attack on this part of the front, and prided ourselves on the fact that at last we should have the chance we had waited so long for, as the 15th division was to lead the attack. The 24th saw us preparing for battle. We were served out with 'iron rations' – hard biscuits, a tin of bully-beef, and a small tin of tea and sugar. Also we received a plentiful supply of ammunition, so that every man carried no less than 250 rounds, which was no light weight to be carting about. We were asked to destroy all letters and papers which might identify us in the event of us being taken prisoner. We were also advised to make out our wills in the space provided in our pay-books, which were then collected and stored away. All finally completed, the battalion moved forward to Philosophe, close to the frontline trenches. Instead of going to rest for a few hours in the usual manner, we gathered in groups talking over our chances in the morning. Then the absolute coolness of everyone was shown by the fact that we commenced singing. All the old favourites were sung one by one, bringing back memories of training days, and old scenes of sunny, southern England. Then friends wished each other 'Good luck', friends who knew that the next day would find many of them among the casualty list. Before dawn we began our journey to the trenches by way of Chapel Alley and Devon Lane. Our progress up the communication trenches was very slow. The air was full of the stifling odour of powder and gas, and once we halted to don our gas masks, reaching the firing line shortly before 5 a.m.

Here I will give a description of our dispositions and various objectives. The attack was being made by the 4th Army Corps under the command of Gen. Rawlinson. The left position was occupied by the 1st Division; men of the 'Old Contemptibles', whose objective was the strongly fortified Hohenzollern Redoubt. On the right was our old friend the 49th Division of London Territorials, a fine fighting force, who were to take the line on the right of the village of Loos. We (the 15th Scottish Division) had the post of honour in the centre, our goal being the village of Loos, and beyond that the now famous 'Hill 70'. The sector was of course familiar to us, and for a long time we had daily watched the shelling of the village, and its familiar steel tower at the pit-head, which was a land-mark for miles around. We were expected to take the village in about three days, and our reinforcements had been arranged for on that allowance of time. It was to be a hard struggle, but surely the general staff must have under-rated the dash and determination of the regiments engaged. Had reserves been lying near, Loos would without a doubt have been a deciding battle.

At five o'clock after gas had been discharged against the enemy, and which through contrary winds was blown back and killed many of our own men, we mounted the parapet of the trench with the aid of short ladders, and so at last we 'were over the top'.

In 'no man's land' we found ourselves in a heavy mist, through which came the whirr and whine of shells and bullets. Men began to fall immediately, and one of the first to be killed was our signal officer, Lt Cameron, shot through the heart as he

clambered out of the trenches. In short rushes we kept on, grim
and determined, through a tangled growth of long grass, till we
came to the enemy front line. With fierce yells, we were among
the 'Jerries' and then ensued some terrible hand-to-hand fighting,
as we showed them the art of using bayonets. Cutting, smashing,
thrusting, we drove them before us to their second line, but even
here they could not keep us back. True, they fought hard, but
could not stand against our determination, and our terrible
bayonets. In spite of growing losses in our own ranks we kept
on driving the Germans before us and soon had them on the run
for the village, and here they set up a desperate defence. Their
machine-guns took a terrible toll from our thinning ranks, but
still we hung on till we were again in hand-to-hand conflict with
them. From house to house, and cellar to cellar, we hunted them.
Machine-gunners slaying us from their hidden posts threw up
their hands crying 'Kamerad' when we got within striking
distance, but these deserved and received no quarter. Cold steel
and bombs did their duty then, and the village was strewn with
dead and running with blood. Hundreds of prisoners, we had
taken in the open, were sent to the prison camps in the rear of
our lines, and at eight o'clock in the morning we were in
possession of the village. In three hours we had accomplished
what had been planned for us to do in three days. As is always
the case in a big battle, there had been a great mix-up of men
and regiments, and now as we tried to re-organise for a further
attack, men were placed under the nearest available officer
irrespective of what regiment they belonged.

Our colonel – Douglas-Hamilton – was still with us, and also
our adjutant, Capt. Milne, a cool officer belonging to the Indian
Army.

Arrangements were now made to push on with the advance
on Hill 70. Meanwhile, on our left, the 1st Division was held up,
owing to the strong defences protecting the Hohenzollern
Redoubt, so that we were suffering heavily from enfilade fire.

On our right the 49th Division was keeping well up with us. Included in that division were the London Irish, who are credited with coolly dribbling a football in front of them as they advanced. Our own division had done well in gaining so much ground, though we had paid dearly for our success. Looking behind, we could see artillery galloping forward in the face of a murderous fire, men and horses and guns being smashed up in strange-looking heaps. Our progress towards Hill 70 was slow, and we had to suffer terrible losses from that terrible cross-fire from the Redoubt, which caught us on the left flank. It was unfortunate indeed that the 1st Div. were held up. Machine-gun bullets mowed down the long grass and weeds in which we lay, as a scythe cuts down corn in a harvest-field, and men on all sides were losing their life blood on that gently rising slope. So far I was unharmed, which seemed a wonderful thing to me. After a time we gathered together and charged the hill. A short fight and we had reached the top, held it for a time and were driven back by weight of numbers. Again we charged, held the top and were forced back. The situation was serious, and anxiously we looked back for reinforcements but no help could we see. A third time we charged on that awful hill-side, but the enemy, with his reserves at hand, were too many for us and again we fell back. Truly we were holding to the motto of the regiment: 'A Cameron never can yield'. We numbered at this stage less than a hundred all told, and for all we knew might be all that was left of the 6th Camerons. As the evening drew near we made a fourth and final attempt to win and hold the ridge. This time we meant to do or die. Led by our brave old colonel, bareheaded and with no other weapon than his walking stick, we made for the top of Hill 70, through a murderous rifle and machine-gun fire, while shells crashed all around us. Our action was a sort of last desperate chance, but in the face of such heavy odds it could only end in failure. The white-haired old man who led us was shot dead, and shortly afterwards Capt. Milne, cool and unruffled to the last, paid a similar penalty. Driven back to the foot of the slope as darkness came on, we dug ourselves in, wondering what was happening around us. We had seen no sign of reinforcements, and now with the darkness came rain, which made our position miserable. All day we had been struggling and fighting, and were glad of the chance to eat a biscuit as we lay in our shallow holes through that awful night, soaking wet and under a never-ending fire from the enemy. Except from cuts and bruises from barbed wire, and the rough and tumble of the battle, I was still alright, though separated from most of my companions, many of whom were wounded or killed. Sunday 26th was a day of heavy shelling along the British front. We made no more attacks, but hung on desperately to our new line and the ground we had gained.

Reinforcements had been hurried forward to support us, but these, men of the 21st Div., had never been in action before, but surely that could be no excuse for the poor fight they made. In many cases officers had to keep them in the trenches at the point of their revolvers, but even then were not always successful in their efforts. It seems a hard thing to say against a British division, and yet only a few weeks later this same 21st Division made a great name for themselves on the very ground where they had failed us so badly. Throughout the day, in the mist and smoke of battle, we lay in our shallow holes with bullets whistling in all directions, with shells dropping and ploughing up the ground everywhere, and men being killed and wounded constantly. We'd had no decent meal since Friday night, and were parched with thirst, but still we kept a vigilant eye in front for the counter-attack that was sure to come. Late at night after all hope of any help seemed to have gone, we were relieved by the Guards Division, and never was relief more welcome. Battered, broken, and weary, we struggled back to the village of Mazin-garbe, in little groups as best we could. So far we knew nothing as to what extent the battalion had lost in numbers, but I thought

there could be few men left. It had been a fight such as the
division had always wished for, and we had left our mark on the
Germans. They would not forget the men in kilts in a hurry. The
Battle of Loos has been mentioned as the 'Camerons' day out',
for there were no less than five battalions of the regiment
engaged – the 1st, 4th, 5th, 6th and 7th. For his bravery on Hill
70, Col. Douglas-Hamilton was posthumously awarded the VC,
and I well remember the pride we all felt when the news became
known. Had he survived I feel sure he'd have been as proud of
his regiment, and the fight it made, as we were of his honour. In
all, the division gained six VCs that day, besides many smaller
distinctions. It was on the Saturday morning that Piper Laidlaw
of the 7th Kings Own Scottish Borderers strode along the
parapet of the trenches playing the battalion into action. On the
27th, after we were rested and cleaned, we had a battalion roll-
call, one of the most touching scenes that can be imagined. What
a little band we seemed to be, in place of the fine regiment of
three days ago, as we gathered in the garden behind
headquarters. Our Regimental Sgt Major, Peter Scotland, began
calling the roll, company by company. There were few responses
as names were called, though what little information there was
about missing men was given by friends. All my friends of the
cycle section had come through safely; Charlie Hutchinson and
Andrew Johnstone were among the missing, but they eventually
turned up slightly wounded. Another good friend, big 'Jock'
Anderson, was missing, and to this day his fate remains an
unsolved mystery, but I have no doubt he did his bit, for Jock
was a whole-hearted fighter. The losses of the division ran into
thousands and our own battalion had lost 700 out of 950 who
went into action. Of the whole forces engaged, the casualties for
the week-end totalled over 69,000 officers and men.

The battle-field presented a wrecked and battered appearance. Dead men and horses lay everywhere, with smashed guns
and wagons piled up in confusion. On the Vermelles–Loos road

a whole supply column, caught by enemy artillery, had been smashed to pieces. From the broken barbed-wire defences streamed pieces of tartan and khaki, torn from kilts and tunics, as men had crashed through the entanglements when charging the enemy trenches.

A story is told in connection with the battle, of a Gordon Highlander, who, making his way back wounded from the fight, with bandaged head and arm in a sling, his kilt and hose all torn and bloody, came across a trooper of the Mounted Police standing in the shelter of the old church at Vermelles. As the wounded man slowly made his way past, the MP, while he gazed at the wounds, the dirt and trickling blood of the 'kiltie', said in a condescending manner – '*Some* fight, Jock!' 'Aye,' said the Gordon, taking the cigarette from his lips, as he eyed the other up and down, from the red band on his hat to the polished boots and spurs on his feet – 'and *some* don't.' On the 28th while fighting still continued near Hill 70, we left Mazingarbe and marched back to Hallicourt, bivouacking in a field near the village during a night of heavy and continuous rain. On the following day we moved further back to the larger village of Labouissere, where we billeted in a barn and were fairly comfortable. For a day or two we had an easy time, and during our stay we were visited by the Corps Commander, Sir Henry Rawlinson, who came to congratulate us on our behaviour in our first battle. We also had an inspection and were addressed in satisfied terms by our divisional commander, General McCracken, who no doubt felt proud of his men. On 3rd October, we left Labouissere and, passing through the large mining village of Marles, we reached Allouagne. Here we were joined by a draft of reinforcements, and were glad to recognise many old friends amongst them; men who had been slightly wounded at Loos and were now returning to us from the Base. We spent a few quiet days in the little country village, while we were being refitted with uniforms and equipments, and our time was passed in light exercises. In spite of the horrors we had passed through in the great battle, we began to pick up again our jaunty devil-may-care ways. This was well, for soon we would be on our way back to the front-line trenches, where it did not do to be depressed, and on 12th October we left Allouagne and marched to Hallicourt.

Sir Harry Lauder
Death of a Son

Sir Harry Lauder's only son John, a Cambridge graduate, was killed on 28 December 1916 while serving with the 8th Argyll and Sutherland Highlanders in the line between Courcellete and Pozieres. The news reached Lauder on New Year's Eve while he was in London starring in a popular revue called Three Cheers *in which he performed his famous wartime song 'The Laddies Who Fought and Won'. Defying the shock of his grief, Lauder returned to the stage a few days later and in 1917 he crossed over to France to give a series of concerts for the troops serving on the Western Front.*

It was on Monday morning, January the first, 1917, that I learned of my boy's death. And he had been killed the Thursday before! He had been dead four days before I knew it! And yet – I had known. Let no one ever tell me again that there is nothing in presentiment. Why else had I been so sad and uneasy in my mind? Why else, all through that Sunday, had it been so impossible for me to take comfort in what was said to cheer me? Some warning had come to me, some sense that all was not well.

Realisation came to me slowly. I sat and stared at that slip of paper, that had come to me like the breath of doom. Dead! Dead these four days! I was never to see the light of his eyes again. I was never to hear that laugh of his. I had looked on my boy for the last time. Could it be true? Ah, I knew it was! And it was for this moment that I had been waiting, that we had all been waiting, ever since we had sent John away to fight for his country and do his part. I think we had all felt that it must come.

We had all known that it was too much to hope that he should be one of those to be spared.

The black despair that had been hovering over me for hours closed down now and enveloped all my senses. Everything was unreal. For a time I was quite numb. But then, as I began to realise and to visualise what it was to mean in my life that my boy was dead there came a great pain. The iron of realisation slowly seared every word of that curt telegram upon my heart. I said it to myself, over and over again. And I whispered to myself, as my thoughts took form, over and over, the one terrible word: 'Dead!'

I felt that for me everything had come to an end with the reading of that dire message. It seemed to me that for me the board of life was black and blank. For me there was no past and there could be no future. Everything had been swept away, erased, by one sweep of the hand of a cruel fate. Oh, there was a past, though! And it was in that past that I began to delve. It was made up of every memory I had of my boy. I fell at once to remembering him. I clutched at every memory, as if I must grasp them and make sure of them, lest they be taken from me as well as the hope of seeing him again that the telegram had forever snatched away.

I would have been destitute indeed then. It was as if I must fix in my mind the way he had been wont to look, and recall to my ears every tone of his voice, every trick of his speech. There was something left of him that I must keep, I knew, even then, at all costs, if I was to be able to bear his loss at all.

There was a vision of him before my eyes. My bonnie Highland laddie, brave and strong in his kilt and the uniform of his country, going out to his death with a smile on his face. And there was another vision that came up now, unbidden. It was a vision of him lying stark and cold upon the battlefield, the mud on his uniform. And when I saw that vision I was like a man gone mad and possessed of devils who had stolen away his faculties. I cursed war as I saw that vision, and the men who caused war. And when I thought of the Germans who had killed my boy a terrible and savage hatred swept me, and I longed to go out there and kill with my bare hands until I had avenged him or they had killed me too.

But then I was a little softened. I thought of his mother back in our wee hoose at Dunoon. And the thought of her, bereft even as I was, sorrowing, even as I was, and lost in her frightful loneliness, was pitiful, so that I had but the one desire and wish – to go to her, and join my tears with hers, that we who were left alone to bear our grief might bear it together and give one to the other such comfort as there might be in life for us. And so I fell upon my knees and prayed, there in my lonely room in the hotel. I prayed to God that he might give us both, John's mother and myself, strength to bear the blow that had been dealt us and to endure the sacrifice that He and our country had demanded of us.

My friends came to me. They came rushing to me. Never did man have better friends, and kindlier friends than mine proved themselves to me on that day of sorrow. They did all that good men and women could do. But there was no help for me in the ministration of friends. I was beyond the power of human words to comfort or solace. I was glad of their kindness, and the memory of it now is a precious one, and one I would not be without. But at such a time I could not gain from them what they were eager to give me. I could only bow my head and pray for strength.

That night, that New Year's night that I shall never forget, no matter how long God may let me live, I went north. I took train from London to Glasgow, and the next day I came to our wee hoose – a sad, lonely wee hoose it had become now! – on the Clyde at Dunoon, and was with John's mother. It was the place for me. It was there that I wanted to be, and it was with her, who must hereafter be all the world to me. And I was eager to be with her, too, who had given John to me. Sore as my grief was, stricken as I was, I could comfort her as no one else could hope to do, and she could do as much for me. We belonged together.

I can scarce remember, even for myself, what happened there at Dunoon. I cannot tell you what I said or what I did, or what words and what thoughts passed between John's mother and myself. But there are some things that I do know and that I will tell you. Almighty God, to whom we prayed, was kind, and He was pitiful and merciful. For presently He brought us both a sort of sad composure. Presently He assuaged our grief a little, and gave us the strength that we must have to meet the needs of life and the thought of going on in a world that was darkened by the loss of the boy in whom all our thoughts and all our hopes had been centred. I thanked God then, and I thank God now, that I have never denied Him nor taken His name in vain.

For God gave me great thoughts about my boy and about his death.

Slowly, gradually, He made me to see things in their true light, and He took away the sharp agony of my first grief and sorrow, and gave me a sort of peace.

John died in the most glorious cause, and he died the most glorious death it may be given to a man to die. He died for humanity. He died for liberty, and that this world in which life must go on, no matter how many die, may be a better world to live in. He died in a struggle against the blackest force and the direst threat that has appeared against liberty and humanity within the memory of man. And were he alive now, and were he called again today to go out for the same cause, knowing that he must meet death – as he did meet it – he would go as smilingly and as willingly as he went then. He would go as a British soldier and a British gentleman, to fight and die for his King and his country. And I would bid him go . . .

Sir Harry Lauder
The Scottish Soldier

In the aftermath of his son's death, Harry Lauder offered to undertake war work by visiting wounded British soldiers, at one stage interrupting a fishing holiday in Aberdeenshire to speak to veterans in a small local convalescent home. This led him to reflect on the indomitable spirit of the Scottish soldier.

No part of all the United Kingdom, and, for that matter, no part of the world, has played a greater part, in proportion to its size and its ability, than has Scotland in this war for humanity against the black force that has attacked it. Nearly a million men has Scotland sent to the army – out of a total population of five million! One in five of all her people have gone. No country in the world has ever matched that record. Ah, there were no slackers in Scotland! And they are still going – they are still going! [The exact figures were rather lower: 668,416.] As fast as they are old enough, as fast as restrictions are removed, so that men are taken who were turned back at first by the recruiting officers, as fast as men see to it that some provision is made for those they must leave behind them, they are putting on the King's uniform and going out against the Hun. My country, my ain Scotland, is not great in area. It is not a rich country in worldly goods or money. But it is big with a bigness beyond measurement, it is rich beyond the wildest dreams of avarice, in patriotism, in love of country, and in bravery.

We have few young men left in Scotland. It is rarely indeed that in a Scottish village, in a glen, even in a city, you see a young man in these days. Only the very old are left, and the men of middle age. And you know why the young men you see are there. They cannot go, because, although their spirit is willing their flesh is too weak to let them go, for one reason or another. Factory and field and forge – all have been stripped to fill the Scottish regiments and keep them at their full strength. And in Scotland, as in England, women have stepped in to fill the places their men have left vacant. This war is not to be fought by men alone. Women have their part to play, and they are playing it nobly, day after day. The women of Scotland have seen their duty; they have heard their country's call, and they have answered it.

You will find it hard to discover anyone in domestic service today in Scotland. The folk who used to keep servants sent them packing long since, to work where they would be of more use to their country. The women of each household are doing the work about the house, little though they may have been accustomed to such tasks in the days of peace. And they glory and take pride in the knowledge that they are helping to fill a place in the munitions factories or in some other necessary war work.

Do not look along the Scottish roads for folk riding in motor cars for pleasure. Indeed, you will waste your time if you look for pleasure-making of any sort in Scotland today. Scotland has gone back to her ancient business of war, and she is carrying it on in the most businesslike way, sternly and relentlessly. But that is true all over the United Kingdom; I do not claim that Scotland takes the war more seriously than the rest of Britain. But I do think that she has set an example by the way she has flung herself, tooth and nail, into the mighty task that confronts us all – all of us allies who are leagued against the Hun and his plan to conquer the world and make it bow its neck in submission under his iron heel.

Let me tell you how Scotland takes this war. Let me show you the homecoming of a Scottish soldier, back from the trenches on leave. Why, he is received with no more ceremony than if he were coming home from his day's work!

Donald – or Jock might be his name, or Andy! – steps from the train at his old hame town. He is fresh from the mud of the Flanders trenches, and all his possessions and his kit are on his back, so that he is more like a beast of burden than the natty creature old tradition taught us to think a soldier must always be. On his boots there are still dried blobs of mud from some hole in France that is like a crater in hell. His uniform will be pretty sure to be dirty, too, and torn, and perhaps, if you looked closely at it, you would see stains upon it that you might not be far wrong in guessing to be blood.

Leave long enough to let him come home to Scotland – a long road it is from France to Scotland these days! – has been a rare thing for Jock. He will have been campaigning a long time to earn it – months certainly, and maybe even years. Perhaps he was one of these who went out first. He may have been mentioned in dispatches: there may be a Distinguished Conduct Medal hidden about him somewhere – worth all the iron crosses the Kaiser ever gave! He has seen many a bloody field, be sure of that. He has heard the sounding of the gas alarm, and maybe got a whiff of the dirty poison gas the Huns turned loose against our boys. He has looked Death in the face so often that he has grown used to him. But now he is back in Scotland, safe and sound, free from battle and the work of the trenches for a space, home to gain new strength for his next bout with Fritz across the water.

When he gets off the train Jock looks about him, from force of habit. But no one has come to the station to meet him, and he looks as if that gave him neither surprise nor concern. For a minute, perhaps, he will look around him, wondering, I think, that things are so much as they were, fixing in his mind the old familiar scenes that have brought him cheer so often in black, deadly nights in the trenches or in lonely billets out there in France. And then, quietly, and as if he were indeed just home from some short trip, he shifts his pack, so that it lies comfortably across his back, and trudges off. There would be cabs around the station, but it would not come into Jock's mind to hail one of the drivers. He has been used to using Shank's Mare in France when he wanted to go anywhere, and so now he sets off quietly, with his long, swinging soldier's stride.

As he walks along he is among scenes familiar to him since his boyhood. Yon house, yon barn, yon wooded rise against the sky are landmarks for him. And he is pretty sure to meet old friends. They nod to him, pleasantly, and with a smile, but there is no excitement, no strangeness, in their greeting. For all the emotion they show, these folk to whom he has come back, as from the grave, they might have seen him yesterday, and the day before that, and the war never have been at all. And Jock thinks nothing of it that they are not more excited about him. You and I may be thinking of Jock as a hero, but that is not his idea about himself. He is just a Tommy, home on leave from France – one of a hundred thousand, maybe. And if he thought at all about the way his home folk greeted him it would be just so – that he could not expect them to be making a fuss about one soldier out of so many. And, since he, Jock, is not much excited, not much worked up, because he is seeing these good folk again, he does not think it strange that they are not more excited about the sight of him. It would be if they did make a fuss over him, and welcome him loudly, that he would think it strange!

And at last he comes to his own old home. He will stop and look around a bit. Maybe he has seen that old house a thousand times out there, tried to remember every line and corner of it. And maybe, as he looks down the quiet village street, he is thinking of how different France was. And, deep down in his heart, Jock is glad that everything is as it was, and that nothing has been changed. He could not tell you why; he could not put his feeling into words. But it is there, deep down, and the truer and the keener because it is so deep. Ah, Jock may take it quietly, and there may be no way for him to show his heart, but he is glad to be home!

And at his gate will come, as a rule, Jock's first real greeting. A dog, grown old since his departure, will come out, wagging his tail, and licking the soldier's hand. And Jock will lean down, and give his old dog a pat. If the dog had not come, he would have been surprised and disappointed. And so, glad with every fibre of his being, Jock goes in, and finds father and mother and sisters within. They look up at his coming, and their happiness shines for a moment in their eyes. But they are not the sort of people to show their emotions or make a fuss. Mother and girls will rise and kiss him, and begin to take his gear, and his father will shake him by the hand.

'Well,' the father will ask, 'how are you getting along, lad?'

And – 'All right,' he will answer. That is the British soldier's answer to that question, always and everywhere.

Then he sits down, happy and at rest, and lights his pipe, maybe, and looks about the old room which holds so many memories for him. And supper will be ready, you may be sure. They will not have much to say, these folk of Jock's, but if you look at his face as dish after dish is set before him, you will understand that this is a feast that has been prepared for him. They may have been going without all sorts of good things themselves, but they have contrived, in some fashion, to have them all for Jock. All Scotland has tightened its belt, and done its part, in that fashion, as in every other, toward the winning of the war. But for the soldiers the best is none too good. And Jock's folk would rather make him welcome so, by proof that takes no words, than by demonstrations of delight and of affection.

As he eats, they gather round him at the board, and they tell him all the gossip of the neighbourhood. He does not talk about the war, and, if they are curious – probably they are not! – they do not ask him questions. They think that he wants to forget about the war and the trenches and the mud, and they are right.

And so, after he has eaten his fill, he lights his pipe again, and sits about. And maybe, as it grows dark, he takes a bit walk into town. He walks slowly, as if he is glad that for once he need not be in a hurry, and he stops to look into shop windows as if he had never seen their stocks before, though you may be sure that, in a Scottish village, he has seen everything they have to offer hundreds of times.

He will meet friends, maybe, and they will stop and nod to him. And perhaps one of six will stop longer.

'How are you getting on, Jock?' will be the question.

'All right!' Jock will say. And he will think the question rather fatuous, maybe. If he were not all right, how should he be there? But if Jock had lost both legs, or an arm, or if he had been blinded, that would still be his answer. Those words have become a sort of slogan for the British army, that typify its spirit.

Jock's walk is soon over, and he goes home, by an old path that is known to him, every foot of it, and goes to bed in his own old bed. He has not broken into the routine of the household, and he sees no reason why he should. And the next day it is much the same for him. He gets up as early as he ever did, and he is likely to do a few odd bits of work that his father has not had time to come to. He talks with his mother and the girls of all sorts of little, commonplace things, and with his father he discusses the affairs of the community. And in the evening he strolls down town again, and exchanges a few words with friends, and learns, perhaps, of boys who haven't been lucky enough to get home on leave – of boys with whom he grew up, who have gone west.

So it goes on for several days, each day the same. Jock is quietly happy. It is no task to entertain him: he does not want to be entertained. The peace and quiet of home are enough for him; they are change enough from the turmoil of the front and the ceaseless grind of the life in the army in France.

And then Jock's leave nears its end, and it is time for him to go back. He tells them, and he makes his few small preparations. They will have cleaned his kit for him, and mended some of his things that needed mending. And when it is time for him to go they help him on with his pack and he kisses his mother and the girls goodbye, and shakes hands with his father.

'Well, goodbye,' Jock says. He might be going to work in a factory a few miles off. 'I'll be all right. Goodbye, now. Don't you cry, now, mother, and you, Jeannie and Maggie. Don't you fash yourselves about me. I'll be back again. And if I shouldn't come back – why, I'll be all right.'

So he goes, and they stand looking after him, and his old dog wonders why he is going, and where, and makes a move to follow him, maybe. But he marches off down the street, alone, never looking back, and is waiting when the train comes. It will be full of other Jocks and Andrews and Tams, on their way back to France, like him, and he will nod to some he knows as he settles down in the carriage.

And in just two days Jock will have travelled the length of England, and crossed the Channel, and ridden up to the front. He will have reported himself, and have been ordered, with his company, into the trenches. And on the third night, had you followed him, you might see him peering over the parapet at the lines of the Hun, across No Man's Land, and listening to the whine of bullets and the shriek of shells over his head, with a star shell, maybe, to throw a green light upon him for a moment.

So it is that a warrior comes and that a warrior goes in a land where war is war; in a land where war has become the business of all every day, and has settled down into a matter of routine.

Eric Linklater
85831 Pte Linklater,
The Black Watch

This account of Eric Linklater's war service was recorded in his first autobiography, The Man on My Back. *Having enlisted in the Yeomanry, Linklater transferred to the infantry in order to see action in France – by then he was a musketry instructor – and was posted to serve in 4th/5th Black Watch. When he joined the battalion, it was stationed in the Arras sector and played a role in stemming the great German offensive of March 1918. During the Allied counter-offensive south of the River Aisne, Linklater was shot in the head on 11 April 1918 and badly wounded. The steel helmet that saved his life became a prized possession and in later life the furrow in his skull left by the bullet was one of his distinguishing features.*

According to the official history of the Black Watch, the remnant strength of the battalion, when the retreat was over, was one officer and thirty men. But we had two or three more than that, I fancy, and one of them a piper. The next day, marching peacefully in the morning light of France along a pleasant road, we encountered the tattered fragment of a battalion of Foot Guards, and the piper, puffing breath into his bag and playing so that he filled the air like the massed bands of the Highland Division, saluted the tall Coldstreamers, who had a drum or two and some instruments of brass that made also a gallant music. Stiffly we passed each other, swollen of chest, heads tautly to the right, kilts swinging to answer the swagger of the Guards, and the Red

Hackle in our bonnets like the monstrance of a bruised but resilient faith. We were bearded and stained with mud – the Guards, the fifty men that were left of a battalion, were button-bright and cleanly shaven – we were a tatterdemalion crew from the coal-mines of Fife and the back streets of Dundee, but we trod quick-stepping to the brawling tune of 'Hielan' Laddie', and suddenly I was crying with a fool's delight and the sheer gladness of being in such company.

They were brave comrades, but they could not speak French. A day or so later we were in a poor little village, and for some reason more hungry than usual. But the villagers were as hungry as ourselves, and though there was a baker's shop in the muddy street, the baker would give us no bread. His people, he said, were rationed like soldiers – the French were a nation of soldiers – and therefore not a loaf could be spared. Absolutely and definitely, he refused to sell. But he had a daughter, a plump girl with fair hair, with pale fat cheeks and little dark brown eyes that looked quickly from one to another of the kilted troops, and saw in them some recondite cause for often giggling.

'Here, you!' exclaimed a lean and hardy private. I turned obediently. 'If you can parly-voo the old man, you can parly-voo the lassie. Away and ask her for a promenade the night, and gie her a bit cuddle, and see what you can do. You'll maybe get twa-three loaves out of her the morn's morn.'

'But I'm on guard to-night,' I said.

'I'll tak your guard. Away you and clean your buttons, and see if you ken the French for square-pushing.'

So in laborious and schoolboy terms I made love to the baker's daughter, and an hour before dawn I was at the bakehouse door, and she came hurriedly, and without another word put half a dozen crisp long loaves into my arms.

I prided myself on a conquest, but so apparently did she, and spread the news of it. For in the afternoon I was walking down the street, and passing two thin and dirty little boys, I heard one say to the other in solemn tones, '*Voilà l'Ecossais qui parle français!*'

It was a very gratifying moment.

We continued marching westward and came to Arques, where we were billeted in what seemed to be a deserted factory. I threw my kit into a corner – the farthest corner from the door – and went out for a stroll; but when I came back my belongings were in the middle of the floor, and in my chosen corner was a black-avised and surly man with a short pipe in his mouth and an air of possession.

'That was my place,' I said.

'Weel, it's mine noo,' he answered grimly.

Everybody, with happy anticipation, was watching us; and sadly I realised that I must challenge him to fight. It was clearing my throat – for the words were curiously slow in coming – when a sergeant shouted through the open door, 'Stand to! Get your kits packed, and on parade. Full marching order.'

'What's the matter now?' they asked him.

'We're going up the bloody line again: that's all!'

It was true, and I was thankful to hear it; for the order came just in time to save me from a thrashing.

For the next two or three weeks the war was in a state of singular confusion. We were in the neighbourhood of Ypres again – at Zillebeke and Voormezeele – and wherever we went we were digging trenches and fighting off an enemy who generally appeared from some entirely unexpected quarter. It was the season for low-lying fog, and on one occasion we refrained, in the nick of time, from opening fire on a battalion of Cameron Highlanders who, in the most mysterious fashion, came charging towards us out of what we thought was the German line. We were now a composite battalion, made from Cambridgeshires, Cheshires, KRRs [King's Royal Rifles], Black Watch, certain Welshmen, and other remnants of the 39th Division; and when, about this time, Haig issued the celebrated order in which he said we were fighting with our backs to the wall, there was laughter from one end of the country to the other; for we had no such illusion of support, and were more likely to be fighting with our backs to the enemy, since the Germans often appeared on both sides of us.

Nothing occurred of any military importance – though a good many lives were lost – but to myself there happened something of startling interest. I nearly became a good soldier. It began with a gumboil and outrageous toothache that swelled my cheek to the likeness of a dumpling, and put me into the vilest temper. When the gumboil subsided, I discovered to my amazement that I had acquired not only confidence, but a new capacity of enjoyment. Rations were plentiful: I ate with good appetite, and swigged my rum with enormous pleasure. I was still afraid, especially of being taken prisoner, and of heavy trench-mortars that shook the earth with the close violence of their explosion; but my fear was under control, and far less tiresome than toothache.

It is true that I never learnt to handle pick and spade very cleverly, and as many of my fellow privates had been miners, my ineptitude was the more apparent by contrast. Once, while we were digging a new line, the Commanding Officer came to inspect our work and stood for a long time behind me. Compared with the deep excavation of my comrades, I had made, I confess, but a shallow hole; and his voice, when at last he spoke, was recognisably unfriendly.

His first question was insulting. 'What are you doing?' he asked.

I turned and stood rigidly at attention: 'Digging a trench, sir.'

'My wife,' he said, 'has a small dog, a Pekinese, that goes out every morning to do its business in the garden. And that little Pekinese dog makes a bigger hole than you do.'

Glumly, amid sycophantic laughter, I waited for the inevitable conclusion. It came. He turned to the NCO beside him and said coldly, 'Take his name, sergeant.'

But I found compensation when, in a rather casual way, I became a sniper. Because of the composite nature of the battalion, organisation was a little sketchy, and appointments were made in a somewhat perfunctory fashion. At stand-to one morning the company sergeant-major enquired for marksmen, and though others kept a prudent silence, I stood proudly forward, exclaiming 'Here, sir!'

'All right,' he said, 'you're a sniper. There's a hole about twenty yards in front of that sap that'll give you a good field of fire. You'd better get into it before the mist rises.'

And then I earned my pay, and in a taut unresting way enjoyed myself. I had found a rifle that was unusually well balanced, and I got the nose of the sear so filed that little more than blood-pressure on the trigger would fire it. It was a good rifle. Twice we were attacked, and the attacks were beaten off; and there were German working-parties within easy range. I earned my rations, and for a few days lived at the full pitch of strenuous excitement.

But my little while of active service was nearly over. Early one morning we were driven out of the ruined village of Voormezeele and, in a most unwilling counter-attack, recaptured it an hour or so later. Pressing hard, and vastly outnumbering us, the Germans came back. They turned our flank, and my platoon was left in an unfinished trench that thrust like a tongue into their midst. I was at the extreme end of it, because from there ran a sap I had used for sniping. They were very close. One could see the agitation of their features, and the shape of their helmets appeared more sinister than ever. I had used all my ammunition – I had been shooting badly – and in any case my rifle was too hot to hold. But I had a box of bombs, already detonated, and I threw one that fell short. I was swinging for the second when I heard a wild shout behind me, and looking round saw the trench was empty save for one man, who had come back to warn me that we were retreating. He was an old regular soldier, and had also been a nurse in a lunatic asylum. He was a big good-looking man, but his cheeks had strangely fallen in. He must have lost his false teeth, I thought.

I threw my second bomb, more usefully than the first, and turned to run. I ran so very fast that, although I was the last by a long way to leave the trench, within two hundred yards I had passed several of those who preceded me; including an officer who was looking back with an expression of reluctance that, in the circumstances, appeared strangely ill-timed.

I continued to run till in a mingling of righteous indignation and utter dismay I felt on my head a blow of indescribable force. It was a bullet, and probably a machine-gun bullet; for the rifle-fire of the German infantry was poor.

When I recovered consciousness, the surrounding landscape appeared entirely empty. But I could not see very well, and perhaps I was mistaken. A few shots, that were evidently hostile, gave me a rough direction, and with clumsy fingers I took from a pocket in the lining of my tunic a little package of field-dressings. I could not undo it, but stuck it whole on the back of my head, where I judged the wound to be, and kept it in position with my steel helmet, that a chin-strap held tightly on.

Scarcely had I made these arrangements when, my sight growing more foggy, I fell into a water-logged trench. It was deep, and full to the brim, and the sides were so well revetted that I had great difficulty in getting out. I was nearly drowned, indeed, and lost my good rifle there. But the cold water revived me, and now my only feeling of discomfort was extreme weariness. So I threw off my equipment and my tunic, and found progress a little easier. Presently, after walking, as I thought, for many miles, someone came to help me, and I saw a cluster of men in kilt and kilt-apron, who looked familiar. I waved my hand to them. It was the very last, the ultimate remnant of the battalion, and already they were forming for the counter-attack.

In the afternoon they recaptured Voormezeele.

My wound was dressed and I was given a coat. I lay for some time among dying men, and grew so displeased with such company that I got up and, joining a party of walking wounded, found something to eat. I was ravenously hungry. Then we were put into an ambulance, and the jolting of that was an agony that drove one nearly mad. The ambulance stopped, and we had to get out and walk to a train. Watching us were thirty or forty men of the Chinese Labour Corps. Moon-faced, thickly wadded coolies like those I had been warder among in the long hut at Calais. The same men, perhaps.

They began to laugh at us. We were a ludicrous company, tottering and misshapen, roughly bandaged; but only the dreadful sanity of China could have seen the joke, I think. Thin of voice, the coolies tittered with laughter; then as their mirth grew, doubled-down and held their sides, or clapped each other on the back. Peal upon peal their laughter rang, and they pointed to the saviours of the western world.

Hugh MacDiarmid
Casualties

Written in France at the end of the war when Hugh MacDiarmid was stationed in Marseilles, the story was sent to his old teacher George Ogilvie and was published in the Summer 1919 edition of Broughton Magazine. *Alan Bold suggests that the story might have been written in response to the death in action in 1915 of MacDiarmid's close friend John Bogue Nisbet.*

————

For three weeks the working hours of the unit had been sixteen out of every twenty-four, and at length, in the centre of that sloppy and muddy field, appeared what was to be known to the Army as the Nth Casualty Clearing Station.

Tired enough from the strain of continued and unremitting road-making, tent-pitching, and the innumerable heart-breaking tasks incidental to the shifting of stoves and equipment, and the improvisation of those diversely essential things which cannot be secured except by indents which take many weeks to circulate through the chain of offices, the unit disposed itself, as units do, to snatch some sleep before the first rush should begin.

None too soon, it shortly appeared, for as we stumbled to the Fall-In, headlights began to appear on the road from Albert, a long trail of ambulance cars stretching back into the rainy dampness which hid the tremendous business so casually referred to as 'The Big Push'. The turn of the first car into the little road found a quietly active camp, for hasty preparations had been carried out in just such improbable corner-grounds many times before.

Here, as always in the track of armies in the Somme region,

the salient element was mud – thick, deep, insistent and clinging mud that the strongest will could not treat as negligible. There it was and it made the smallest errand an exacting fatigue. The cars manoeuvred through it with the casual air that comes of much experience. Even London taxi-drivers might have learned something from the dexterous and undelaying way in which Red Cross cars were juggled over that boggy land. One by one the cases were slid out by stretcher-bearers working deftly and surely with a sort of tired ease. Car after car rolled up – just the price of 'strengthening the line and solidifying positions in the neigh- bourhood of—', as it would appear from the day's official report. Men of all units, tired, pale and dirty, were carried into the hut that a party of engineers had finished feverishly that very day. Their khaki barely showed through the encrusting mud save where it had been slit to rags to allow of temporary dressings being put on at Field Ambulances and First Aid Posts and now showing in curious patterns of white and red. Among them were some to whom this station would be something more than a wayside resting-place, men to whom the doctors up the line, working in dugouts where immediate attention to all could not be given, had given a desperate last chance. They died on the way or slipped off without fuss in the Receiving Room, but one or two were pulled through by efforts and methods that would stagger civilian practice.

All night the slow heavy labour of stretcher-bearing went on. And great grey cars pulled up with loads of less seriously wounded who straggled brokenly into the room, muddied and shivering, hatless and coatless often, and with that complete apathy of look and bearing which tells of strain that has gone beyond endurance.

The detached onlooker might have found it moving enough, but here, fortunately, there were not detached onlookers. Lady friends, of the type we all know, were compelled to find stimu- lants for their sentiment somewhat further down. But, here, a man who had been shovelling mud from the road during a back-breaking afternoon was now booking particulars of the arrivals. But some stared blankly through the interrogator, deaf and speechless, shaking and quivering, and that matter-of-fact fellow entered them as 'Shell-shock – No particulars available', and they were led off in that new world of theirs to a mattress, and ultimately who shall say to what strange and undesirable destiny.

The slightest cases walked or limped casually up to the keen deft-handed doctor and his alert assistants with the air of men to whom this was but one more incalculable phase of a business whose immensity made all impressions unseizable. To them, indeed, it had been overwhelming, and many of them were so youthful that one felt that the first instinct of their mothers, could they have seen them, would have been to reprove them for being out without overcoats on such a night!

The lashed rows of marquees that had been dignified by the name of 'wards' received these exhausted men on straw palliasses and blankets, and even, for serious cases, cot-beds. Casualty Clearing Stations belong not to any particular division but to an army, and therefore hither came representatives of most of the troops of an Army – Canadian, New Zealanders and South Africans, as well as famous British regiments and new raised battalions, and sick from locally quartered West Indians, Artillery, Engineers, and billeted troops. And there were men in mud-stained grey, stoical as our own, who somehow seemed mere ordinary men again and enemies no longer!

Serious cases speedily filled every available cot and an overflow lay around on stretchers. From all sides came the accustomed moaning for water and the close and heavy breathing of those past even moaning. A strapping sergeant of New Zealanders, gasping out his last unconscious moments, was the first to go. There was no more than time for a quick laying-out (with the boot which was hanging so unnaturally to one side, the foot came off too, despite bandages). His transit must have been a desperate gamble from the start – a wrapping in a rough blanket with scrawled particulars attached, and the big fellow who had travelled so far to his fate was taken on a stretcher to the marquee that served as a mortuary.

Many joined him that night. With these hopeless ones there was no time even to stop to watch by the ebbing life, so many bedside fights there were where a forlorn hope still remained. Work went on without respite, changeless save for the occasional sudden appearance of officers who would leave a few hasty directions for the special treatment of cases which had just left their hands in the operation theatre. Those worst hours before the dawn passed in hectic attendance – the tiredness of the body had perforce to be treated merely as a clogging dream – and the day-staff came to the relief of worn-out men.

The peaceful dawn-wind smote the workers as they stooped to pass through the low canvas doorways and the first faint flush of red showed behind a tree on a far ridge.

Up to that ridge wandered the indescribable waste of the countryside, trenched and pitted and ploughed until it had become a fantastic and nightmarish wilderness. On this dreary tract nothing remained of the gifts once showered by nature. But the grim legacies of man at war were countless – chaotic and half buried heaps of his machinery, munitions and equipment, and the remains of his hasty meals. And he himself lay there, shattered in thousands, to give a lurking horror to a treacherous and violent surface of mud and slime and unlovely litter. The very weeds which might have graced the desolation refused such holding-ground.

Pale now beside the compelling splendour of the reddening day showed the yellow stabs of our guns, flashes that had lit the sky in the night watches, and only the long road, never varying, told that the unspeakable harvest on the Somme was still being gathered in.

Hugh MacDiarmid
Letters from Salonika

While serving on the Salonika front, MacDiarmid kept up a regular correspondence with George Ogilvie, his former English teacher at Broughton Junior Teaching Centre in Edinburgh. The third letter was published in the Christmas 1917 edition of Broughton Magazine. *The Kerr mentioned in the fourth letter is Roderick Watson Kerr, whose poetry was published in* War Daubs *(1919), and in the same letter Nisbet is John Bogue Nisbet, another friend from Broughton. MacDiarmid's plans for a volume of poems to be entitled 'A Voice from Macedonia' never came to fruition, although some of his war poetry was published in* Broughton Magazine.

Somewhere in the East
2 September 1916

Dear Mr Ogilvie

Why it should be vitally necessary for me to write you tonight I can no more indicate that [than] I can indicate, why, having unaccountably delayed in writing to you, I found it increasingly and finally absolutely impossible to write to you again. The loss has been mine, and an incalculable one. One of the chief considerations in the psychological tangle from which I have never freed myself is undoubtedly the fact that I have never done anything worthwhile. I have nursed my ambitions, dreamed my dreams – and grown older, that is all! Never a day has passed however but what I have thought of you. Never a day but what I have said, 'Tomorrow I will write the Fine Thing – then I will write to him again.' But the tomorrow has never come. I have written and written and great are the piles of my MSS – but they have never taken the one shape I keep on hunting for. Someday yet perhaps – !

But in the meantime picture me lying here in the mouth of a tent on a Balkan hillside; looking out over the ancient city of Salonika and its crowded waterways, across the sun-smitten gulf to high Olympus (not so very high, after all – only some 3,000 feet).

And despite my booklessness, the total absence of such company as in pre-war days I would have found congenial – despite the ravages of mosquitoes which have paid me marked attentions since I came here (indeed marked me all over), the huge heat, and the fact that the ground beneath me is one mass of ant-hills – a very moving scene! – I am as healthy as ever I was, and happier than I had ever thought to be.

It is a big hospital, that down below there to which I am attached on the Quartermaster's Staff – a cushie job! – and it will be to say enough concerning the life here, or rather the difficulty of living here, to say that business is brisk.

It is a wonderful place this ancient city with its huge new population of soldiers. So many Scotsmen are here that it has been suggested that it should be called not Thessalonica, but Thistleonica. But that would not be just to our allies. East and West meet and mingle here in an indescribable fashion. Soliders of half-a-dozen different nations fraternize in canteens and cafés. Naturally and necessarily one picks up an incredible polyglottery. Even the coins in one's pockets are representative of almost every nation in Europe.

One wearies here for letters in an unspeakable way. Perhaps you will understand and forgive and write me sometime – that is to say if you can make head or tail out of this extraordinary scribble. My address is 64020 Sergt C.M. Grieve, RAMC, 42nd General Hospital, British Salonika Force.

Now I must close. At least I have managed to write again. I

earnestly hope that this letter will find you in good health and
spirits, and that you will be interested a little to hear once more,
after a long lapse of time, from your old pupil.

C.M. Grieve

———————

Salonika

4 December 1917

Dear Mr Ogilvie,

I have written you several letters at spaces in the great interval
since I last heard from you and in the absence of any reply can
only conclude that all of them have been turned into fish-food
by the fortunes of war, the only alternative being a fear, which I
will not give house-room to, that something has happened to
you. But once more in the hope that this time I may circumvent
the conspiracy of circumstances – or, alternatively, lay that
persistent little ghost of unformulated anxiety (perhaps after all
it is your letters to me which have gone astray) – I must scribble
a few lines to wish you in time the old old wish of a merry
Christmas and a happy New Year.

My malaria which ruined my summer is once more
quiescent. It hibernates and is unlikely to give further trouble
until the hot weather returns, but another of the endemic diseases
of this unnatural country has been playing havoc this last
fortnight or so with my debilitated constitution and I am only
just pulling myself together and accomplishing what is really one
of those feats of physiological acrobatics in which lies the real
significance of the 'survival of the fittest'. A few more such
successes – and I will be able to survive anything. In a Balkan's
Who's Who I could safely put down my recreation as 'patho-
logical equilibrism'.

Day succeeds day here in a monotony of existence in which
an accident or an air raid is a God-sent diversion. The anato-
mical side of life is appallingly obtrusive. Conversation is practi-

cally monopolised by indecent discussions of 'how one feels today'. I share to the full 'Erewhon' Butler's revulsion from the tendencies of modern science.

Fortunately I am not without books and paper. Turgenev, Henry James, J.M. Synge, the Georgian Poets, Galsworthy's *Fraternity*, Gilbert Murray's Greek translations, and a few others make me little worlds in my spare time that carnal considerations cannot violate – and for myself I have actually committed to paper in rough draft (which nothing will induce me to put into any more final shape as long as I am in khaki) two one-act plays, some seventy poems, and the first volume of a trilogy of autobiographic novels somewhat of a cross in nature between Gorki's [My] *Childhood*, and Wells' *Tono-Bungay* – eheu! I shall arrive yet if I come scatheless out of the holocaust into civil life, where there are personal rights again.

I hope time is being good to you and that I shall have news of you again some happy day at no too great distance.

I wish you all good and desirable things and ascribe myself in affectionate respect,

Your old pupil,
C.M. Grieve

Please remember me seasonably to Dr Drummond should you be seeing him.

———

Christmas 1917

Dear Mr —— [Ogilvie],
Camped on a high and airy promontory jutting out into the blue Aegean, across which, a day's sail away, my usual station is on a very clear day dimly discernible on a further coast. I am at present enjoying a rest-cure and write in a holiday mood for the first time in close on fifteen months.

A recent recurrence of malignant malaria left me deplorably

reduced in physique and stamina and, noting my debility, the authorities took compassion on me and sent me hither to this 'change of air camp' for a ten-days' spell, of which four or five days have still to run.

There are caller air[s] which would revive me more speedily and thoroughly, I know, but failing these yet awhile (the wheels of the chariots of Mars stand badly in need of oiling), the change here is doing me a world of good – I feel a different fellow already – and by the time my holiday is over I should be quite built up again for the winter. Now that the colder weather is setting in I need fear no further recurrence of the fever till next summer by which time I hope to have shaken the dust of Macedon off my Army Pattern boots finally and forever – but one never can tell.

In the meantime, however, I have little to do but eat, sleep, bathe and remember old friends. The bathing is splendid, along a long sweep of beach (reached by a break-neck goats' track down steep cliffs) in waters clear to a great depth and with a fine smooth, sandy bottom. On walking along the shore one may see some quaint native fisheries, with two rickety ladder erections sticking up out of the water like the skeletons of stupendous cranes. From seats on the top of these the fishermen can see their prey entering their nets some distance out. They then haul up the nets until they go out and secure their yield in a primitive old boat. Red mullet, for the most part, and an eel-like fish with silver belly and bright green back, and curious thin sword-like mouths, like a snipe's bill.

More curious still is a chance encounter with a lonely but well-contented Scots highlander, line-fishing with an old cod-hook, baited with the entrails of mussels (with which the adjacent rocks are plentifully bestruck). He has a true highland knack of casting – power to his elbow! – and is doing great damage to a school of pink-and-silvery, flounder-like fish. But as he says, no doubt he'd be 'nane the waur o' a wheen worms'.

But mostly I lie on the cliff-top – the climb back from the beach liking me not – lie in the sunshine on almost bentless terrain, watching the crafts go up and down the shining waterways. All kinds and conditions of vessels are here. Modern men-of-war and motor-craft: old-fashioned sailing-ships and native boats, Trireme and Submarine, galleon and collier, schooner and motor-yacht pass and repass in striking epitomes of naval history.

Behind, the ground rolls endlessly in almost desert stretches. Scarcely a tree is to be seen. But all that Masefield in his *Gallipoli* says of Mudros and the Dardanelles, and the magic colours, which the powerful sunlight draws out of the rocky barennesses [sic] there, is true also of my present location – and even Masefield's pen has not done full justice to the subtle wonders of these unsuspected colours that make it seem as if the wizardry of the slanting rays of the sun turned grey stone and brown clay into gold and silver and ruby and emerald.

And in such settings I lie and dream.

Your old pupil,

C.M. Grieve

_____

Macedonia
13 February 1918

Dear Mr Ogilvie,

My state of mind at this writing can be best indicated perhaps by the following quotations from my current Suggestion Book: viz 'NB – See October 1917, *Little Review*, not allowed to be issued in America, on account of Wyndham Lewis's "Cantleman's Spring Mate". The case of "Cantleman" was taken into court in New York and brilliantly and humorously defended, but to no avail. The soldier Cantleman and the girl he met in the forest are still most damnably "wrapt in mystery"' – Scots Bureau, 27/7 (a reference number, which must go as merely adumbrating an extraordinary system I have evolved for not losing sight of workable material concerning Things Scottish – similar systems cover my other interests) – Mr J.A. Ferguson, sportsman, dramatist, novelist and poet. *Campbell of Kilmohr*.' – 'NB T.W.H. Crosland's *The English Sonnet*.' – There are thousands of such entries now in these suggestion books of mine, each indicating some line of creative endeavour, or journalistic intention. Will I ever be free to develop them? Looking over them I can only ejaculate Eureka, Zeugma, Catachresis and all abominable things. I feel like a buried city.

The first thing I must do when I get into civilian clothes again is to go into a comtee [committee] of Ways and Means. Then, if the way is clear, I must first of all, however intriguing other speculations may be, dispose of my trilogy of novels. I could complete them in a year. My brother is now 1st Clerk in the 4th Inland Revenue Division, Edinburgh – I will live on him for that year, probably. After that I can work up these Suggestion Books – and my Catholic Adventures – and the one-act plays and poems. – The appalling thing is that there are additions every day to these Suggestion Books, new impulses for lyrics, new motifs – and I can finish nothing under present circumstnaces – and I have already mortgaged more than my allotted span several times over. Verily as someone said, 'Life is a predicament in which we find ourselves before death.'

I was glad to get your last letter. (I forget whether I have written you since receiving it or not). I remember Roderick Kerr well – He succeeded me as editor of the Mag didn't he? – and went in for punning verse after Thomas Hood. I should like to see his *English Review* stuff. If you should be writing to him please congratulate him on my behalf on his 'arrival'. I shall hope someday to meet him, as you suggest the fates may allow, chez vous. Other Edinburgh news is scanty. Nisbet's sister has just been married. I am afraid that by the time I get back all the nice girls will be bespoken. Still we have our compensations here.

One Maregena, a Spanish girl hailing from Barcelona, would
interest you. Only a Turgenev could write her up. Incidentally
she writes herself. Curiously poignant little songs they are,
somewhat like Heine's or Emily Dickinson's. I am collecting all
she will permit to pass into my hands. One day I shall translate
them perhaps. – There are others. – Miss Murray is teaching
down in Essex now. A friend of mine, a *New Age* writer and
poet, lives there too in the same village – G. Reston Malloch.
And Miss Cecilia Murray is down in Bucks.

I am in excellent health just now and having a fairly lively
time. We had a champion Burns' Night, the 'Immortal Memory'
devolving upon me. I do a lot of talking and speechifying.
Modern musical tendencies was the theme of a lively discussion
the other night: but when we got off generalities and down to
names and motifs, I found that Rimsky-Karasov [*sic*], Stravinsky
and Debussy did not enter into the scheme of things for the
others, so I dropped out. The general ignorance of recent
stringed-instrument experimentation is abysmal – and yet a
fellow who can sing 'Annie Laurie' or has heard of Chopin and
Handel contests my right to argue, seeing I do not like music and
am tone deaf. A mad world!

It is a terrible thought, shutting me in most horribly on
myself, that of a list of say twelve people in whom I am for the
moment pre-eminently interested, not one of them is known to
any other member of the mess – these are Paul Fort, the Sitwells,
Rebecca West, Serge Asanoff, Remy de Goncourt [Remy de
Gourmont] (whose posthumous papers I am dying to read),
Joyce Kilmer (an admirable appreciation of whose works I have
just read in *The Month*), Theodore Maynard (quotations from
whose *Drums of Defeat* – and *in extenso* his fine tribute to
Pádraic Pearse – I find in the latest *Dublin Leader*, the Sinn Fein
paper, to hand) – and so on.

Still one can always read. Under my pillow just now I have
Chesterton's *The Club of Queer Trades*, Alpha of the Plough's

Pebbles on the Shore, E.V. Lucas's *A Little of Everything*, some *English Review*s containing stories by Caradoc Evans, some copies of *Everyman* and of *The Month* and *The Tablet* and *The New York Saturday Post* and *The Sydney Bulletin* and *Life* and *La Revue Franco-Macedoniene*, and some *National News*, copies with instalments of Wells' *The Soul of a Bishop* – on the whole I cannot complain.

I have a letter from the Rev. T.S. Cairncross – did I ever mention him to you? He has published several volumes of pleasant prose and two volumes of poetry: *The Margin of Rest* (Elkin Matthews), written largely under the influence of Heine on the one hand and Bliss Carman on the other, and *The Masters' Return* (Scott), a volume of rhymeless rhythms reminiscent of Henley. He could not be omitted from any adequate anthology of modern Scottish poetry. Several of his vernacular ballads are wonderfully good. But the great bulk of his stuff is still in MSS. He is just back from chaplaining in France and is likely to contribute something good to the literature of the War. I should like to send on some of his stuff to you – but must wait till I get home. I should like your opinion of him. He writes most delightful letters.

Excuse this paper and scribbling hand. I shall hope to hear from you again soon. It was fine of you to will my safe return. Any psychological force I can support the suggestion with, will be devoted to making you an effective master of Nietzschean methods.

Au revoir, then, with all good wishes.

Yours etc.

C.M. Grieve

PS Please remember me to the Rev Dr Drummond.

———

Macedonia
28 April 1918

Dear Mr Ogilvie:–

Yours of date a month ago today just to hand by a mail which yielded me nothing else. The postal authorities have been dealing hardly with me lately. I have had no letters from home since 2/3/18. Imagine then the doubled joy with which I welcomed your letter.

I do not think I have ever felt better since the malaria microbe invaded my veins way back in September 1916 than I do at this writing. During the past fortnight or so I have been constantly in the open sharing all the strenuousness that is involved in the establishing of a new camp. I have experienced the sundry travails of a heavy porter, a navvy, a general contractor's ganger – and, if the weather has been progressively hot, well the good brown ale at intervals has been all the more refreshing. Our labours are nearly over. Soon we will resume the ordinary routine. But it has been good while it has lasted – hard work, long hours, willing comrades, a little period of hard playing and riotous fun, and then, the soundest of sleep.

Beneath my newly reissued solar topee my face is of a deep good-natured brown and there are no dark rings under the eyes which are clearer and livelier perhaps than lately they were. Something deep in me has been stirred by the sensation of striving muscles and the sight of spaded clay that never responds to the disciplined system of more settled periods. Once but for my father (and that was after I had been to Broughton a year or so) I would have become a gardener – but that was so many centuries ago!

I wish I could lay my hands just now on Maurice Hewlett's *Epic of Hodge* [properly *The Song of the Plow,* in which the central character is named Hodge]. I am just in the mood to appreciate it. As it is I shall be surprised if I do not find it to my

hand any moment. I nearly always do. You comment on the
strange way in which I seem to keep in touch. I suppose it is the
operation of some law similar to that which makes birds of a
feather flock together. Seek and you shall find – such urgent need
as mine cannot be denied. Just now I have in my little Nestlé's
Milk Box library a recent number of the *Dublin Review*, Viola
Meynell's *Lot Barrow*, Stella Callaghan's *Vision*, Turgenev's
Rudin in Constance Garnett's translation, Austin Dobson's
Fielding, a monograph on Landseer, Archibald Marshall's
Richard Baldock, a presentation copy autographed by the author
to his friend, Dion Clayton Calthorp [*sic*], whom we also know,
and a copy of the *Englishwoman* containing a very delightful
review of the poems of George Reston Malloch (erstwhile the
G.R.M. of the 'Ham and Meat' corner of the *Glasgow Herald*)
who is one of my own correspondents too. – It is strange, but it
could not have been otherwise if I had been in the middle of the
Sahara. At the worst I would have written (or more probably
dreamt) my own library. – And it may further interest you to
know that most of my reading comes from 'The Soldiers' Recreation Fund, 29 Drumsheugh Gardens, Edinburgh'.

I am in one of my buoyant moods. When I wrote that last
letter in which I despaired of ever producing anything I was in a
'Rudin' mood – but today! No, I will not be snowed under in
any mental sense. What I do most desperately fear is that my
physique will not carry me through, or that the free expression
of myself will be inhibited by family and economic cares before
I get a chance to establish myself in a monetary sense – which I
must do before I can labour uninterruptedly and successfully at
my work. – But today I am well in body and in mind and all my
diverse purposes are grouping themselves harmoniously into a
delectable life's work with no confusion or failure anywhere: –
If only the war would end soon and let me get begun in real
earnest!

In a day or two per registered post I shall send on to you a series of poems designed to fill a gap in the Soldier Poets' series published by Erskine MacDonald, which so far has mainly consisted of the work of men serving on the Western Front and at all events has not so far included anything from Salonika. I suggest calling the little collection 'A Voice from Macedonia'.

They represent the work of three consecutive days, except one or two written earlier and at isolated times. Probably they might be the better of having more time spent on them but that would be rather against the idea of 'soldier-verse' – essentially a hasty and spontaneous thing. But I send them to you, rather than directly to Erskine MacDonald's, confident that I am not trespassing too far on your kindness in asking you to read them first and make any little alterations or corrections you deem good. Will you please then submit them to Erskine MacDonald for me? I can guarantee a circulation of at least 100 among my own immediate friends here – and advts. in the *Balkan News* and the *RAMC Corps Magazine* would be profitable, while of course I have at least fifty personal friends at home who would have a copy.

Whatever happens to them I feel sure you will find some interest in these Active Service effusions and that in itself will amply redeem the few leisure hours they took to write. I heard that you utilised my Karabouroun letter for the *BM* and if any of these poems can be similarly used I shall be only too happy. It was, by the way, with remarkable indirectness through a Miss Mabel Leighton, now teaching at Ayton in Berwickshire, that I heard of my reappearance in the *BM*. She it seems knew me at Broughton. I do not remember her at all – but how nice to be remembered after all this time!

I have been definitely passed for invaliding home as a chronic malaria subject. The scheme was temporarily hung up but has just restarted. So expect a surprise call from me sometime during this summer!

I shall ask my mother in my next letter to post on to you

two or three volumes of Cairncross's work I happen to have lying at home.

You refer to my letters showing a 'serene detachment from the War' – but please remember the strictness of the Censorship. However loyal I may be to certain ideals bound up in the Allied Cause I was never to say the least of it an Anglophile – and when I am free of his majesty's uniform again I shall have a very great deal indeed to say and to write that I have not nearly enough desire for premature and secret martyrdom to say or write until then.

In a postscript you ask me to give you my full denomination and address in this reply but your doubts seem to be groundless – you have correctly addressed me on this last envelope.

By the way if you hear anything about Miss Murray – more particularly in regard to her health – please tell me. We write – but the intervals are always long and irregular. The last time I heard from her she was teaching down in Essex. I have not heard from her now for more than usually long – which generally means that she has had another breakdown. She scarcely ever alludes to such matters herself and after inexplicable silences resumes as casually as if she had never left of[f] writing. I am not now in touch with anyone who is in the way of hearing anything about her, but at Broughton you may be. I am afraid my relations with the other sex are incredibly complicated and that between Nelly and I, if it could be written up, would be voted quite impossible, but it is nevertheless although so sketchy and haphazard vital in different way [sic] to both of us – and part and parcel, as you say, of a group of associations I would not willingly let die.

Now I must cease. I shall post the poems on as soon as I can get them censored. Hoping to hear from you soon again – and ever with the kindest regards.

Yours,
C.M. Grieve

Compton Mackenzie
The Dark Night of the
Suvla Landing

Following the failure of the naval operation to force the Dardanelles, ground forces were landed on the Gallipoli peninsula in April 1915 to attack the heavily defended Turkish positions. In August General Sir Ian Hamilton, the commander of the British Expeditionary Force, made his second attempt to gain control of the Gallipoli peninsula. It involved a double strike against the Turkish positions at Ari Burnu (Anzac Cove) and a night attack on Chunuk Bair. At the same time a new landing was made at Suvla Bay, a few miles to the north. By the time the British assault began, the Turks had brought up fresh reserves and the landings ended in failure. It was clear that the Gallipoli operations had been a disaster and Hamilton was replaced by General Sir Charles Monro, who ordered a complete evacuation at the end of the year. Of the characters mentioned by Mackenzie, Captain C.F. Aspinall was to become the official historian of the campaign, Major (later Major-General) Guy Dawnay was one of Hamilton's senior staff officers, Captain (later Brigadier) Wyndham Deedes was head of counter-intelligence and George Lloyd (later Lord Lloyd) was a Member of Parliament and another of Hamilton's staff officers.

At half-past three on the afternoon of the sixth of August the thunder of the guns on Helles travelling across the clear air to Kephalo proclaimed that the general attack ordered there had begun. This was intended to occupy the Turks in the Southern

Zone and prevent their moving northward to reinforce the
defenders above Anzac, where the Australians and New
Zealanders launched their attack at half-past five. The gunfire
pulsated on the still air, and by seven o'clock the whole length
of the long line of tawny cliffs was twinkling with starry shells.
All through the afternoon the troops of the Eleventh Division
had been embarking in the new armour-plated motor-lighters
that from their appearance were known as beetles. Ten thousand
troops embarked at Imbros; six thousand were on their way
from Mudros. From Mytilene four thousand more were steering
northward into the unknown out of the unknowable, for half an
hour after the last trawler had left Port Iero *Canopus* had deliberately fouled the cable so that no news of their departure could
be signalled from enemy agents in Lesbos.

The evening was brilliantly clear: the sea was calm. About
half-past seven I stood above the GHQ camp and looked down
across the waters of Kephalo to where on the level land beyond
K beach hundreds of evacuated tents clustered like ghosts in the
twilight. The roadstead was thronged with shipping; and the
smoke of many funnels belching into the clear air and making
turbid a sky slashed with the crimson of a long slow sunset
suggested the glimpse of a manufacturing town in a hollow of
the Black Country beheld from some Staffordshire height. One
after another the ships moved out of the harbour: great liners
like the *Minneapolis* with the newspaper correspondents on
board, destroyers, trawlers, beetles, battleships, and many
others. By half-past seven the roadstead was empty. The metallic
blues and greens and blood-reds in the water had turned to a
cold dull grey. Eastward the ever increasing surge and thunder
of the guns: here an almost horrible quiet. At ten o'clock the new
landing was due to begin. Hardly anybody spoke at dinner. Jan
Smith had gone over to Suvla, so George Lloyd, Deedes and I
drew lots for the three shifts of sitting up for Intelligence signals.
Lloyd drew ten to one, Deedes four to seven, and I to my great

pleasure the middle shift from one to four. This was the time, we reckoned, when we should be hearing of important events at Suvla. By now the heavy presentiment of failure had vanished. I was feeling positive that during my shift great news would come through which I should remember to my dying day. I was too much excited to go to bed, and from ten to twelve I worked on that absurd memorandum on the Müller family in Mytilene, and my proposed scheme for their elimination. At midnight I went across with George Lloyd to the O tent where we drank cocoa. No news of any kind had yet arrived; but we told ourselves that we really must not expect any quite as soon as this. Lloyd was listless and downhearted. I urged him to go to bed, such a headache had he, and as I walked with him to his tent he told me how much he hated being here and doing nothing while the push was on.

'I'm no good at GHQ to anybody,' he said bitterly. 'If I were with my regiment, I should feel more respect for myself.'

It was difficult to reassure George Lloyd when he succumbed to these self-searching moods of despair. I left him and walked back to the O tent after telling the orderly in I to bring across any telegrams. By one o'clock there was nobody left in the O tent except Guy Dawnay, Cecil Aspinall, Barttelot and the Cipher-major Orlo Williams with his code books. Sir Walter Barttelot was a Coldstreamer who had joined the staff while I was at Mytilene. He was a quiet attractive man, the head of one of the most ancient families in England. His father had been killed in South Africa: he himself was to be killed in 1918. I felt that depression was setting in here under the strain of waiting for news, and I tried to amuse them by enacting a series of imaginary scenes between various members of the General Staff. Apparently I was successful in being funny, for Orlo Williams told me the other day that one of his memories of Suvla night was trying not to laugh, because in the bruised condition of his bones after falling from his horse two days before every laugh was an agony. However, I could not go on being funny indefinitely, and we were soon sitting anxiously waiting for news.

Two o'clock went by without further news. Guy Dawnay and I walked out to listen for firing northward. The night was utterly still. General Birrell had gone back to his disturbed sleep. Over the Peninsula the blood-red horn of the waning moon just risen was clawing up at the sky. A rocket flamed on the horizon. A ship was hooting mournfully while it waited to be allowed in through the Kephalo boom. At half-past two somebody in O tent produced a bottle of Horlick's Malted Milk Lozenges, and we all started sucking them in a melancholy. Aspinall must have drawn forty ladies by now, each one becoming a little more wooden than her predecessor. I tried to cheer up things by reading out my scheme for kidnapping the Müller family. Guy Dawnay suggested that I should submit a scheme for kidnapping some of the Brigadiers of the new Divisions.

'Good God!' Aspinall rapped out suddenly. 'They must be ashore by now.'

A telegram came in to say that the fouled cable had been mended. That brigade and a half from Mytilene should be nearly off Suvla at this moment.

At half-past three I went outside again to listen for gunfire. The moon, clear of the mirk of the Peninsula heights by now, was shining very yellow in the eastern sky. But there was no news yet of the Ninth Army Corps, though the first grey of dawn was perceptible.

Then at ten minutes to four an orderly came in with a signal.

'At last,' cried Aspinall, tearing open the envelope. Then 'Damn!' he groaned, tossing the piece of paper down.

'*Bamboozled 800 punctured*,' said the message.

It was only a code message for the Quartermaster-General's department; but it sounded as if some mocking demon had chosen those two words to tell us that the Suvla Landing had failed.

'But they must be ashore by now,' said Aspinall miserably.

It was now four o'clock and time to wake Deedes for the shift from four to seven. But before I woke him I ran down under the paling sky to the Signals tent and asked the sergeant in desperation if there was still no news from Suvla.

'Only this, sir,' he said, 'from the signaller on the New Landing. It was in reply to us, for it seemed so funny not hearing anything from over there.'

He wrote out on a form that the signaller of the New Landing reported he could now hear hot musketry and the sound of bursting shells behind him.

I hurried back with this message to the O tent.

'Well, they've landed anyway,' said Guy Dawnay grimly.

'Yes, they've landed,' Aspinall agreed. 'But this is what we ought to have heard three hours ago.'

I left him to discuss for the twentieth time what could have been holding up the operation, and went along to wake Deedes, whose tent was at the top of the Lines. The moon was now much higher, a frail silver slip of a moon turning to ivory in the pale eastern sky. The little wind of dawn was lisping through the withered herbage and ruffling the sand here and there with cat's-paws. The guns had started to growl again. I found Deedes already in his dressing-gown, and as he moved nattily about his tent he would stop from time to time to listen if the kettle on his spirit-lamp was beginning to boil. In the glimmering twilight of dawn he looked more than ever like a pious church-worker getting up to attend early Service. I told him about the disappointments of the night. He made no comment but advised down me to get off to bed. So I left him and walked down through the rows of tents which stood out against the wan air of dawn as black as the night fast receding into the west.

It was a long time before I fell sound asleep, for I kept waking to clutch at phantoms. There was no vestige of hope left in my mind that the Suvla Landing could now succeed. I felt as

if I had watched a system crack to pieces before my eyes, as if I
had stood by the deathbed of an old order. The guns I could hear
might have been a growling that foretold the murderous folly of
the Somme. The war would last now until we had all turned
ourselves into Germans to win it. An absurd phrase went singing
through my head. *We have lost our amateur status to-night.* It
was foolish for me who had been old enough to appreciate the
muddle of the South African War to go on believing in the
practical value of the public-school system. I had really for long
mistrusted it, but since coming out here I had fallen once more
under its spell as I might have fallen under the spell of a story by
Rudyard Kipling. Yes, the War would go on now. I must
remember to write home to-morrow for more woollen under-
clothes. We should be here indefinitely now. Queer that a man
like Sir Ian Hamilton so perfectly cut out to ride into Constantinople at the head of a victorious army should be thwarted of
his hope. He would appear so Wellingtonian, charging up Achi
Baba on a black horse and looking over his shoulder to wave on
. . . the picture faded as I woke up again fully . . . and then I
trembled once more upon the verge of sleep with a vision of Sir
Ian Hamilton standing beside a drum, the smoke of battle
beyond his slim eager form, a field marshal's baton grasped
tightly in one hand, the injured hand by his side lending an added
dignity to his appearance like Nelson's missing arm . . . the
smoke of battle . . . and along the horizon the domes and
minarets of Constantinople. People years hence would stare at
the heroic picture and never know what the man himself would
have suffered before he could stand proudly up like that as a
conqueror . . . once more I was fully awake, and that heroic
battle-piece had faded. There were no domes and minarets along
the horizon. There was only the long line of tawny cliffs and the
sun fast overtaking a frail moon in the bland sky of morning.
There were only the flies wandering over my mosquito-net, and
an overwhelming desire to sleep while the day was still cool. Last

night must somehow be separated from any other night by sleep. It had been too profoundly moving an experience to melt inevitably into another dusty day. It must be enshrined in sleep and remembered all the rest of my life as a dream in which I had beheld so many other people's dreams topple over and crash. And away in London they would be getting up presently, unaware that during the night the old London had vanished.

John Maclean
The Clyde Unrest

The phenomenon of 'Red Clydeside' was triggered in Glasgow in 1915 by the confrontation between engineers and the Ministry of Munitions over the issue of dilution [employment of women] and by the rent strikes, but it also took place against the wider context of the emergence of an anti-war and pro-peace movement within the city. The first stirrings had been heard a few days after the declaration of war with a demonstration on Glasgow Green and the city soon became the focus for the largest and most vocal working-class opposition to the war experienced in wartime Britain. Many of those who spoke out against the conflict were also involved in the heavy industries, either as workers or trade union leaders, so that when the term Red Clydeside came into common usage in 1919 it embraced both the anti-war campaigners and the trade unionists who were agitating for higher pay and to preserve their trades. Very often their aims and ambitions overlapped, although as with any informal political grouping there were differences of approach. The following articles were published in the magazine The Vanguard, *which was suppressed in 1916.*

The situation in the Clyde area is just as interesting as it was recently in South Wales, and as it is presently in Dublin, where the Transport Workers have paralysed work at the Docks. Unrest and dissatisfaction manifest themselves in many directions, but principally in opposition to the Munitions Act, the raising of rents, and the threat of conscription. We think it necessary to deal with these in the order mentioned.

The Industrial Slavery Act

Since the introduction of the infamous Munitions [of War] Act [July 1915], in the output of which the leaders of the trade unions have played their treacherous part, the workers of the Clyde have found themselves bullied and ordered about by foremen and managers as never before. Men, seeking to leave one factory for another, have found themselves detained to suit the interests of the employers. Others, wishing to stay, have been dismissed without a clearance card and have thus been kept six weeks out of work to satisfy the desire for revenge of some vicious foremen or managers.

Silly, irritating impositions in the interests of greedy capitalism have ruthlessly cut across use and wont, or definite trade union regulations, to the utter disgust of even 'patriotic' workmen with sons and other relatives at the front. Men, meeting to discuss new exactions and the concessions that might safely be granted to the masters, have been brutally ordered back to work, whilst supposed ring-leaders have been suspended.

In such circumstances the men stop work, and of course, in due course, become victims under the vile Slavery Act. Penalty after penalty, always against the workers, has convinced the workers on the Clyde that the purport of the Munitions Act was not increased supplies to the soldiers, but the crushing of trade unionism. In that we think the workers right.

The Germans, because of better education, established an eight hour day in Krupp's, gave an increase of 20 per cent on wages, and supplied good dinners free. In that factory, or rather series of factories, the workers have received increasing control over the production. So we find it also in other branches of German industry, with the wonderful results in the war apparent to the intelligent worker who refuses to swallow the rubbish printed in the stupid British capitalist press.

With German practice and experience before us we are

convinced the Munitions Act has been a very clumsy weapon to
crush trade unionism in the industries vital during the war.

The February [1915] Clyde Engineering Strike was a revolt
against the trickery of the masters, who thought they would get
the men to work for a very obsolete rate of wages even during
the war with its rising cost of living and increased output of
material. The fright the Government got showed itself in the
farcical attempt to stop the men drinking, and placing new slave
chains upon them in order to get, as they said, a greater and a
greater output.

The capitalist class seized on the [Peter] Marshall case to
demonstrate that the men were doing their utmost to hold back
production, and the presiding Sheriff gave a savage sentence to
frighten others who might be thought guilty of the ca' canny
policy, although Marshall was simply charged with an ordinary
assault.

Things did not turn out as the silly old Sheriff and his class
expected. The Beardmore workers, aroused by his vile spleen,
rallied round Marshall and obtained a large sum for the benefit
of the dependents of Marshall and his family. At the same time
they prepared to strike if he was not liberated. He was liberated.

This Marshall case revived the unofficial committee of shop-
stewards in the engineering works, and as luck would have it the
Fairfield shipwrights' case arose as the Marshall one faded away.

The unofficial committee decided to widen its borders so as
to include unofficial representatives from all allied trades in the
engineering and shipbuilding shops. Now railwaymen and miner
are admitted – and even a teacher – to show the solidarity of
brawn and brain workers.

This wise provision entitled and enabled the Committee to
consider the Fairfield case and decide upon action, if need be.

A manager, passing some shipwrights, saw one or two
standing by waiting to do their work. He got two dismissed. The
men all struck. Seventeen were fined in £10 by a joke of a

Munitions Tribunal for the first time under the absolute control of the Munitions Department bossed by that 'friend of the people', Lloyd George. The fine was paid on behalf of fourteen of the men, but three Socialists preferred to go to prison for a month as they rightly believed that payment of the fine implied their recognition of the Act and that they were criminals.

A move began among the Fairfield and other Govan workers to prepare a strike for the release of the three brave and good men.

The unofficial committee also roused itself to the occasion, and resolved that if the shipwrights and other workers in Fairfield struck the whole Clyde area would be paralysed.

The shipwrights' officials getting wind of this, and acting under instructions from the spineless [Alexander] Wilkie MP [Labour, Dundee], staved off action in Fairfield. At the same time they got the allied trades officials to act with them. They had in existence a committee that had been formed to deal with non-unionism only, the Clyde Shipyards joint Trades' Vigilant Committee by name.

This committee was used to issue a circular to the rank and file, pointing out that the Minister of Munitions was going to hold an immediate enquiry into the Clydeside workers' grievance with regard to the unjust operation of the Act, and this enquiry will open to-morrow, Friday, the 15th inst. (October) at 12 noon, and steps are being taken by this committee to present the case of the men. You may, therefore, rest assured that everything possible will be done to establish our claims. Meantime it is absolutely essential if we are to succeed that we should have the whole-hearted co-operation of the men in our efforts, and this can best be secured by each and every workman absolutely refusing to take drastic action of any kind without first consulting the responsible officials of his 'Trade Union'.

A 'patriotic' appeal winds up the slippery official dodge.

Here it must be stated that the Govan Trades Council played

a very important part, for by its instructions and in its name, its energetic secretary, Harry Hopkins, issued over 700 explanatory circulars about the Fairfield case and forms of resolutions that might be sent to the proper personage.

Munition officials came to Comrade Hopkins to find out all they could, but failed to get the lead expected.

The Government enquiry was a farce, as the officials well knew, and was protracted so long that it was hardly worthwhile striking to release the men. The officials played the game splen- didly – and consciously. At the proper moment they broke off negotiations with the Government officials, and instead of declaring a strike they summoned a conference of officials and stewards in the Christian Institute on Saturday, October 23, with Mr Sharp, of the Boilermakers, in the chair.

Everything was prepared so as to tic up opposition. This our comrade, William Gallacher, saw right away, and so he set himself to the task of making the officials show their hand. This he did effectually – to the satisfaction of our big meeting in the Panopticon [music hall, the Trongate] the following evening at any rate. A resolution mildly suggesting a strike was passed, but no preparations were made to meet again to carry the resolution into effect, although Gallacher firmly raised the matter.

It is no surprise, then, to learn that the three men were released on Wednesday, October 27, after three weeks in prison, the fine having been paid. We know the imprisoned men did not pay the fine and did not consent to its payment. Either the official gang or the Government did it to save their dirt-stained faces. They have not, however. The men were in three out of the four weeks; the men were still firm. Cowardice and weakness charac- terise the officials and the Government.

The insult is still on the workers, and the shame, too, that they lie down to a vicious attempt to make criminals of them – the only class that counts.

Grey [Sir Edward, Foreign Secretary] is a fossil who has

bungled his department; Asquith [H. H., Prime Minister] can only 'wait and see' while the Germans spread themselves around; and Kitchener [Field Marshal, Secretary for War] is only good for re-killing dead dervishes; Lloyd George [David, Minister of Munitions] is a good jumping-jack, and most of his other colleagues would do very well in a Berlin museum. It is men of this kidney who would make criminals of our class.

It is up to the unofficial committee now to forge ahead, refusing to recognise officials who have betrayed the workers (as Highland chiefs and Indian princes have betrayed their peoples in the past to the English), and are equally ready to again do the trick. The withdrawal of the charge against our Comrade Bridges, of Weir's, by the Minister of Munitions, shows that fear of a strike is the only thing recognised by the Russo-Prussians who rule this country. The very fact that Bridges was summoned because, as shop-steward, he approached a man to join the union, is further proof that the attempt is to crush the unions and to continue: the stupid methods of irritation started under the protection of the Munitions Act.

Unless the Clyde men act quickly, determinedly, and with a clear object in view they are going to be tied up in a knot. We know that the Glasgow press was threatened with the Defence of the Realm Act should it make mention of strike had one broken out. We know that the military authorities had engineers and allied workers in the army at home ready to draft into the Clyde works in the event of a strike. We know also that, despite the clamour for munitions, young men are being dismissed from all the Clyde works in order to force them into the Army. When the occasion arises they will be re-instated in their old jobs, but now as military slaves – worse even than munition slaves. Quick and firm action is needed if slavery is going to be abolished and conscription defeated. We must now fight boldly for the common ownership of all industries in Britain.

The Vanguard, November 1915

John Maclean
Rent Victories

In May 1915, the first rent strike was held in South Govan, close to the Fairfield shipbuilding works, and by the end of the year at least 25,000 tenants had joined the movement, including a number of Labour councillors. Mass meetings were held to support the rent strikers and local women's housing associations were set up to galvanise support for the rent strikes and to back those who faced court orders. Inevitably, with men at work, the bulk of the organisation fell to women, who formed tenement and kitchen committees to protect their localities. In that sense the movement had a political aspect, but its emphasis was more anti-profiteering than anti-war. When munitions workers were taken to court in the middle of October for refusing to pay rent increases, their defence counsel explained to the court that they were not troublemakers but men engaged in essential tasks helping to win the war: 'They are not working for the proprietors of their homes. They are working for the purpose of turning out munitions.' Outside in the streets women carried placards stating that while their menfolk were fighting in France or working in factories and shipyards, 'We are fighting the Huns at Home.'

Through the tireless energy, of Mr [Andrew] McBride, Secretary of the Labour Party's Housing Committee, and ardent support of the Women's Housing Committee, an agitation was started in the early summer against rent increases in the munition areas of Glasgow and district. Evening and mid-day work-gate meetings soon stimulated the active workers in all the large shipyards and engineering shops.

Emboldened, the organisers by demonstration and deputation tried to commit the Town Council to action against increases. As it acts as the Executive Committee of the propertied class the Council shirked the responsibility of curbing the greed and rapacity of the factors and house-owners.

Enraged, the workers agitated more and more until the Government intervened by the appointment of a Commission of Inquiry – Dr Hunter [Lord Hunter] and Professor [W.R.] Scott [Professor of Political Economy, Glasgow University]. This was the signal for all the factors in the city to give notices of increase of rent. They anticipated that this united front would influence the Commissioner (as it did), and that the Government would compromise the situation by allowing half the demands to be made legal.

They all calculated without consideration of the awakened anger of the whole working class. People in the previously unaffected areas saw no objection to munition workers paying more but when they themselves became liable to increased rent they adopted the aggressive. Encouraged by the universal working class support, and irritated by the operation of the infamous Munitions Act, the Clyde workers were ready to strike. This several yards did when 18 of their comrades appeared before Sheriff Lee. Beardmore's workers at Dalmuir sent a big deputation to tell the Sheriff that if he gave an adverse decision they would at once down tools. We have been favoured with a report of the proceedings in the Sheriff's room from the principal spokesman. It is intensely interesting as described by one of the spokesmen. In the circumstances the Sheriff wisely decided against the factor's demand for an increase. This was the first victory for working class solidarity. We state the cause of triumph in these terms advisedly, for it really was due to joint action and not to the justice of the case (and there could be no juster) that success came to our side.

The strike having taken place, the workers were bent on

letting the Government know that out they would come again unless it restored rents to their pre-war level. It now transpires that a Rent Bill will be passed, forcing all factors of houses, rented at £21 and under (£30 in London), to reduce the rents to the level prevailing immediately prior to the outbreak of the Great Slaughter Competition.

To soothe the factors and the house-owners it is intended to force bond-holders and mortgage-holders to reduce the interest on their bonds and mortgages to the old rates. If this Bill is passed, it will be a full victory for the mass action of the working class.

It should be noted that the rent strike on the Clyde is the first step towards the Political Strike, so frequently resorted to on the Continent in times past. We rest assured that our comrades in the various works will incessantly urge this aspect on their shop-mates, and so prepare the ground for the next great counter-move of our class in the raging class warfare – raging more than even during the Great Unrest period three or four years ago.

Bear in mind that, although the Government has yielded to enormous pressure, it must do something to balance the victory. Remember how Lloyd George came out with the Munitions Act as a reply to the victory of the striking Clyde engineers, and let that put us all on our guard.

We are of opinion that the reply will come in the form of an attempt to compulsorily hold back a bit of each worker's wage to finance the war; all the more so in view of the engineers' timely demand for an increase of wages owing to increased cost of living. The argument will be that if the Government is penalising house-owners and bond-holders, why ought it not to detain a portion of the workers' incomes to help their trench-mates to win the war. Workers, beware!

Our contention is that thrift should begin at the top amongst those who live on 'unearned income'. These people are living as luxuriously as ever they did, and intend to do so as long as circumstances let them. Just the other day we read that furs selling for fifty guineas at the beginning of the year are now fetching about eighty guineas. This means that, scarcity apart, an increasing demand is being made for such luxuries. This further means that the wealthy are more spendthrift than they were earlier on in the war, and that they are of opinion that all sacrifices ought to be made by the poor, whose wages are so low that they cannot be other than thrifty.

Readers ought to know that three years ago a report was issued of an investigation into the living of about a hundred families in working class wards in Glasgow. The investigators found that one out of every three families had to live under starvation conditions, on the assumption that every penny was put to the utmost use. These same conditions prevail to-day, with an infant mortality now deplored by wealthy ladies who themselves refuse to bear youngsters enough to fill up the gaps of war, and who consequently are anxious to keep up the balance of population by amateurish attempts to save the kiddies who, by misfortune or mistake, happen to enter this devilish world. In the circumstances it would be preposterous, as well as impolitic from a capitalist standpoint, to hold back anything from wages. We well know that an attempt will at first be made to limit deductions to those earning £2 and more per week. When once the 'principle' has been established, the process will be gradually applied to all workers by the same piecemeal method as Lord Derby intends to use to force conscription.

It is up to the workers to be ready, and resist with a might never exerted before. Whether the Clyde Workers' Committee as constituted to-day is able or willing to cope with the situation is doubtful; but it is just as well to give it a further chance with the added support of miners and railwaymen. However, just as this unofficial committee views with suspicion the official committees of the various unions, and attempts to act as a driving force, we warn our comrades that they ought to adopt the same attitude towards the unofficial committee and see that it pushes ahead. If it still clings on to academic discussions and futile proposals, it is their business to take the initiative into their own hands as they did in the case of the recent rent strike. Remember that the only way to fight the class war is by accepting every challenge of the master class and throwing down more challenges ourselves. Every determined fight binds the workers together more and more and so prepares for the final conflict. Every battle lifts the curtain more and more, clears the heads of our class to their robbed and enslaved conditions, and so prepares them for the acceptance of our full gospel of Socialism, and the full development of the class war to the end of establishing Socialism.

A victory at football, draughts, or chess is the result of many moves and counter-moves. We do not lie down and cry when our side loses a goal. No, we buckle up our sleeves and spit on our hands, determined to get two goals in return, or more. So in the game of life. It advances from move to move, ever on grander and grander scale. Let us be up and doing all the time, never giving the enemy time to settle down to a peaceful enjoyment of victorious plunder. Prepare, then, for the enemy's counter-stroke to our victory on the rent question!

The Vanguard, December 1915

Naomi Mitchison
Bad News from France

Naomi Mitchison received the news of her husband's injury while staying with her parents-in-law in London. With her brother Jack Haldane – at home on leave – she had just attended a matinee at the Alhambra Theatre starring the Bing Boys and the dancer Gaby Deslys. Her husband Dick Mitchison was suffering from a fractured skull and was being treated at the Le Tréport military hospital near Boulogne. Earlier Mitchison had transferred from his regiment, the Queen's Bays, to serve in the Royal Signals, as 'it was clear that there would be no more cavalry charges'.

Mr Asquith says in a manner sweet and calm, 'Another little drink won't do us any harm.'

We went back in high spirits to the Mitchison house on the Embankment and there was a telegram. Dick had gone on his motor-bike on some errand for the Signals mess. At Gamache crossroads a French army car ran into him and left him for dead with the motor-bike on top and burning him. A British car which was following them picked him up unconscious and took him to the base hospital at Le Tréport. Here they found he had a fractured skull. The administrative wheels began to turn. I as next-of-kin was sent for; this was done in that war when possible for seriously wounded cases. His father came with me; it should have been a chance for him and me to get to know one another, but it didn't work out that way, which was a pity and mostly my fault. I kept a diary for this period which somewhat shows me up. It is written in pencil on a flimsy block of paper which I must have bought at Le Tréport, but is quite legible.

When I started it I was already extremely impatient with Dick's parents and yet felt guilty about my feelings towards them. The diary is very competently written with sharp and intelligent descriptions of people and places, and knowledge of myself trying to keep calm by thinking that now I knew how the heroine of a novel, which I was already trying to write, was going to feel. This habit of taking notes on one's own behaviour in periods of emotional stress is rather dangerous if people catch you at it.

At the beginning I was getting my main support from Jack (still called 'Boy' throughout). Here it starts, as we came back from the theatre to the house on the Embankment. When I was going back upstairs, my father-in-law

> '. . . caught me by the wrist and half dragging me up to the stairs, said in a harsh and painful whisper "We've had a telegram. Dick is hurt." Then I, "How badly, my God, how badly?" "Very dangerous." I thought suddenly that he was breaking it to me that Dick was killed. "Give me the telegram. Where is he hurt?" "The head. Dangerously." I was in the dining-room by this time; Mrs M was sitting on a chair; she got up and kissed me and I thought to myself – the skull; probably he's dead now. And tried to remember about the respiratory centre and the vagus – suddenly all reality was sucked away from things and there was no way of telling whether I was dreaming or not. "Let me tell Boy," I said, but Mr M went to tell him leaving me and Mrs M in the dining-room: I still had the tune of one of the songs tinkling somewhere back in my mind; but the rest was completely a dream. I wanted Boy very badly. Mrs M was crying; she was all shrunk up and her emotion was catching at mine and breaking down my self-control. I looked at the telegram – dangerously ill – they wouldn't

say that unless it was very bad indeed . . . Mr M came in, he was looking very old and both of them almost hopeless . . . I thought I should never see Dick again . . . Boy came in, and he was very calm and strong, but a little white and already thinking what to do . . . I felt very sick and clutched at the edge of the table and choked . . . I was being shaken by the certainty that Dick was dead; every few minutes I felt that suddenly and bit my hand but couldn't stop myself crying . . . the day went by and I can't remember exactly, only some things isolated . . . Boy alone with me in the dining-room when the crest of one of these waves of fear and longing for Dick caught me and I clutched at his arm with both hands and he was so perfectly and splendidly sane and spoke fairly sharply like cold water . . . and the queer feeling that I was acting and must do the thing expected of me in my part . . .'

Then there were all the arrangements to make and clearly I became reasonably calm and efficient and annoyed at the general assumption that I must be looked after. The night before we left, 'I dreamt that it would be all right and woke wondering whether that would be a good sign.' Goodbye to Jack and would I see him again before the end of the War – or then? We went down to Folkestone in a Pullman car – I for the first time – then embarkation, 'beautifully smoothly worked'. I looked about me.

'The lower deck of the boat was thick with soldiers, sitting or standing about, with their equipment and a haversack full of things. On the upper deck were officers – a lot of red tabs, and some French, sitting on ship's chairs, and a few like us, civvies, anxious looking. Everyone wore life belts, uncomfortable as they could

be, but looking less stupid over khaki than over mufti
. . . We started in half an hour or so, with a faint and
not inspiring burst of cheering. A little spray came onto
the decks; below a few of the men were singing *Michigan*
and *Tipperary* spasmodically and with no great heart
. . . I had recovered my *aequanimitas*, saying to myself:
we shall find Dick better; in a little I shall be laughing at
my fear now and wishing I had known that it was going
to be all right, so as to be able to enjoy this crossing;
therefore let me enjoy it now. I was also saying: if Dick
is dead, what shall I do? I must have some plan; I think
I shall take Greats or be a doctor . . . But still I was a
little stunned and the clock of reality seemed to have
stopped twenty hours before.'

At Boulogne Dick's poor father fussed and tried to hurry things
'which was of course no earthly use. There was a crowd of
RAMC people, a sturdy little woman, a canteen worker, very
much pleased with her khaki, a tall, gaunt lady in black, dishevelled from the voyage, also trying to hurry her papers through
... It was all very simple though; our things were not even looked
at in the *douane*; an officer herded us through; we went off to a
hotel in a car, Mr M hurrying me on when I wanted to change
my money and then being late himself.'

By that time I had made friends with Mrs Johnstone, the
dishevelled lady in black, whose boy was wounded in the leg and
arm in hospital at Abbeville; she lent me a motor veil; one needed
them in those days. Lunch was served by VADs in uniform – no
doubt older than me, as one wasn't allowed out of the country
until at least over twenty. The RAMC captain saw us into an
official car and off we went through the cobbled streets of
Boulogne, past a sentry onto a road with barley growing at each
side, while the lady with the wounded son and I talked together,
finding we were fellow Scots; the son was only twenty-one.

'I thought the harvest seemed very thin and poor; there were few boundaries and cattle grazed tethered . . . sometimes a girl, straight bodiced and barefoot, driving a cow; a few gleaners, old men and women, each with a ragged bundle of corn . . . villages with straggling houses, painted white or blue and usually an *estaminet* with the French soldiers in their pretty and unfamiliar horizon blue standing about. Along one stretch every village was full of zouaves, bronzed and handsome people with red fezes and baggy knickerbockers, who grinned at us as we went past bumping on the *pavé*, hooting wildly before corners . . .'

For we were driving at the unprecedented pace of fifty miles an hour with the wind beating and booming in our faces and ears.

After two tyre bursts, and my admiration for the RAMC chauffeur who changed wheels so quickly, we got to Abbeville and found the hospital where Mrs Johnstone's boy was, and waited.

'After a time the chauffeur came out saying, "That lady's had bad news; they say her son won't live." It depressed Mr M visibly but I thought it might be the natural delight in horrors – even after two years in France at war – of that class. And so it was, for after a long time she came out, more than ever dishevelled with her eyes bright, but saying he might have to have a leg off but would live. We left her things at the YMCA building in a little courtyard . . . It came on to rain, torrents all in a minute beating along the streets . . . we put up our canvas hood; I noticed how very many house pipes leaked.'

But by now I was worrying and wondering as we got nearer Le Tréport. I had

'. . . a picture in my mind: a long ward, just getting dark,
a few yellowish lights along the walls, the evening grey
outside; rows of white beds, a grave sister; red screens
and two round one bed; inside a little light, on the pillow
a head bandaged; eyes shut; perhaps a little muttering
or a vague toss about of hands, not conscious life. I
elaborate the picture; put in a basin or two on a locker
by the bed – ice in a flannel bag – hear myself ask the
sister how it goes – the watch through the night . . .'

About this time I began taking omens from the magpies in the
fields. But Dick's father had no such irrational consolation. We
got to Le Tréport and I put down every detail of the place.
'Suddenly I feel very queer.' We pulled up in front of the hospital,
I jumped out and ran up the steps, asking the cheerful-looking
RAMC sentry for Lieutenant Mitchison – Queen's Bays. 'Surely
he would have known if there had been a death among the
officers.' Then the doctor came, quite young, nice-looking,
speaking to Mr Mitchison who seemed more upset than ever and
couldn't speak. 'How is he?' I said. 'You are the wife, aren't you?'
I nodded. He explained that Dick was slightly better, but the
condition was still very dangerous. We went up three flights of
white stone stairs, which I was to know very well. The hospital
had been a grand hotel, as I write later 'the sort of hotel one has
never been to oneself, bathrooms to every bedroom and landings
one could dance on'.

'I wait outside, while Sister goes in, leaving the door ajar.
Suddenly a voice, so strong and familiar I can hardly
believe it. "What, my wife? Bring her in at once, Sister."
I go in. It is a small white cheerful room, a bed with a
silk quilt. Dick, looking very well and normal, but for a
very unshaved chin: "Hullo Nou!" Sister leaves us for a
few minutes. I try not to talk or let him, but he, talking

rather too loud, asks questions, is very cheerful, moves
his head about, is sorry he is such a wretched sight but
he can't get his shaving things. There is a slight smell of
paraldehyde . . .'

After that his father and I settled into the Hotel des Bains, 'a
quaint place with a twisty stair . . . my room is small but has
three windows that swing open like doors. One looks towards
the *place* and the harbour with grey-sailed fishing boats, the
other two onto a narrow street, very crowded in the evenings
with poilus and their girls. I expect Mr M is writing letters in the
salon or reading the Continental *Daily Mail* – a bad paper but
with good news. His letters take three times as long to write as
mine. '

At this point, we were going up to the hospital twice a day,
though only I was allowed in.

'I see him every day for an hour or two . . . his head
aches of course, very badly   I think it's a great pity
they don't tell him more; as it is he is always trying to
get up, even when I am there, and when I prevent him
calls me all kinds of stupid fool, which I'm sure I am,
but not for that. Mostly he is quite sensible, and even
when delirious very rational, arranging a dinner party,
talking about the Signal Troop or leave; he even wrote
out a telegram to the Paris Hotel . . . The usual thing is
five minutes normal though in pain, talking sensibly and
not very restless; then a few minutes while the pain
comes on, very restless, perhaps trying to get up, with
his body and arms rigid, mouth open and eyes shut,
cursing his headache or complaining of the pain, calling
on himself to stop it, and then five minutes lying back,
quite exhausted, often with one arm thrown over his
forehead . . . His date memory has stopped the day of

the accident; sometimes he asks how old I am . . .
hearing all right, though eyes are not yet.'

I give a run-down on the doctors, who sound efficient and on
the whole cheering, but my real praise is for Sister Holbeach,
charming and sympathetic, 'not un-necessarily professional . . .
as becomes a nurse, optimist'. I had told her about my nursing
experience at St Thomas's and she said that she had spoken to
Matron and I would be allowed to nurse Dick more of the time.
What I don't say in the diary, and yet now I remember most
vividly, is that, at the first interview, the doctor said he would
probably not live, but conceded that he was in very good
condition and might recover. I know I dug my toes in about this;
it was just not going to happen; that is why I didn't put it into
the diary. When it didn't happen I was told that he would
probably never recover intellectually and might live in a
somewhat crippled condition. I expect they were quite sorry for
this eighteen-year-old, faced with a life sentence of this kind. But
again, I refused to believe it and that is why it isn't in the diary.
I was fighting to win, as Janet fought for Tam Lin.

Meanwhile I was taking in Le Tréport. By this time I was
reasonably fluent in French, and, from looking at a notebook I
kept for years with quotations in it, it is clear that I normally
read quite a lot of French poetry. So now I looked about me:

'The blue French soldiers in the streets are slightly more
untidy than their English *confrères* – a step nearer the
battle-field – many of them wearing one or two medals.
I never can tell the ranks apart. Some very fine horses . .
. and there is khaki among the blue, officers mostly,
either RAMC or from the regiments near here – come
in mostly as far as I can see for a drink and a bath,
possibly for a little distracting society . . . the ladies of
the place are mostly bourgeoisie – a quantity of flappers,

less obvious and more subtle than the same type at, say, Bournemouth . . . short skirts, bright coloured blouses and caps or veils tied over their hair.'

There were families staying at the hotel.

'A very nice French colonel with grey moustache and grey kind eyes; he has a boy of seventeen and one of about eight, delicate looking, both of them . . . a young mother and a charming little girl of five or six with masses of yellow hair, blue jersey and shorts and long bare legs . . . a good lady with hair in a tight knob who has a horrid snivelling son in a tight brown suit whom she is always looking after very carefully; I think French boys of that sort of age are particularly horrible . . . at the *table d'hôte* a group of VADs in their blue caps, cheerful and English, sometimes a single lady in a velvet tamoshanter and a short coat edged with fur who looks incomplete without an officer . . . the hotel people are charming and friendly . . . but I find everybody's nice to me.'

We walked to the hospital every day through the middle of the market, and sometimes I bought a few flowers. There were 385 steps to the cliff top. 'We probably meet Mr and Mrs Sassoon, very Jewish, friendly and good folk, but somehow one cannot imagine her pearl necklace, which is probably extremely valuable, to be anything but rather a bad sham.' We filled in the day somehow; I still have two pottery animals I bought then. There was a shop which had about two dozen one-franc classics, which I bought; I read a lot of Guy de Maupassant at this time. But I daren't buy a copy of *La Vie Parisienne*, because Dick's father would be shocked. Clearly we get on dreadfully badly, and I realise that it is largely the generation gap, but that didn't help.

'He's very English (doesn't shake hands when I, as a Scot, would) and when some of Dick's superior officers came to find out how he was ... he was very formal and a little nervous and, when one of Dick's Signal troop came to find out too, he tipped most adequately, but it was I who did the talking ... I wonder how much I misjudge him and myself; it's partly shyness with him; I'm not shy in the same way.'

It was early September and sometimes there was a storm which made bathing more exciting. I bathed usually in the early mornings when there was no crowd and one could run down from the hotel.

'There are long flat shadows on sea and sand; the sun is bright but not hot and when one is knee-deep in the smooth grey water, rhythmically stirred by long slow ripples, it makes a pathway; but there is no-one to go with. I have a comic French bathing-dress with scarlet trimmings and two blue anchors on the collar.'

There was shopping, trying to get some silk to make silk pyjamas for Dick. 'Sometime perhaps, I shall go into Eu, or walk along the beach to the rocks, but one wants someone to go with who will enjoy it in the same way.' But the days went by. Dick saw another specialist, Gordon Holmes, and was said to be out of danger. But the fight had to go on and was sometimes curious.

'Today for instance he didn't even know me. In the morning he had a long talk with me, calling me Lindsay – a Signalling Officer. I think he enjoyed it very much, for, by a curious coincidence, this Lindsay knew many people at Oxford, Willie for instance, and Joseph. He had known Heath [Heath had been killed earlier that year] and on his saying that he was the finest man he had known, he and Dick gripped hands. Dick also told him about his "missus" and her family and finally they shook hands and Lindsay went away promising to come back soon. A few minutes after, Dick called Sister to ask me to go to him, and when I was there told me what a nice man was this "Lindsay" – poor Lindsay who only existed for ten minutes. Then in the afternoon, after a sleep, Dick woke up to say that he was going off at once to East Hertford to contest the seat with Pemberton Billing. He sat up and was not put off long by my saying there was no need for him to go for a fortnight. Then, for I didn't want him to struggle to get up, I tried to make him remember where he was. "No," he said, "I'm in hospital at Bethnal Green; I must telephone to the other hospital; how did I get here? Please fetch my clothes, I must go to Hertford." I reminded him of who I was, but he was politely incredulous, a little surprised at my wearing his wife's rings. "Admit, nurse, that you have stolen them!" and utterly shocked – the picture of virtue! – at this strange nurse kissing him! "My good girl, I've never met you before; I quite like you, but I wish you'd go away." I couldn't stop him getting up, so I called the orderly and finally Sister who managed to quiet him, taking his orders about telephoning to Hertford with the greatest calm. Then, as she was going away, Dick remarked, "Oh Sister, will you please ask this nurse to go; I don't know her," implying that she wasn't a credit to any hospital. Exit me!'

Once we went up to the hospital and found a big convoy had come in and there was a correspondingly big evacuation of patients well enough to go back to Blighty.

'We found all the back part of the hall covered with stretchers, on each an officer in a brown blanket, a woolly cap, and labelled. Most of the MOs were there, giving orders, looking at the labels, bending over to talk to their patients. The Sassoon boy was there, also Major Cripps. A long string of ambulances, all driven by women, came up to the door, one by one. The first row were picked up one after another, two orderlies to a stretcher, with sometimes a man in front shifted so that they could get one out from behind, like a great game of patience. It all went wonderfully smoothly . . . The next day the Sassoons and Miss Cripps left, which I'm sorry for. We used to see the Sassoons every day up at the hospital . . . once I went in to see the boy – a typical young Eton Jew, who will probably get on in the world very well.'

But could this have been Siegfried?

I had gone swimming and walking with Miss Cripps; we said '*bon soir*' but disengaged ourselves from the poilus. Often there were a few officers in for two-day leave from the division near us.

'Two evenings ago, after dinner in the salon, Mr M was reading, I was playing patience. We heard three or four officers come in and begin talking to Madame . . . they wanted to know about bathing; then they began to talk to one another about some particular incident at Delville Wood. Finally I chucked my patience, got up and said I was going to give them chocolates; Mr M seemed somewhat surprised and said it would embarrass them. However I ran upstairs and came down with my choco- lates and offered them; they were really pleased and began talking to me, all at once, and before Mr M came out of the salon – very shy – I knew their names and some of their histories, where they'd come from, what they'd been doing, and how very particularly pleased they were to get back to real dinners and beds and bathing . . . They were KSLI 5th Battalion . . . Last night about half a dozen came into the salon and started a conversation as soon as they possibly could. They were awful TGs [Temporary Gentlemen] mostly, but they'd just come from fighting the Boche in Delville Wood . . . we had a long talk about Syndicalism . . .'

Another was an Australian ranker, who told me about holding a trench for thirty hours in an advanced position; he was recommended for the Military Cross.

I try to type them.

'They're all conscientious fatalists and they all try to talk about England or after the war, but always after a little you get back to shop. There was a Major and several others, also a nice little Canadian doctor up at the Hospital, whom we had seen several times before, and he was quite drunk; I think he often is: not a good thing for a doctor . . . Here am I, sitting on a table in the middle of the stuffy salon of a third-rate French hotel, being as charming as I can to an audience of TGs, all to give them the memory of a pleasant evening to take back to the trenches by Givenchy; that's why I wear pretty frocks and hats and do my hair just not anyhow, but to look nice; it's probably as much worth doing now as it ever will be again in my life. I would give a lot to be able to sing.'

At this time another specialist, Meyers, saw Dick, said he was to go to Netley Hospital, where most people with brain damage went, and apparently thought that ultimate mental recovery was only a matter of time. But, as I write, 'It's certainly rather disconcerting that he's still just as bad mentally.' I describe another incident:

'He gets violently angry with both me and the orderly when we stop him, calling us both dirty cads and damned liars; he also hits out like anything, and when the orderly has gone reproaches me bitterly for having called him, saying it's the sort of low thing I would do and often, which of course is the best thing, turning over and being offended till he falls asleep. But often I leave him to the orderly, particularly when he says "*Enlevez cette femme là, c'est la mienne, mais enlevez la.*" And then as a parting shot when I'm going out "I don't ever want to see you again." He forgets all about it by next time, but I'm so afraid it will stay in some sort of distorted image in his subconscious memory. Yesterday morning he told me how the doctors and orderlies had lured him to an opium den and nearly killed him, but how he had fought them all.'

Clearly this was fairly exhausting, especially as one could not be quite certain about ultimate recovery. But I had a last evening with two VAD nurses, Miss Duval and Miss Tozer.

'We went off in a car to the Forêt d'Eu . . . the most lovely evening . . . the Forêt still full of wild flowers and very green . . . long stretches of slim tall beech trees, sudden rises among birch and chestnut with a steep white bank at the roadside, trailed over with honeysuckle, small roads under an arch of beeches and a deer leaping across, a clearing with a reaped cornfield and back through high woods of straight thin trees and the pink sunset blinking behind the stems like jewels. I don't know whether they were lovelier when it was growing dark or before, when you get broken patches of sunlight lying across the road and clear, sudden greens, almost spring-like. We stopped at a little farm, in the middle of the wood like a fairy tale, a square court-yard, an orchard of apple trees covered with small red fruit and the forest closing in all round. In the quiet of the wood we heard twigs snapping, a bird, a dog far off, and then listening closer, every few seconds a thud, less sound than vibration, as if the earth were snoring a long way under, and that is the guns. When the wind is right they are quite loud and on dark nights they see from the hospital the horizon all lit with flashes.

'We had a perfect French dinner, omelette, chicken, haricot beans stewed in milk, cider, jelly and cream and bowls of thick soft coffee. And we all told one another our life histories and made friends and deplored the badness of a girl's schooling and how hard it is for her to make her way to any really educated work. Both the girls are scientists . . . it seems an awful waste that they should be VADs here in the position of privates under sisters who may or may not be nice, but anyhow discourage questioning and are very jealous. No chance of rising from the ranks or learning any more than they know now. They work for a twelve and a half hours' day, with three hours off and short meal times; once in two months they get a whole day off and once in eighteen months a week's leave. They're both going to chuck it when their terms are up and I think they'll be quite right.

'They were telling me one thing which must be particularly annoying to Miss Tozer, who was doing brain research before the war – that there are any amount of splendid head cases here which die, and it would be the chance of a century if there was anyone here to note symptoms and do a PM. Of course if she were to suggest such a thing – which she could probably do perfectly – the authorities would first faint and then kick her out. But it is stupid.'

So there was the magic again, but also the proper concern of the scientist. Miss Tozer, Miss Tozer, what happened to you? I looked you up in *Who's Who* just in case, but as we agreed, it is so hard for a girl to get up to the top – if that *is* the top.

We left the next day. There had been no more forty-eight hour leave people. But plenty of rumours. I add, 'Poor old Dick will be sick if the cavalry, as seems likely, get through in three weeks.' So, apparently, we thought!

There the pencil diary ends, with only a few more guilt feelings about my father-in-law. Typically, I never managed to arrive at what to call either him or Dick's mother. I couldn't think of them as parents and they were the wrong generation for first names.

So there we were, waiting very anxiously in London, where it had somehow been arranged that, before going to Netley, Dick should come to the Clock House hospital. It seems odd that these private arrangements could have been not only possible, but were not disapproved of. One only asks oneself whether the treatment of wounded officers was very different from that given to ordinary private soldiers. That wasn't a question I had asked, so far. One took certain things for granted. But Dick's parents and I were all in a rather agitated state, totally unsure of how he would be.

But something very odd had happened. For three weeks Dick had been in a strange country, usually in a hurry with something important he had to do. Sometimes he met people he knew, but often he was alone, or chased by non-human entities. Then he was on a boat in mid-channel and there were creatures crawling about the decks, sea snakes and whatnot. Then 'something clicked', and he was back in the ordinary world, gradually realising where he was and why. And that was how he was when he came to us in London, very weak, but himself. He never quite recovered his sense of smell, though this is never strong with fairly heavy smokers as he was. But smell is supposed to come into taste, especially of wine, and this never left him. And quite soon he stopped being able to draw maps of the strange country.

Neil Munro
Rumours of War

This is the final part of a collection of 'Random Reminiscences'
written by Neil Munro and originally published in the Daily
Record *and edited after his death by his friend and fellow writer*
George Blake. It was published in 1931 under the title The Brave
Days *and in his introduction Blake made the astute point that*
Munro was 'the master of a most enviable journalistic style:
crisp, colourful, and yet gracious, and these qualities could be
discerned in the slightest thing he wrote, even in a two-line
paragraph'. Munro's mention of 'Dora' is a reference to the
Defence of the Realm Act, which was introduced in August 1914
to give the government wide-ranging powers for securing public
safety, including censorship.

I

The selection of Loch Doon for an aviation centre during the
years of war was one of the many costly blunders that had their
origin in ignorance and fear. Any intelligent young airman of
today may well find it incredible that no further back than a
dozen years ago the idea of making the shores of a little inland
loch far among the hills the arsenal and training ground for an
aerial fleet could be seriously entertained. It was a project
hatched in a mare's nest. Consideration was given to nothing but
remoteness and privacy.

There was an equally absurd though more inexpensive
attempt to make Glen Tilt a secret aviation depot. The Marquis
of Tullibardine had little difficulty in closing this depopulated

glen against all prying visitors, and what testing and training in aircraft was furtively done there has never been revealed so far as I know. 'Dora', in her time, kept dark all such sensational new Highland Games. Tourists and cameras were strictly interdicted. And the ghost of 'Dora' still seems to haunt the newspaper offices.

I confess I know nothing directly about the Glen Tilt experiments. The rumours of its mysterious secret activity may possibly have been all lies or grossly exaggerated. But I think not. Glen Tilt is exactly such a place as would be chosen for secret experimental flying stunts by the same innocent people who picked Loch Doon.

They had – we all had – the most guileless notions of the power of the enemy and what his plans should be. Immediately on the outbreak of war, and becoming a conviction as months went on, was, apparently, the feeling that the Germans were super-men who during pre-war years had taped off every parish and by-path in this country and left behind them a stupendous system of espionage, with all the equipment needed to bring it into action on 'Der Tag'. The unquestioned courage and intellect of spies and other enemy agents in our midst to strike immediately at vulnerable parts of a nation of congenital idiots and poltroons was implicit in our rumours and alarms.

On Sunday, 2nd August, 1914, two days before our declaration of war, rural telegraph offices were kept open all day and night. I was in Argyll at the time, and thought this ominous. The day was spent by me in motoring to the nearest railway stations – Dalmally and Arrochar. I am ashamed when I recall now what silly patriotic and romantic elations were stirred in me when I found that already there were armed guards on every railway viaduct, on reservoirs, and the Loch Long torpedo testing station. All along the Callander-and-Oban and West Highland Railways, the fiendish ubiquity of German spies, and their readiness to start immediately blowing up culverts and railway bridges, or poisoning us at our kitchen-taps, were already taken for granted!

Every nation at war had the same illusion – that the enemy was brainier and more far-seeing than itself, and possessed of mysterious scientific resources greater than its own, which it had overlooked in its devotion to sport, love, rearing a family; to work and business, mumps in the household, conviviality, cinemas, or church-going.

That was the unusual temperature in which mares began to nest in Britain. 'Dora' every day and many times each day, throughout the war, poured telegrams into the newspaper offices prohibiting any allusion to this, that, or the other thing, and so struck dumb the only agent the public has today for deciding – though it takes skill to use the medium correctly – what elements of fact are in the gossip and chatter of every week.

Quite unmistakably, 'Dora' herself, having read many novels of William Le Queux and Seton Merriman, either guilelessly believed in a Britain hotching with alien enemies, taped out, riddled with secret ammunition stores, and provided with magical systems of communication and co-ordination with Berlin, or craftily took advantage of that popular delusion and made the most of it to buck up our national *morale*.

'Dora' – small blame to her! – in the early years of the war knew as little about aviation as about television or electric greyhound coursing. It was her ignorance that made her so complaisant about silly schemes like these of Loch Doon and Glen Tilt – in which many precious lives would have been uselessly lost had the projects ever come to a practical test.

The ideas that battleships can be built and tested in the wide, open estuaries of Great Britain without the observation of foreign visitors, or that a gully in the hills is a fine discreet place in which to train seaplane and airplane pilots and bombers, are equally childish. But such notions are not quite so foolish as the assumption that outside of the trivial aggregate space occupied

by London and the other big cities in the Kingdom, the populace
in England, Scotland and Ireland is so blind and incurious that
enemy organization can flourish in its midst without suspicion.

Nowhere in these islands could the illusions of fear and false
rumours have been more ludicrous than in the West of Scotland,
where never an enemy spy was discovered nor a single shot of
the enemy heard. The men of the shipyards, engine-shops, and
munition factories of the Clyde, though working all those war
years with more passion for their job than ever they knew before,
were suspected by London of a tendency at any moment to
sedition and bolshevism. William Le Queux – of all men in the
world! – was sent to Glasgow more than once to nose around the
docks and workshops and apply his renowned acuteness as an
international crime investigator to the discovery of possible
bombs in ships' coal-bunkers, or disguised Russian ex-grand-
dukes in our hotels. He lived *en prince* himself in the Central
Station Hotel, looked occasionally through a knot-hole in a
workshop gate with the most penetrating scrutiny, without seeing
anything to write home about, and thoroughly enjoyed himself.

One year, about this season, the rumour was that enemy
aeroplanes and submarines working round our coast were
getting petrol supplies for re-fueling from secret dumps in the
hills of Galloway! Even that preposterous yarn was swallowed.
Many active mountain-climbers from Glasgow and elsewhere
scoured the hills and lochs of the Crockett country in small
parties, no doubt equipped with automatic pistols, and later,
members of the Scottish mountaineering clubs combined in the
holiday season to quarter systematically the whole suspected
area. Nothing has been heard of them since.

Very wisely and promptly, a boom was thrown across the
estuary from the Cloch to Dunoon to exclude enemy seacraft,
either surface or submarine. In one respect it was a great success.
Nothing tangible or inimical ever broke through or even tested
a barrier backed up by constantly patrolling tugs and the forts

behind them, but mare's-nest fledglings were strong on the wing and not to be held up by a boom of any kind. They flocked very thickly about Greenock and the Tail of the Bank.

Several times a day during 1914–1916 I was rung up on the 'phone to listen to the most startling reports from Greenock. They were conveyed to me, not only in all seriousness, but with circumstantial detail and genuine alarm by a well-known gentleman holding a highly responsible position in the shipping trade whose sanity and judgment in ordinary times I would never have questioned.

After two or three false alarms from him that German submarines had got under the boom and were now hanging about the Tail of the Bank, my scepticism and unpatriotic calm began to irritate him. It was with considerable elation, as one whose earlier scares were now justified, he came to me personally one day with the news that a U-boat of large dimensions had, the previous night, been stranded at Inverkip, and was at the moment lying there in a helpless position, visible at low tide. Crowds from Greenock, he assured me, were flocking to Inverkip to see her.

The Torpedo Factory near Fort Matilda was, at all times, supposed to be liable to enemy attack, or to overt attempts to pry into its secrets. It was screened off from the Greenock to Gourock tramlines by iron network, and surrounded by sand-bags. All passengers on the top-decks of the tramcars had to come down and crowd into the inside of the cars while passing the factory. Any lady passenger taking home a bag of tea-cakes from the shop was subject to suspicious examination; she might have bombs. Pedestrians were diverted off the main road where it bordered the Factory and shunted on to a roundabout road.

In spite of, or perhaps because of, all those precautions the Torpedo Factory occasioned the most startling rumours every other week. Spies, it appeared, could hardly be kept out of its sacred precincts. They were, of course, dealt with summarily –

'put up against a wall and shot' was the inevitable phrase for prompt and drastic measures. One morning, as a particularly frenzied story went, no less than six spies were lined up against the fatal wall and thus disposed of *en bloc*. The theory of the Tail of the Bank was that this unpleasant job was done by a platoon of defaulters from the adjacent training camp.

2

Of all the absurd rumours that swept the British Isles during the war, the most unaccountable was that which convinced at least nine-tenths of the population that a Russian army from Archangel was being transported over the railway systems of Scotland and England to attack the Germans from the Channel ports. Where, and with whom, did this fantastic story originate?

How came it that, in the autumn of 1914, London was quivering with excitement over daily reports (not, of course, in the newspapers) that mysterious and darkened troop-trains were nightly streaming south from the Moray Firth to the English Channel, revealing in brief stoppages at places like Inverness, Perth, Leuchars Junction, and Wigan, that they carried the hairiest of Cossacks with the snow of the Siberian steppes still on their boots?

I was in London when this fairy story first 'broke', as they say in American journalism. To my amazement, everybody, including the most knowing and cynical journalists, believed it, rejoicing greatly at the imminent smack in the jaw that was coming to Fritz from an unexpected quarter, and regretting only that the censorship made it impossible to allude to it in their journals. The only sceptic newspaper man I met at the time was Charles E. Hands, old war correspondent of the *Daily Mail*.

There is a certain club in Adelphi Terrace, whose membership is supposed to be almost exclusively of world travellers, big-game hunters, explorers, Bohemians, crafty men-about-town up to every dodge of *chicane* and intuitively aware of what is what. They gulped the 'spoof' yarn like a cocktail. To express in their presence the faintest doubt of its veracity stamped you as a pro-Hun and surrounded you with the atmosphere of a Frigidaire.

Charlie Hands was the only man in that club I could speak to, assured of sympathy and reason. To us, at least, every new day's rumours confirmed our impression that the Russians were being conjured up out of Northern mists to stimulate British morale, or delude the Germans.

In a few days, it looked as if we were mistaken. The war correspondent of, I think, the *Daily News*, cabling from France, stated that he had actually seen the vanguard of the Archangel Russians on the battlefield. But, from that day, he ceased to be known as a war correspondent.

About the same time, the editor of one of the oldest and most dignified morning papers in London came into the club one evening with a story that he had just had the assurance of the manager of the Hotel Metropole that Cossack officers off a troop train from Scotland had put a severe strain upon his accommodation the previous night. This editor was an old friend and compatriot of my own whom, in normal circumstances, I should have implicitly trusted for an accurate report of anything, but I was convinced that in this instance he was mistaken.

An inquiry of the management of the Hotel Metropole failed to discover any confirmation of his story other than that some foreign guests in furlined coats had been there the previous night.

My business was to telegraph a London Letter each morning to Glasgow. Each day's Letter had to be submitted to the Censor, to make certain that I was not betraying any military secrets, such as the movement of troops, etc., within the Kingdom. This, at the time, could obviously apply only to British troops; the soldiers of no other nation were expected to land in Britain. There could, therefore, I argued to myself, be no censorship upon reasonable allusion to the rumours of this phantom invasion from Archangel.

One day, accordingly, I included in my Letter some paragraphs referring to those silly rumours about Russian troops being carried surreptitiously by rail from the North of Scotland to the South of England during night hours. I ironically made it clear that the story was entirely fictitious.

Those were the only paragraphs deleted by the Censor from any correspondence of mine throughout the war! The implication was obvious. The Government did not want to have the Russian yarn contradicted, or even smiled at. It was deliberately invented and disseminated to keep Fritz guessing.

Who thought of it? Somebody in Intelligence in London perhaps. It could hardly have been a suggestion from Intelligence in France, where by that time something had been learned of rural psychology, some recognition of the fact that one single Russian, Chinaman, or Negro cannot traverse a parish without arousing curiosity and speculation.

Any idea that the Germans were to be misled by those rumours of a rear attack by Russia through Britain could have been entertained only by an office-boy.

It has, I think, never been admitted that the Russian fiction was concocted or deliberately disseminated by the War Office, but a post-war speech by a British General who had been at the head of Intelligence in France confessed the responsibility of his department for that other extraordinary rumour about German 'corpse-factories'.

Thousands of British soldiers went to their death convinced that the atrocious story of the Germans cremating the dead for the sake of the fat in them was true. I was more than once seriously assured in France by responsible officers that they had actually seen 'corpse-factories' with the German dead put up in wired bales for incineration.

That was not entirely incredible, but when a field officer of a Glasgow regiment held me up one day in the streets of St Pol to tell me he had just seen, that morning, a factory with vats and

casks for the economic disposal of cadavers, I was horrified at
his credulity.

The lie persisted till the day of Armistice. In October, 1918,
I witnessed the retreat of the Germans from the Hindenburg Line
on the St Quentin Canal. They were being pushed back by the
Australians. The canal, which ran underground for three miles,
had been utilized by the enemy as a gigantic 'dugout'. Great,
roomy barges moored stem to stern extended throughout the
tunnel and had been used as living-quarters. At frequent intervals
shafts had been sunk and galleries cut for communication with
the surface.

While approaching the south end of this tunnelled canal at
Riqueval, where it lay at the bottom of a huge ravine, the story
went from front to rear of the attacking Australians that the
biggest 'corpse-factory' ever seen had been found at the mouth
of the tunnel.

I was in the company of several Australian statesmen and
well-known English writers, including Sir Gilbert Parker and 'Ian
Hay' – all in civilian clothing – and it was Australian badinage
the marching 'diggers' had for us as we drew near the ravine at
Riqueval. They recognized Sir Joseph Cook, their own Naval
War Minister; called him 'Joey', sang 'Oh! oh! it's a lovely War',
and advised us on no account to miss 'the Chamber of 'Orrors'.

The 'Chamber of 'Orrors', otherwise the 'corpse-factory',
when we got down the ravine proved to be a building at the
mouth of the tunnel in which was machinery for working the
sluices. A platoon of German soldiers had taken refuge in it when
the Australian artillery began to bombard the tunnel; two shells
had exploded in its interior, made scrap of the entire engineery,
and strewed it with fragments of men.

The first Australians to explore this *macabre* chamber were
convinced it was a 'factory'; as such it was seriously regarded by
a whole Australian Division, and, naturally, few went into it to
correct the ghastly impression.

3

But those Russians. . . . Following the publication in a newspaper
of my sceptical views on their reality every post brought me
letters which showed that the North of Scotland is still convinced
of the tangible presence of that army from Archangel in its midst
in 1914. South of Inverness, apparently, there is, to judge from
my correspondence, not the same conviction – merely the
repetition of the rumour of the time about darkened troop trains
sweeping night after night through railway stations.

From south of the Forth and Clyde to the Border I got only
one letter whose writer looked likely to make a useful contribution to the elucidation of what remains a provoking mystery.

There is probably no other serious Scottish vocalist on the
popular concert platform today whose name has been so long
familiar to Scotland as J.M. Hamilton. He is now a septuage-
narian, but, with voice and vigour unimpaired, he still seasonally
tours the whole country, a favourite exponent of our genuine
native minstrelsy.

In September, 1914, Mr Hamilton, tenor, and Miss Nellie
McNab, mezzo-soprano, with their 'Scotch Song Scena', had a
week's engagement in a hall at Invergordon. During the same
week the late W. F. Frame, the well-known Scottish comedian,
with his touring company, was appearing in another hall in the
same town.

Invergordon had already wakened up from the quietude of
a fishing village to noisy animation as a result of the war and its
railway propinquity to the Cromarty Firth. Its mole and harbour
were manifestly destined to play an important part in the
Admiralty's plans for the Fleet. There was sufficient of an influx
of naval ratings and soldiery to fill at least two concert halls for
the week, though Invergordon was not yet the extraordinarily
bustling place it was to be before the war was ended.

One afternoon, three troopships came into the Cromarty

Firth through the narrow channel between the Sutors and anchored off Cromarty, where they lay all night in the roadstead. Very quickly the rumour went through Invergordon that they were filled with troops from Russia, to be landed the following morning and entrained for some unknown destination in the South of England.

Hamilton and Frame, who were always great friends, were afoot at an early hour next morning and found the populace of the burgh excitedly watching the debarkation. Cameron Highlanders acted as guard at the wharf, and their band played up to the railway station what Mr Hamilton describes as the dirtiest and most unsoldier-like troops he had ever set eyes on.

They carried no arms, neither rifle nor bayonet, and wore a miserable uniform – misfit, torn, and stained tunics half-unbuttoned; trousers apparently made of jute or canvas; clumsy heavy top-boots midway to the knee, and nondescript caps. The officers carried swords, and were more smartly attired than the rank and file.

Uniformed nurses accompanied them, and a number of padres who, later, were identified as Russian priests of the Greek Church from the fact that little medallions they presented to bystanders who pressed cigarettes and other kindly attentions on the soldiers were ecclesiastical charms of the Greek Catholic Church.

Frame and Hamilton all day shared the excitement of Invergordon, and, with members of their concert parties, provided themselves with copious supplies of cigarettes which they distributed among the foreigners, who were not permitted to break ranks till they got into the trains. The latter left behind them as souvenirs a good deal of Russian paper money of infinitesimal value.

Disembarkment started about 9 a.m. on a pier strictly guarded by soldiers and police, the latter including a good many London Metropolitan policemen wearing the characteristic striped armlets of the force, which were to be conspicuous in Invergordon throughout the whole war period. The first train-load cleared out of the station at 10 a.m., the second at noon, and the last at 3 p.m. They were exceptionally long English trains, and the general estimate of the people at Invergordon was that they each carried about a thousand men.

The entire baggage of this force had to be carried from the wharf to the station by the Cameron Highlanders, who not very cheerfully undertook this fatigue for an alien body of husky-looking men who seemed quite fit to undertake it for themselves. Though the utmost secrecy was maintained as to the exact character of those troops, or their destination, and though they spoke a language never heard before or since in Invergordon, it was taken for granted, and never afterwards disputed, that they were indubitably Russians.

Such, at all events, remains the conviction of Mr J.M. Hamilton, a sensible man who adds no picturesque or romantic frills to his narrative of an event which could not at the time be even hinted at in the Press.

'You have only to write to the Provost or Town Clerk of Invergordon, or the stationmaster, to confirm my story,' he says. 'The people of Invergordon must be astonished to find doubts cast on the report that Russians from Archangel or somewhere else went south through Scotland and England in train-loads from the Moray Firth.'

I have no doubt Mr Hamilton's recollection of the circum-stances is strictly accurate. It is, in less detail, confirmed by letters from ex-Service men who seem to have been about the Cromarty Firth at the time. It should be remembered that from practically the outbreak of war, the North-east Coast was 'out of bounds' to civilian intrusion and curiosity.

Permits to travel north of Inverness by rail or road were only to be secured by passengers with valid excuses for butting into what had become an important naval and military zone between the Highland capital and Thurso. I went round the naval bases and army training camps in that area myself in the winter of 1915–16, but it was as an official correspondent, provided with passes and other papers which had to satisfy RTOs, Commandants, and the sleuths of the London Metropolitan Police.

From nowhere else in the North-east area of the coast than Invergordon has any suggestion come of a Russian landing. I suspect that Frame and Hamilton saw the only Russians who ever landed there, and that upon the southward transport by rail of those three train-loads the amazing rumours with which London cheered itself up were wholly founded.

Between what Invergordon calculated was about three battalions, and the Army Corps of the public imagination, there is a mighty difference! Train-loads of our own troops were, at that time, being moved nightly up and down the country; those three trains from Invergordon, passing south to their unknown destination, and of peculiar interest to the public on account of the rumours preceding them at every station, were not readily to be distinguished from the others.

It was, in the circumstances, not surprising that by the time they reached the South of England the 3000 (estimated) Russians had multiplied to at least an Army Corps in the public imagination.

What, exactly, was this force landed at Invergordon? I don't know. It is a remarkable thing that up till now no newspaper has taken advantage of the abolition of the censorship to trace back to its source a *canard* so extraordinary.

My impression is that those presumptive Russians landed in Scotland may have been intended for Labour battalions. Russia at that time was reputed to have only one rifle for every five men mobilized, but in any case the absence of arms would not be surprising in a corps destined for non-combative work with an allied army.

John Reith
Marching off to War

While training to be an engineer in Glasgow, Reith had joined the Territorial Force and in 1911 was commissioned in 5th Scottish Rifles, a Territorial battalion of the Cameronians. At the outbreak of war, he was appointed the battalion's transport officer but his prickly personality led to quarrels with his commanding officer and adjutant over matters of discipline and dress – he insisted on wearing the wrong colour of shirt and ate in the Sergeants Mess – and shortly before the Battle of Loos in September 1915 he was transferred to the Royal Engineers. In common with other Territorial battalions, 5th Scottish Rifles mobilised on the outbreak of war and moved their first station, in this case Larbert near Stirling, before proceeding to Broughty Ferry in Angus for coastal defence duties.

Various styles have at various times been appended to one's signature: British Inspector – this in the United States of America, 1916–17; Major, RE; Controller of various things in the Ministry of Munitions in 1919; General Manager, Managing Director, Director-General, even Chairman since. But none has given such satisfaction as when first one signed over a rubber stamp in a foundry stores shed at Larbert.

> Lieut
> Transport Officer 5th SR

Nor, things being as they are, is any title or designation likely to give more; for this was my first real job. The Transport Officer was a somebody; an object of mystification, envy and even respect among his brother officers. He was not, as they, subject to routine parades and orderly duties. He was a power in the land; one with whom it was expedient to be on friendly terms; he could perform or withhold all sorts of services . . . Transport Officer. Magnificent – like the gold star.

The major issues of war are in the hands of God, politicians and the general staff. The regimental officer, realising his helplessness, is not greatly concerned about them. Apart from discharging to the best of his ability the particular little task allotted to him he is not exercised with schemes for the rout of the enemy. Beyond satisfying himself that there is an appropriate depth of sand or earth on his dugout roof, and choosing when available a cellar instead of an attic (or at any rate a room before reaching which a shell would have to pass through at least one other) the chances of his own survival and the general progress of the campaign do not figure much in his mind. He has too much else to do, and in the doing of them the Transport Officer is often of determining importance. A horse and cart at the right moment, or a few cubic feet of space in a cart, may make all the difference to his outlook on life. They may make war tolerable and perhaps, for the time being, enjoyable. A mighty and beneficent power to wield. Transport Officer, 5th SR.

And well it was that we little people did not, in the main, realise how little we were. Marionettes on strings. Well that we saw only our own tiny stage and what happened thereon – though often enough things happened there which were not conducive to confidence or peace of mind. The dominant sentiment today on war? Tragedy, ghastly tragedy of death and wounds and incapacity; of sorrow-stricken homes and incon-solable bereavements. Yes. The fatuity of war as an instrument of peace; the train of complications, economic, social and political; all manner of problems which it aggravates rather than solves. That also. But to such as I more than anything else the appalling inefficiency of its conduct. Inefficiency in result is obvious; less has been said or written of its general management.

Efficiency is primarily an engineering or a commercial term. It implies that a machine does its work to a certain standard, that a bridge carries its load with a reasonable factor of safety; that, in an elementary way, the value and performance of the product are commensurate with the cost of making it. Prime and overhead costs must not merely be sufficiently lower than the selling cost of an efficient and useful article to enable proper wages to be paid and good materials to be used; they must allow for a profit on the operation as well. There is no cost accounting in war; the criteria of efficiency are never applied. St Luke wrote that one king going to war against another king first sits down and consults whether he be able with ten thousand men to meet him that comes against him with twenty thousand; otherwise while the other is a great way off he sends an ambassador desiring conditions of peace. Clausewitz says that the first and gravest strategic decision is rightly to understand the war and not to try and make of it something which in its relations it cannot possibly be. Here are implications of efficiency in the engineering sense; the study of object and possibilities first and then of the machinery and its operation. The percentage relation between the two constitutes the efficiency factor but too often war history approaches the object by way of the machinery.

Tactics change with armaments and ancillary equipment. Efficiency in this field implies a right economic proportioning of effort between the three services, and in each service between its major subdivisions. Efficiency is involved in the relations between front and maintenance armies; and in the relations between trench warfare (with continuous strain in the line and comparative ease behind) and open long-range warfare with relatively low battle stress and relatively great privations. Efficiency must be thought of in the objective sense – the relation of effort to object, as well as in the subjective sense – the best effort per se in which it is ordinarily used.

Strategy is more or less permanent in the formal and professional sense, but its efficiency varies in relation to the varying configurations of society and politics, and is subject even more than tactics to the necessity of right estimation.

Maybe some day someone will write a treatise on the comparative efficiency (or inefficiency) of great naval and military and air operations. Examples of wars and battles in the past may be judged coolly in the way an engineer judges the efficiency of his machine. Frederick the Great at Rosebach and Leuthen in 1757; Napoleon in the Jena campaign of 1806; Wellington at Salamanca, 1812; India in 1843; Kitchener in the Sudan. Of accurate and inaccurate strategic estimating there are examples with Prussia and Holland in 1787 and with Prussia and France in 1792.

Efforts and costs of all kinds in the Great War were utterly disproportionate to results, and for a variety of reasons. Compare, for instance, the Palestine campaign with that of Mesopotamia. Consider as a simple issue a sphere where too much was asked for too little to be given, as in Gallipoli; and too much given for too little gained, as on the Somme. Many of the practices and devices of efficient business management are applicable to the preparation and conduct of war. If another should come let us hope that the board of directors will be able at its conclusion to submit a satisfactory, audited balance sheet. It is still well to die for one's country; the sacrifice of a hundred lives to achieve a particular object may be fitly made, something worthwhile being bought at an economic price. What proportion of those whose names are commemorated on the hundred thousand memorials which star the land gave their lives, in fact less for God, King and Country, than simply to stupidity, jealousy, managerial incompetence. Must war be inefficient in life and in money?

Leaving cloud-wrapped Olympian heights peopled by politicians and generals for a single field occupied by horses and ordinary men – it has been mentioned that in times of peace Territorial infantry had no transport at all – men, horses or carts. The men necessary were obtained either by new enlistments, the great majority of whom had never before been subject to any sort of military discipline (and some of whom seemingly did not propose ever to be so subject) or by the process of detailing by officers commanding companies, who not unnaturally sent to Transport as many as possible of their less desirable members. In the former category there were a few with some knowledge of the horse; in the latter a few with some experience of military procedure. But whether in general it is more difficult to super-impose the practices and habits of a soldier on a civilian groom or cab-driver, or those of a horse tender on a stock-broker's clerk or a tradesman mechanic, it is impossible to say; it depends on man and horse. At any rate we had to essay both tasks.

I sought out the Transport Officer of the 8th SR and in a sequestered field, under his kindly tuition I acquired sufficient self-confidence to enable me to parade a few days later, mounted and spurred, at the head of the Transport column in a Brigade route march. It was an anxious and embarrassing experience; and once in the saddle I dared not dismount lest I be unable without ignominious assistance to regain it. I had also acquired various army manuals and other literature on the subject, and working at them through succeeding nights I became theoretically pretty well up in the subject. On appointment I had of course ordered two pairs of riding breeches and leggings, and, with ineffable delight, had procured a gigantic pair of spurs. But in the matter of apparel, I was to my chagrin not only forestalled but outclassed by the Machine Gun Officer. He had known that he would be mounted on mobilisation, and had certainly equipped himself for it.

Quick attention had to be given to personnel; and without leave of anyone I annexed several of the best of my old viaduct party. OC Company was naturally incensed, but instead of simply instructing me to return them, he protested to the orderly room *post factum*. Being summoned to account, I submitted the urgent need of a few reliable men as leaven in what was already known to be an undisciplined lump, and was allowed to keep the men; but I do not remember feeling myself to have had more than ordinary justice. I presumed further on this clemency to return some of the most obvious misfits, including the Transport sergeant, to the companies from which they had been ejected. I did not expect them to be welcomed, but neither had I anticipated such a storm of indignation among officers commanding; they would not have these men back. Neither would Transport; they could do what they liked; send them to the Doctor's unit perhaps; or to the Machine Guns. I was certainly not popular, but it was a respectful unpopularity.

One of the most efficient viaduct corporals was made Transport sergeant. It was taking a risk as he knew nothing about horses, but he was intelligent and efficient; I hoped he would learn. In any event what was immediately required was proper disciplinary control, expert knowledge being already to some extent available. He did well enough, discovering some reliable fellows for promotion – Whitelaw, clerk in a Glasgow shipping office but brought up with horses, was one; Anderson, a stockbroker but formerly in the yeomanry, another. The Adjutant urged my attention to an ex-regular with Boer War ribbons and already carrying a lance-corporal's stripe; he thought he would make a good Transport sergeant; he gave us a lot of bother before we were able to get him moved. MacLelland, a Glasgow Academy boy a few years younger than I, volunteered for service as my groom; there could have been none better.

A week later Whitelaw and Anderson asked me to speak to one Wallace, as they found he knew something about horses and they thought he might be useful. His name was known to me; year after year it had figured high in shooting competitions even at Bisley – Lance-Corporal R.B. Wallace. I knew him by sight: considerably older than most of us with a heavy black moustache; strongly built; discontented of expression. I assumed that he was only in the 5th for the shooting facilities thereby afforded. Prima facie he was no good, for his company commander had sent him to Transport on mobilisation. But we were hard up for NCOs, and as a lance-corporal he was an embarrassment if he could not be given a job. Sitting on the high stool of a foundry foreman's desk, I sent for Wallace and watched him coming down the long storeroom where the men were quartered. He had a heavy, slightly rolling gait. He favoured me with a salute and stood awkwardly and it seemed suspiciously to attention. 'Good morning, Wallace,' I said, and felt neither friendly nor hopeful. I spoke of the state of Transport, enquired what his civilian occupation was, what he knew about horses and whether he were content to look after a pair of them and nothing more; whether he would like some responsibility. He had the clear green-blue eyes of a shot. He was a foreman joiner, but he knew a good deal about horses, having been brought up on a farm. I was watching him closely; became more friendly and made him smile. He was no longer standing to attention, his hands were playing with the ink pot on the desk. I did not then, as in later years, take much pride of myself in the article of the judgment of men; but I was drawn to this man in the course of a ten minutes' conversation as I had never been to anyone before, nor, I think, since. I sought out his company commander. 'What sort of fellow is Lance-Corporal Wallace?' I asked. 'Oh, a pot hunter; I don't much care for him; I don't think he's any use.' 'Hence your sending him to Transport,' I remarked. But I thought then, as I knew later, that he had made a profound mistake. Bob Wallace.

With him, the sergeant, Whitelaw and Anderson, I began to get some sort of order into the party of about fifty men. A surprised and rather resentful section found itself for the first

time under orders to clean up and parade for church with the
rest of the Battalion. There were all sorts of troubles: negligent
grooming; gear and equipment 'lost'; absences without
permission sometimes accompanied by insobriety. Light relief
was afforded by such incidents as a driver reporting that there
was 'something wrong with one of the front paws' of his horse.
I made no effort to cultivate the Adjutant or my brother officers;
I was very busy and got into the habit of cutting meals in the
mess. When there was an hour to spare I would ride off into the
pleasant country with one or other of the Transport staff. Until
we were clear of Larbert my companion would be a length in
rear as propriety demanded, but he would then draw level and
until nearly home we would converse amiably about our job
among the glorious autumn colours of Stirlingshire.

A night alarm showed that Transport was in tolerably good
shape. It came at 1.15 a.m. on October 9th and we were on
parade with all our carts and wagons and ammunition ponies
within fifteen minutes. This was the last occasion on which I was
not entirely in command of my mount. My report of 'all present'
to the Adjutant was delayed by some ten minutes, owing to a
difference of opinion with the animal which I was unable
summarily to determine. Even so we were ahead of the last
company and were considered to have performed something of
a feat. A few days later we were complimented on our turn-out
by the Commander-in-Chief, Scotland. For this affair I had
acquired a new mount, a large mare of seventeen hands, the
gentle but somewhat obstinate animal inherited from my predecessor being relegated to the shafts of the doctor's cart.

My father and mother came twice to see me, and the
Minister brother – who had been a missionary in India for five
years – called for advice prior to service with Indian troops in
France. My mother was particularly interested in the horses, as
in her youth she had been as much at home in the saddle or
driver's seat as on the ground. Five weeks at Larbert passed easily

enough and we were beginning to wonder how long we were to be here. With the other units of the Lowland Division we had little contact. I did not know what was going to happen about foreign service; I assumed that sooner or later we should be on our way overseas.

At 10.00 p.m. on Tuesday October 27th I was sitting at the high desk in the Transport office with the NCOs and one or two others around when a cyclist orderly arrived with a message that I was wanted at once in the mess. 'A ticking off,' I thought, probably inter alia on my non-appearance for dinner. I found the Brigade Major with the CO and Adjutant. News at last. The Battalion had to relieve a Black Watch lot at Broughty Ferry on the Tay by 3.00 p.m. next day. This was good. To start with it meant a period of much activity, with Transport the master of the situation; and at the end Broughty Ferry was a congenial spot to me, good country and several friends.

I hurried back to Transport and wrote out orders for the collection of gear from the companies, Quartermaster's stores, HQ and officers' billets. We stowed away our surplus and unauthorised stores in an enormous wooden box purloined a fortnight earlier, loaded it on to a wagon with our own kit, and then all through the night were busy moving stores of all kinds to the railway station, entraining horses and wagons as each had done their allotted tasks. Beds and bedding and kit came last at 10.00 a.m. I was in the saddle from midnight till 8.00 a.m. and Anderson likewise as galloper; it was such an occasion as we both thoroughly enjoyed. We thought we had done really well when, about midday, an enormous train pulled out of Larbert carrying the Battalion and all its horses, wagons and stores.

On arrival at Broughty Ferry I took forty-nine men to a baker's shop for tea, and presumably somebody paid the bill later. We got the horses detrained and on to ropes slung across the Castle Green. That night I slept happily in the goods yard office and next morning made for one of the mansions on the outskirts of the town where I had frequently spent the weekend, where I knew the owners would be glad to put me up, and where in addition several horses could be stabled. To my sorrow the family was away so I had to decide which of various alternative billets to try. I presented myself at the West Manse and explained to the Minister and his wife my desire to partake (with batman) of their hospitality, but of course they could claim billeting and ration allowances for both of us. Being recovered from their astonishment and, so soon as they had comprehended the latter part of the offer, indignation, they made me very welcome. They were old friends of my family; there was a son, a three striper, in the Navy, another in the Church but he had already joined up; a third in his last year at Rugby was at home, but obviously eager to go to war. Our Battalion made such an impression on him and on his parents that he enlisted at the depot shortly afterwards and in due course was killed.

Next day all horses were satisfactorily stabled and all men billeted, and we settled down to a comfortable routine. Late on Saturday night Transport was ordered to fetch some stores from the railway station at Dundee; most of the men had turned in, but in any event I liked going on these jobs myself. Wallace accompanied me. I had already come to have an admiration and something like affection for him. Rattling along by the Tay we discussed the war – our war. A good war so far, we agreed; and we hoped we should be allowed to stay where we were for quite a time. He was surprised at my management of the spirited pair of horses, but on returning to Broughty Ferry there was an accident. The town was in a droll state of defence against German landing; fortifications on the heights above, barbed-wire entanglements and barricades even in some of the main streets. These latter, with two adjacent right-angle turns, required some negotiation. I took one of them at the trot; the corner of the lorry dislodged a plank of wood and a cascade of shingle roared down into the street. We thought it great fun.

Sunday – church parade, to which even the grooms had to go, and the service taken by the Minister from Barry nearby in the uniform of a padre. I still remember his text. Impressive. How many more services of this sort at home? I thought to make the most of the opportunity so went on to the ordinary morning service in the West Church and in the evening to St Luke's where also the Minister and his wife were old friends, and who had bid me to supper afterwards. Kitty, their daughter, was alone in the Manse pew; she signalled to me to come beside her and this I speedily did. I had known her for some years, but only slightly. She was eighteen and very pretty. As we sat at supper the Transport sergeant arrived. His message was obviously urgent; and it was terrific. 'The Battalion,' he announced, 'is proceeding overseas at once.'

I should have been very pleased; it was a tremendous honour to be sent out so quickly; it was what we had been hoping and training for. But, as with the outbreak of the war itself, it was inconvenient; I was getting on nicely in Broughty Ferry and could have done with a few weeks more. I remember the hush that came over the supper table; a dramatic moment. Sunday supper in the manses of Scotland has always been something of an occasion; the labours of the day are over and there is usually a visitor or two; the so familiar, peaceful scene. Overseas at once. To the Front.

I thought of home, of Father and Mother. Weekend leave had been given from Larbert, and the previous Sunday had been Communion in the College Church. I had wanted to go; I might never have the chance again. Several of the officers were going off and I asked the Adjutant if I might go too, and told him why. 'Come and see me about it,' he replied. I did not know what he meant but a few minutes later concluded that it was reprimand for asking him in the mess anteroom instead of in the orderly room. I was too proud or too silly to pursue the matter; now of course I wished I had.

I went off to a night's glorious activity similar to that at Larbert less than a week before. At midnight I went to the West Manse; the Minister had had the news from Tudhope, my batman. It had upset him; over sixty years of age, I remember him before his study fire, head in hands: 'I must go and drill or do some mortal thing to ease my mind.'

At 12.30 a.m. I was speaking to my father on the telephone. 'We're going to France tomorrow,' I said. There was a silence before he replied. I knew it would be a shock to him and to my mother; they had still thought that Territorials would not be sent overseas. They commended me to God's care. It was awful; but perhaps as well to have the parting thus. Sleep would be long in coming to them that night.

The Battalion left at midday for Southampton, but Transport orders were to go to Deptford and 'refit'. At four o'clock we were entrained. I had sent a note to Kitty saying there was no chance of my getting along to bid them farewell, and asking her to come to see me off. They all came and waited for over an hour; her father and mother felt that they were acting *in loco parentium*, as indeed they were. Kitty sat with me in the compartment for a few minutes. Politely I asked if I might kiss her. She nodded. I kissed her on the cheek; I knew no better, nor did for long years after that.

It was an eventful night; the horses were restless; at each stop we visited the boxes and did our best with them. At Berwick we found one aged animal on the floor and before we could get it up the train moved on and we had to clamber back along the running boards. At Newcastle it was dead and we hauled the carcass out on to the platform. 'You can't leave that horse here,' the frenzied officials said; a London express was due at the same platform a few minutes later. What did they expect us to do with a dead horse?

With our civilian equipment we had only six double-horsed vehicles and we had only six men capable of driving two horses.

One of them went sick in the night so I had to take his pair. I am glad to have driven an old-fashioned two-horse dray through the traffic of London from King's Cross to Deptford. It was a hazardous journey, and an odd sight we presented to the Army Service Corps. Some hours later we debouched from the depot with seventeen two-horsed wagons of one kind or another. In addition we had five single-horsed carts, nine riding horses, eight spare and nine tiny pack horses – sixty-five animals in all.

We arrived intact at Waterloo but I wondered what police on point duty and bystanders generally had thought of us. I did not myself drive one of the new teams; what was the use when a dozen drivers were coping for the first time with a pair of horses. I was more usefully employed going up and down the long column averting major disasters on that extraordinary passage. The entry into Waterloo was rather impressive and quite a crowd gathered to watch it. A steep incline had to be negotiated and most of the vehicles came up it at a hand gallop, but surprisingly there was no mishap. I was standing on the edge of the crowd watching the performance, my horse's reins over my arm and feeling – albeit somewhat anxious about the parade – very professional and pleased with myself, when I heard a voice behind me: 'Well, John.' It was a friend to whom I had wired the approximate time of our departure. Having set the entraining in motion we went off for a quick meal in the station restaurant. 'You haven't told me anything about Kitty,' he said. 'Kitty,' I said. 'What do you know about her? There's been no time to tell you.' He handed me a telegram which had been sent to me at his home. 'Happy here,' she wired, 'but happier with you.' A very nice message, I thought. But I never saw her again.

We reached Southampton about 2.00 a.m. and it was 7.00 a.m. before Transport was all detrained and established at the rest camp beside the Battalion. We had been two nights without sleep and had very little to eat since Sunday night at Broughty Ferry. What I most wanted, however, was a bath. A brother had newly come to those parts on ship survey work and I had procured his address from home. Outside the house, I gave the family whistle and he appeared at his bedroom window. At 8.00 he sent a telegram to my father: 'John is in our bath. His horse is rolling on the lawn.' It was quite true. Coming down to breakfast I saw the mare by that time placidly clipping grass, but with saddle and all its appendages under her belly.

We could have done with a day or two to become accustomed to our new wagons and horses, but we were going overseas at once and the same afternoon embarked ourselves, horses and wagons in ss *Huanchaco*, destination unknown. On the way to the docks a fine heavy draught horse from some other unit strayed in our direction and we annexed it. It was the first of many acts of unauthorised acquisition at which we were soon to become expert. On board I found a parcel of clothes and several letters and wondered how they got there. I wanted to telephone home from the hotel by the docks, but there was no time; all I could do was to send them a telegram: 'France tonight. Much love to Father and Mother. Take care of yourselves.' How extraordinary it seemed. The Battalion aboard ship for war; our labours and self-denials justified after all; the siren of the *Haunchaco* told us that if nothing else. The 5th SR, taken from its Brigade and Division because of what it was, was going overseas.

A ship alongside is part of the land to whose bollards she is made fast. The hawsers are cast off and soon there appear those few inches of black water which put her and all she contains at an infinite distance from the dock and those who stand thereon. Tantalisingly close; infinitely far. Under any circumstances a critical time; war bound, supreme. Very proud of ourselves. The Transport men and horses were as comfortable as could be expected. I wrote up my Diary to date and fell asleep on a truss of straw beside the mare.

David Rorie
The Pity of War

The attack on the Beaumont Hamel Ridge on 13 November 1916 was the last major action of the Battle of the Somme, which had begun almost five months earlier. Most of the men who took part in it were New Army Service battalions or Territorials, as well as Dominion troops from Australia, Canada, India, New Zealand and South Africa. Amongst their number were men of the 51st (Highland) Division, which had been assessed by German military intelligence as one of the most formidable fighting formations in the British Army. Four days later, after some fierce hand-to-hand fighting, the Scots had taken the heavily defended German positions in Y Ravine below the ridge. They suffered 2,200 casualties. In the aftermath of the battle Royal Army Medical Corps personnel of the Field Ambulances treated both Allied and German casualties. Amongst them was David Rorie's 1/2nd Highland Field Ambulance, which was responsible for collecting, treating and evacuating casualties, and Rorie was to say of the men under his command that 'None was stouter-hearted than the stretcher-bearer; none carried out his job more steadily and efficiently during the campaign.'

And now came the inevitable stage of clearing up the battlefield and searching all possible places where wounded, either British or Boche, who had not been picked up in the actual battle, might have sought shelter. At daybreak an MO [Medical Officer] and a party were sent to work from Y Ravine towards White City; while another party, including two Jocks with rifles (as the dug-outs with which Beaumont Hamel was tunnelled were not yet clear of whole-skinned Huns), worked across to meet him, an officer of the 6th Seaforths acting as guide. A further object was to search for a wonderful legendary underground Hun dressing station of the Arabian Nights variety, which, incidentally, we failed to locate.

It was drizzling wet and vilely cold, the trenches in places thigh deep in clay and an awful mess of smashed barbed wire, mud, disintegrated German dead and debris of all sorts. In one trench our occupation for half an hour was hauling each other out of the tenacious and bloodstained mud; and during our mutual salvage operations we had evidently made ourselves too visible, as the enemy started shelling. There was nothing for it but to take to the open and make for another trench, which we promptly did: doing a hundred yards in rather good time.

Now, the Jocks and I were of the Julius Caesar, Napoleon and Lord Roberts type of physique, while our guide was a tall man, whose greatcoat – which for some obscure reason he had put on before starting – blew out as he led us, doubled up on account of the *phut-phut* of bullets, across the open; and it struck me with a great feeling of irritation as we ran that we must be providing excellent comic effect for any of the enemy observing us through glasses, by suggesting an alarmed hen and three chickens on the run. (I had the opportunity of being in a gunner's OP [Observation Post], near Cambrai in 1918 and seeing four Germans doing a sprint under similar conditions. For once I felt a definite kinship to the Hun; I, too, had been at the wrong end of the telescope.) In the next trench we again set about searching the dug-outs and placarding them, to catch the eye of the stretcher-bearers who would follow, as containing so many wounded for removal; but again the Hun gunners got on to us in an exposed place and we had a second sprint across the open for another trench, where we had to stay below in a *sous-terrain* for an hour till things got quieter.

This dug-out was typical of the many with which Beaumont

Hamel was honeycombed. On descending about forty steps one was in a large floored and timbered chamber some fifty feet long; and at the further end a second set of steps led to a similar chamber, one side of each being lined with a double layer of bunks filled with dead and wounded Germans, the majority of whom had become casualties early on the morning of the 13th.

The place was, of course, in utter darkness; and, when we flashed our lights on and the wounded saw our escort with rifles ready, there was an outbreak of '*Kamarad!*' while a big bevy of rats squeaked and scuttled away from their feast on the dead bodies on the floor. The stench was indescribably abominable: for many of the cases were gas-gangrenous. Any food or drink they had possessed was used up, and our water bottles were soon emptied amongst them. After we had gone over the upper chamber and separated the living from the dead, we went to the lower one where the gas curtain was let down and fastened. Tearing it aside and going through with a light, I got a momentary jump when I caught a glimpse in the upper bunk of a man, naked to the waist, and with his right hand raised above his head. But the poor beggar was far past mischief – stark and stiff with a smashed pelvis. Some twenty other dead Germans lay about, at the disposal of the rat hordes. The romance of war had worn somewhat thin here.

When the shelling had eased up and we quitted the place, the wounded firmly believed they were being left for good; although we had repeatedly assured them that in a short time they would all be taken to hospital. But to the end of the campaign the wounded Boche could never understand that he was not going to be treated with the same brutality as he had meted out to others at the outset of war; so it was amidst a chorus of shrieks, wails and supplications that we made for the welcome open air, ticketed the dug-out as containing fourteen wounded for removal, and renewed our search in similar surroundings for fresh casualties.

One other memory of Beaumont Hamel is still vivid. Parallel to Wagon Road, and on its Auchonvillers side, ran a *chemin creux* in which were several dug-outs where we – and the Division on our left – had Battalion RAPs [Regimental Aid Post]. It had been severely shelled and the sides of the road had fallen in, reducing the cart track to a foot-path knee deep in mud. Going up it one morning soon after daybreak, I saw a headless corpse lying on a stretcher at the path side. From the neck a trickle of blood ran to the feet of a man outside a dug-out who was calmly frying some ham in his canteen lid over an impro-vised oil-can stove. His mate – fag in mouth – was watching him. What was beside them had ceased to be worth comment. They were surfeited with evil sights. And they were hungry.

On the 16th, Tenderloin in White City became our HQ for forward evacuation; and there with two MOs and a hundred and twenty bearers we stayed until the 19th, searching all possible locations in the field for any cases possibly missed, and clearing a large quantity of wounded for the Division on our left, who were stunting and whose RAPs could not be cleared without our help. All this time White City and the roads into Beaumont Hamel were distinctly unhealthy, and the weather was vile; while the atmosphere inside our dug-outs – one long chamber with over a hundred and twenty occupants – was almost palpable. A wash was an unknown luxury, of course; but though lousy we were cheerful – even tuneful at times, thanks to the corporal's penny whistle and a veteran gramophone – as our job was nearly done.

By the 22nd our unit had still twenty-four bearers in the RAPs at Beaumont Hamel, twenty-four at Tenderloin, thirty-six in reserve at Auchonvillers, and a tent sub-division at the ADS [Advanced Dressing Station] at Mailly-Maillet; while, in addition, we were running the MDS [Main Dressing Station] at Forceville, handed over to us by the 3rd HFA [Hospital Field Auxiliary], which had left for Puchevillers; so our hands were fairly full. But, on the 23rd, we handed over, and started overhauling equipment in view of our next move.

What Field Ambulance officer does not recall overhauling equipment after a push? The counting of stretchers, blankets, wheeled carriers, etc., etc.; the exploring of Field Medical and Surgical panniers to check missing 'unexpendables'; and the inevitable and unanimous finding of all concerned that what couldn't be found had certainly been destroyed by shell-fire! However, on this occasion we had increased and multiplied exceedingly; for we came away from Beaumont Hamel outstandingly to the good in the essential matters of blankets, stretchers, and especially wheeled stretcher carriers; so that the soul of the ADMS [Assistant Director Medical Services] rejoiced within him, until at the first DDMS [Deputy Director Medical Services] conference he had to meet his suffering and blood-thirsty colleagues who had been on our right and left flanks.

Four days later we moved from Forceville to Senlis, and took over a set of hutments on top of a windswept hill above the village from a Canadian Field Ambulance, finding the place – to be quite honest – in a most unholy mess. He was a good man, the Canuck, right enough, and a 'bonny fechter': but he had a way of his own all through the campaign. Our advance party officer was taken round the show by a Canadian *confrère* (in shirt sleeves, breeches and gum-boots) who, on giving an order to a sergeant *en passant*, received the reply: –

'You go to ——, John!'

The officer's only comment was a grieved: –

'Well, now! He shouldn't say that, should he?' – and the matter apparently ended!

Here, then, we stayed for several uncomfortable cold and wet weeks while the Division was in the line at Courcelette; thence for some weeks of severe frost to the Buigny-St Maclou area near Abbeville, where we were not far from historic Crecy. Later, we were once more at the hutments of Haute Avesnes: and

marched thence to Caucourt, on the other side of DHQ
[Divisional Headquarters] at Villers Chatel, to run a Divisional
Rest Station and prepare the forward medical posts for the next
push, the famous Vimy Ridge battle, where the 51st were on the
right of the Canadians.

Saki (H.H. Munro)
Birds on the Western Front

*Written while Munro was serving on the Western Front, this is
one of the finest pieces of observational writing produced during
the conflict. Throughout his life, Munro had a marked interest
in wildlife, often viewing animals as agents of revenge on
mankind and frequently introducing birds and beasts into his
narratives to the discomfort of the human characters.*

Considering the enormous economic dislocation which the war
operations have caused in the regions where the campaign is
raging, there seems to be very little corresponding disturbance
in the bird life of the same districts. Rats and mice have
mobilized and swarmed into the fighting line, and there has been
a partial mobilisation of owls, particularly barn owls, following
in the wake of the mice, and making laudable efforts to thin out
their numbers. What success attends their hunting one cannot
estimate; there are always sufficient mice left over to populate
one's dug-out and make a parade-ground and race-course of
one's face at night. In the matter of nesting accommodation the
barn owls are well provided for; most of the still intact barns in
the war zone are requisitioned for billeting purposes, but there
is a wealth of ruined houses, whole streets and clusters of them,
such as can hardly have been available at any previous moment
of the world's history since Nineveh and Babylon became
humanly desolate. Without human occupation and cultivation
there can have been no corn, no refuse, and consequently very
few mice, and the owls of Nineveh cannot have enjoyed very
good hunting; here in Northern France the owls have desolation

and mice at their disposal in unlimited quantities, and as these
birds breed in winter as well as in summer, there should be a
goodly output of war owlets to cope with the swarming generations of war mice.

Apart from the owls one cannot notice that the campaign is
making any marked difference in the bird life of the countryside. The vast flocks of crows and ravens that one expected to
find in the neighbourhood of the fighting line are non-existent,
which is perhaps rather a pity. The obvious explanation is that
the roar and crash and fumes of high explosives have driven the
crow tribe in panic from the fighting area; like many obvious
explanations, it is not a correct one. The crows of the locality
are not attracted to the battlefield, but they certainly are not
scared away from it. The rook is normally so gun-shy and
nervous where noise is concerned that the sharp banging of a
barn door or the report of a toy pistol will sometimes set an
entire rookery in commotion; out here I have seen him sedately
busy among the refuse heaps of a battered village, with shells
bursting at no great distance, and the impatient-sounding,
snapping rattle of machine-guns going on all round him; for all
the notice that he took he might have been in some peaceful
English meadow on a sleepy Sunday afternoon. Whatever else
German frightfulness may have done it has not frightened the
rook of North-Eastern France; it has made his nerves steadier
than they have ever been before, and future generations of small
boys, employed in scaring rooks away from the sown crops in
this region, will have to invent something in the way of super-
frightfulness to achieve their purpose. Crows and magpies are
nesting well within the shell-swept area, and over a small beech-
copse I once saw a pair of crows engaged in hot combat with a
pair of sparrow-hawks, while considerably higher in the sky, but
almost directly above them, two Allied battle-planes were
engaging an equal number of enemy aircraft.

Unlike the barn owls, the magpies have had their choice of

building sites considerably restricted by the ravages of war; the whole avenues of poplars, where they were accustomed to construct their nests, have been blown to bits, leaving nothing but dreary-looking rows of shattered and splintered trunks to show where once they stood. Affection for a particular tree has in one case induced a pair of magpies to build their bulky, domed nest in the battered remnants of a poplar of which so little remained standing that the nest looked almost bigger than the tree; the effect rather suggested an archiepiscopal enthronement taking place in the ruined remains of Melrose Abbey. The magpie, wary and suspicious in his wild state, must be rather intrigued at the change that has come over the erstwhile fearsome not-to-be-avoided human, stalking everywhere over the earth as its possessor, who now creeps about in screened and sheltered ways, as chary of showing himself in the open as the shyest of wild creatures.

The buzzard, that earnest seeker after mice, does not seem to be taking any war risks, at least I have never seen one out here, but kestrels hover about all day in the hottest parts of the line, not in the least disconcerted, apparently, when a promising mouse-area suddenly rises in the air in a cascade of black or yellow earth. Sparrow-hawks are fairly numerous, and a mile or two back from the firing line I saw a pair of hawks that I took to be red-legged falcons, circling over the top of an oak-copse. According to investigations made by Russian naturalists, the effect of the war on bird life on the Eastern front has been more marked than it has been over here. 'During the first year of the war rooks disappeared, larks no longer sang in the fields, the wild pigeon disappeared also.' The skylark in this region has stuck tenaciously to the meadows and croplands that have been seamed and bisected with trenches and honeycombed with shell-holes. In the chill, misty hour of gloom that precedes a rainy dawn, when nothing seemed alive except a few wary water-logged sentries and many scuttling rats, the lark would suddenly dash skyward and pour forth a song of ecstatic jubilation that sounded horribly forced and insincere. It seemed scarcely possible that the bird could carry its insouciance to the length of attempting to rear a brood in that desolate wreckage of shattered clods and gaping shell-holes, but once, having occasion to throw myself down with some abruptness on my face, I found myself nearly on the top of a brood of young larks. Two of them had already been hit by something, and were in rather a battered condition, but the survivors seemed as tranquil and comfortable as the average nestling.

At the corner of a stricken wood (which has had a name made for it in history, but shall be nameless here), at a moment when Lyddite and shrapnel and machine-gun fire swept and raked and bespattered that devoted spot as though the artillery of an entire Division had suddenly concentrated on it, a wee hen-chaffinch flitted wistfully to and fro, amid splintered and falling branches that had never a green bough left on them. The wounded lying there, if any of them noticed the small bird, may well have wondered why anything having wings and no pressing reason for remaining should have chosen to stay in such a place. There was a battered orchard alongside the stricken wood, and the probable explanation of the bird's presence was that it had a nest of young ones whom it was too scared to feed, too loyal to desert. Later on, a small flock of chaffinches blundered into the wood, which they were doubtless in the habit of using as a highway to their feeding-grounds; unlike the solitary hen-bird, they made no secret of their desire to get away as fast as their dazed wits would let them. The only other bird I ever saw there was a magpie, flying low over the wreckage of fallen tree-limbs; 'one for sorrow', says the old superstition. There was sorrow enough in that wood.

The English gamekeeper, whose knowledge of wild life usually runs on limited and perverted lines, has evolved a sort of religion as to the nervous debility of even the hardiest game birds; according to his beliefs a terrier trotting across a field in which a partridge is nesting, or a mouse-hawking kestrel hovering over the hedge, is sufficient cause to drive the distracted bird off its eggs and send it whirring into the next county.

The partridge of the war zone shows no signs of such sensitive nerves. The rattle and rumble of transport, the constant coming and going of bodies of troops, the incessant rattle of musketry and deafening explosions of artillery, the night-long flare and flicker of star-shells, have not sufficed to scare the local birds away from their chosen feeding grounds, and to all appearances they have not been deterred from raising their broods. Gamekeepers who are serving with the colours might seize the opportunity to indulge in a little useful nature study.

Charles Hamilton Sorley
Letters from an Infantry Officer

Throughout his short life Sorley was an inveterate corre-
spondent, writing long and lively letters from school at
Marlborough College, from Germany where he studied at the
University of Jena and latterly from his new life as an infantry
officer in the 7th Suffolk Regiment fighting on the Western Front.
After his death his father Professor W.R. Sorley collected the
letters and published them in 1919 and in the Preface he claimed
that his son 'speaks for himself in these letters; and they have
been selected so as to let him be seen as he truly was.' The other
correspondents were two school friends, Alan Hutchinson and
Arthur Hopkinson, and Arthur Watts whom he had met in Jena.
The first letter to Hutchinson describes the journey which Sorley
made back to Britain after the declaration of war.

––––––––––

To A.E. Hutchinson, Cambridge, 10 (?) August 1914

I daresay that, after the three years that Lord K[itchener] has
allotted for the war, they'll forward me from Jena a letter from
you written to me about this time. Howbeit, even supposing you
sent one loose into that delightful land, I naturally never received
it. For, after I had spent three splendid days trying to make
Hopper drunk with Mosel wine in the Mosel valley (I never got
him further than the state of 'not drunk but having drink taken'),
they took us up as spies and put us into prison at Trier. To be
exact, the 'imprisonment' only lasted 8½ hours; but I was feeling
a real prisoner by the time they let us out. I had a white cell, a
bowl of soup, a pitcher of solidifying water, a hole in the wall

through which I talked to the prisoner next door, a prison bed, a prison bible: so altogether they did the thing in style. We had also a hissing crowd shouting '*Totschiessen*' [shoot dead] to accompany us from the barracks to the prison. It couldn't have been arranged more finely: and the man who had occupied the cell before me had just been taken out and shot for being a Frenchman. But the English were in high favour, and I started a rumour that England had declared war on Russia; so they readily gave us a dismissal at our examination, and a free pass calling us unsuspicious. We travelled slowly to Cologne all through Sunday night: but a sad thing happened there, and Paul and Barnabas parted. Barnabas went on in the same train to Amsterdam hoping thereby to reach Hook; while Paul (ravenous for breakfast) 'detrained' at Cologne and had a huge meal. I, of course, was Paul. Meanwhile your post-card has arrived and many thanks. I explain. Your letter probably reached Jena after I had left and was forwarded to the Poste Restante, Trier, as I had directed. But the only three public buildings I was allowed to see were the barracks, the prison, and the station. So, as I have said before, I shall send for the letter and post-cards in three years. They have probably read your letter at Trier and cut out with scissors the words they consider improper.

To proceed, as Sergt-Major Barnes says. I took a train to Brussels, but they turned me out at a deserted village on the Belgian frontier. I walked to the next town and took the train sorrowfully to Brussels. At Brussels I had 'financial difficulties' and had to call on half the consuls in the place to solve them, and then I travelled sordidly on to Antwerp. The last ship had sailed for Harwich so the English consul chartered an old broken-down sad ship called the 'Montrose'. It was being embalmed in Antwerp Harbour because Miss le Neve had been taken prisoner on board it four years ago. They gave us Capt. Kendall, who was last seen going down with the 'Empress of Ireland', to take command. And after three days' journey with commercial travellers of the most revoltingly John Bullish description, I got home on Thursday and was mistaken for the gardener. He always wears my worn-out clo's, so we are constantly interchanged. But mark. Hopper, who arrived triumphant at Harwich two days before I did, had to pay for his crossing. I got a free passage as far as London, where I borrowed money from my aunt's butler to take me on to Cambridge; and my aunt repaid the debt.

Now, have you ever heard a more commonplace and sordid narrative? At least I found it so in experience merely dull, after I had left Hopper. The only bright star was a drunken Austrian, with whom we travelled from Trier to Coblenz, who seated himself opposite to us and gazed in our faces and at last said lovingly: *'Ihr seid gewiss Hamburger Jungen.'* [You are clearly young men from Hamburg.] The poor man was trying to go from Kiel to Vienna, and, perpetually drunken, had travelled via Brussels, Paris, Marseilles, and Metz, which even you must know is not the shortest way. After he had flung Hopper's cap out of the window, he said that Hopper was a *'feiner Mann'* [fine man], but said nothing about me, which just shows how drunk he was. But otherwise it was dull. Now, behold, I cannot stir out of the house, but some lady friend of my mother's, whose mind is upset by the present business, rushes up and says 'O, you're the boy that's had such *adventures*. Been in prison too, I hear. You must come and tell us all about it.' Then there's aunts to be written to. I shall probably be driven into writing a book 'Across Germany in an OM [Old Marlburian] tie' or 'Prison Life in Germany by one who has seen it', followed shortly by another entitled: 'Three days on the open sea with Commercial Travellers' or 'Britannia Rules the Waves'. And so I am simply nauseated by the memory of these five very ordinary and comparatively dull days. The preceding days in the Moselthal were far nicer: only Hopper was so provincial, and, when I entered a Gasthaus with a knowing swagger and said 'I wish to

sample the local Mosel here; what vintage do you recommend?'
Hopper would burst in with '*Haben Sie Munchener Bier*?' [Do
you have Munich beer?] and a huge grin on his face: unwitting
what a heinous sin it is to order beer in a wine district. So we
generally compromised on hot milk.

Having proved my identity at home as distinct from the
gardener's, I investigated my (a-hem!) 'papers' and found, among
old receipts for college clothes and such like, a lovely piece of
paper, which I daresay you have got too, which dismissed me
from the corps. Only mine had EXCELLENT written (in the
Major's hand) for my General Efficiency. Yours can have had, at
most, 'very good'. I took this down to a man of sorts and said
'*Mit Gott für Kaiser und Vaterland* [With God for King and
Fatherland], I mean, *für Konig und Mutterland* [for King and
Motherland]; what can I do to have some reasonable answer to
give to my acquaintances when they ask me, 'What are you
doing?' He looked me up and down and said, 'Send in for a
commission in the Territorials. You may get something there.
You'll get an answer in a fortnight's time, not before.' Compromise as usual. Not heroic enough to do the really straight
thing and join the regulars as a Tommy, I have made a stupid
compromise [with] my conscience and applied for a commission
in the Terriers, where no new officers are wanted. In a month's
time I shall probably get the beastly thing; and spend the next
twelve months binding the corn, guarding the bridges, frightening
the birds away, and otherwise assisting in Home Defence. So I
think you were sensible to prefer your last term at Marlborough.
Only I wish you could come and join the beastly battalion of
Cambridgeshire clerks to which I shall be tacked on: and we
could sow the corn and think we were soldiers together.

But isn't all this bloody? I am full of mute and burning rage
and annoyance and sulkiness about it. I could wager that out of
twelve million eventual combatants there aren't twelve who
really want it. And 'serving one's country' is so unpicturesque

and unheroic when it comes to the point. Spending a year in a beastly Territorial camp guarding telegraph wires has nothing poetical about it: nor very useful as far as I can see. Besides the Germans are so nice; but I suppose the best thing that could happen to them would be their defeat . . .

――――――――

To A.J. Hopkinson, Shorncliffe, October (?) 1914

I thought the enclosure from [your] Uncle peculiarly interesting and return as you must want to keep it. He put the case for Prussian (as distinct from German) efficiency far more fairly than I had ever thought of it before. I think his transatlantic criticism of England's 'imaginative indolence' and consequent social rotten-ness most stimulating in this time of auto-trumpeting and Old-England-she's-the-same-as-ever-isms. Also I suppose he is to a certain extent right that we have temporarily renounced all our claim to the more articulate and individual parts of our individu-ality. But in the intervals of doing and dying let's speak to one another as two pro-Germans, or nearly so, who have tramped her roads, bathed in her Moselles, and spent half-a-day in her cells.

The two great sins people impute to Germany are that she says that might is right and bullies the little dogs. But I don't think that she means might qua might is right, but that confidence of superiority is right, and by superiority she means spiritual superiority. She said to Belgium, 'We enlightened thinkers see that it is necessary to the world that all opposition to Deutsche Kultur should be crushed. As citizens of the world you must assist us in our object and assert those higher ideas of world-citizenship which are not bound by treaties. But if you oppose us, we have only one alternative.' That, at least, is what the best of them would have said; only the diplomats put it rather more brusquely. She was going on a missionary voyage with all the zest of Faust –

Er wandle so den Erdentag entlang;
Wenn Geister spuken, geh' er seinen Gang;
Im Weiterschreiten find' er Qual und Gltick,
Er, unbefriedigt jeden Augenblick!

– and missionaries know no law. As Uncle Alder says, her Kultur (in its widest sense) is the best in the world: so she must scatter it broadcast through the world perforce, saying like the school-master or the dentist, 'Though it hurts at present, it'll do you no end of good afterwards.' (Perhaps she will even have to add at the end of the war 'And it's hurt me more than it's hurt you.')

So it seems to me that Germany's only fault (and I think you often commented on it in those you met) is a lack of real insight and sympathy with those who differ from her. We are not fighting a bully, but a bigot. They are a young nation and don't yet see that what they consider is being done for the good of the world may be really being done for self-gratification like X who, under pretence of informing the form, dropped into the habit of parading his own knowledge. X incidentally did the form a service by creating great amusement for it, and so is Germany incidentally doing the world a service (though not in the way it meant) by giving them something to live and die for, which no country but Germany had before. If the bigot conquers he will learn in time his mistaken methods (for it is only of the methods and not of the goal of Germany that one can disapprove) – just as the early Christian bigots conquered by bigotry and grew larger in sympathy and tolerance after conquest. I regard the war as one between sisters, between Martha and Mary, the efficient and intolerant against the casual and sympathetic. Each side has a virtue for which it is fighting, and each that virtue's supple-mentary vice. And I hope that whatever the material result of the conflict, it will purge these two virtues of their vices, and efficiency and tolerance will no longer be incompatible.

But I think that tolerance is the larger virtue of the two, and

efficiency must be her servant. So I am quite glad to fight this
rebellious servant. In fact I look at it this way. Suppose my
platoon were the world. Then my platoon-sergeant would
represent efficiency and I would represent tolerance. And I
always take the sternest measures to keep my platoon-sergeant
in check! I fully appreciate the wisdom of the War Office when
they put inefficient officers to rule sergeants . . .

———

To A.E. Hutchinson, Shorncliffe, 14 November 1914

. . . England – I am sick of the sound of the word. In training to
fight for England, I am training to fight for that deliberate
hypocrisy, that terrible middle-class sloth of outlook and
appalling 'imaginative indolence' that has marked us out from
generation to generation. Goliath and Caiaphas the Philistine
and the Pharisee pound these together and there you have
Suburbia and Westminster and Fleet Street. And yet we have the
impudence to write down Germany (who with all their bigotry
are at least seekers) as 'Huns', because they are doing what every
brave man ought to do and making experiments in morality. Not
that I approve of the experiment in this particular case. Indeed I
think that after the war all brave men will renounce their country
and confess that they are strangers and pilgrims on the earth.
'For they that say such things declare plainly that they seek a
country.' But all these convictions are useless for me to state since
I have not had the courage of them. What a worm one is under
the cart-wheels big clumsy careless lumbering cart-wheels of
public opinion. I might have been giving my mind to fight against
Sloth and Stupidity: instead, I am giving my body (by a
refinement of cowardice) to fight against the most enterprising
nation in the world . . .

———

To A.E. Hutchinson, Shorncliffe, 25 January 1915

How are you getting on? I can imagine it is not quite heaven.
But neither is this. Heaven will have to wait until the war's over.
It is the most asphyxiating work after the first fine glow of seeing
people twice your age and size obey and salute you has passed
off, as it does after a fortnight. The only thing is that the pay is
good. The rest, as you are probably finding already, is complete
stagnation among a mass of straps and sleeping-bags and water-
bottles. War in England only means putting all the men of
'military age' in England into a state of routinal coma,
preparatory to getting them killed. You are being given six
months to become conventional: your peace thus made with
God, you will be sent out and killed. At least, if you aren't killed,
you'll come back so unfitted for any other job that you'll have
to stay in the Army. I should like so much to kill whoever was
primarily responsible for the war. The alarming sameness with
which day passes day until this unnatural state of affairs is over
is worse than any so-called atrocities; for people enjoy grief, the
only unbearable thing is dullness.
    I have started to read again, having read nothing all the
closing months of last year. I have discovered a man called D.H.
Lawrence who knows the way to write, and I still stick to
[Thomas] Hardy: to whom I never managed to convert you.
    We talk of going out in March. I am positively looking
forward to that event, not in the brave British drummer-boy
spirit, of course, but as a relief from this boredom (part of which,
by the way, is caused through Philpott having been away the last
three weeks in hospital).
    We don't seem to be winning, do we? It looks like an affair
of years. If so, pray God for a nice little bullet wound (tidy and
clean) in the shoulder. That's the place . . .

_____

To Mrs Sorley, Aldershot, March 1915

We are off for a wild game this week-end under the eyes of
Kitchener. But going out still remains an uncertainty as to time,
and has become a matter of the indifferent future to most of us.
If we had gone out earlier we would have gone out with a thrill
in poetic-martial vein: now most of us have become by habit
soldiers, at least in so far that we take such things as a matter of
course and a part of our day's work that our own anticipations
can neither quicken nor delay.

I talked a lot (in her native tongue) to the hostess with whom
I was billeted, and her sensible German attitude was like a cold
bath. She saw the thing, as German hausfraus would, directly
and humanly and righteously. Especially sensible was she in her
remarks against the kind ladies who told her she ought to be
proud and glad to give her sons to fight. After all, war in this
century is inexcusable: and all parties engaged in it must take an
equal share in the blame of its occurrence. If only the English
from [Sir Edward] Grey downwards would cease from rubbing
in that, in the days that set all the fuel ablaze, they worked for
peace honestly and with all their hearts! We know they did; but
in the past their lack of openness and trust in their diplomatic
relationships helped to pile the fuel to which Germany applied
the torch.

I do wish also that people would not deceive themselves by
talk of a just war. There is no such thing as a just war. What we
are doing is casting out Satan by Satan. When once war was
declared the damage was done: and we, in whom that particular
Satan was perhaps less strong than in our foes, had only one
course, namely to cast out the far greater Satan by means of him:
and he must be fought to the bitter end. But that doesn't alter
the fact that long ago there should have been an understanding
in Europe that any country that wanted *Weltmacht* might have
it. The Allies may yet score a victory over Germany. But by last

August they had thrown away their chances of a true victory. I remember you once on the Ellerby moors telling us the story of Bishop What's-his-name and John-Val-John [Jean Valjean] from *Les Miserables*. And now, although we failed then of the highest, we might have fought, regarding the war not, as we do regard it, as a candle to shed light upon our unselfishness and love of freedom, but as a punishment for our past presumptuousness. We had the silver candlesticks and brandished them ever proudly as our own, won by our own valour. Germany must be crushed for her wicked and selfish aspiration to be mistress of the world: but the country that, when mistress of the world, failed to set her an example of unworldliness and renunciation should take to herself half the blame of the blood expended in the crushing.

To Mrs Sorley, Aldershot, 28 April 1915

I saw Rupert Brooke's death in *The Morning Post*. *The Morning Post*, which has always hitherto disapproved of him, is now loud in his praises because he has conformed to their stupid axiom of literary criticism that the only stuff of poetry is violent physical experience, by dying on active service. I think Brooke's earlier poems especially notably *The Fish* and *Grantchester*, which you can find in Georgian Poetry are his best. That last sonnet sequence of his, of which you sent me the review in the *Times Lit. Sup.*, and which has been so praised, I find (with the exception of that beginning 'These hearts were woven of human joys and cares, Washed marvellously with sorrow' which is not about himself) overpraised. He is far too obsessed with his own sacrifice, regarding the going to war of himself (and others) as a highly intense, remarkable and sacrificial exploit, whereas it is merely the conduct demanded of him (and others) by the turn of circumstances, where non-compliance with this demand would have made life intolerable. It was not that 'they' gave up anything of that list he gives in one sonnet: but that the essence of these things had been endangered by circumstances over which he had no control, and he must fight to recapture them. He has clothed his attitude in fine words: but he has taken the sentimental attitude.

———

To Arthur Watts, 16 June 1915

The sight of your handwriting was a call back to another world characters which I first saw (and marked as English) on the blotched and peppered lecture-board in the Jena lecture-rooms: '*Im Sommersemester 1914 gedenke ich zu lesen*,' [in the summer term of 1914 I intend to read] etc. 'Twas a drenching day – a soaked sack of tweeds on my back and luggage lost – so I went in search of the writer, ploughing through the marshes of Heidenstrasse. But I disliked the look of the house pictured an elderly Englishman and fat, accustomed to extension lecturing, sitting over weak tea and sponge-cakes with a German wife and turned back. I returned however in half-an-hour.

But this is scarcely current. Only, in a job like this, one lives in times a year ago – and a year hence, alternately. *Keine Nachricht* [no news]. A large amount of organised disorderliness, killing the spirit. A vagueness and a dullness everywhere: an unromantic sitting still 100 yards from Brother Bosch. There's something rotten in the state of something. One feels it but cannot be definite of what. Not even is there the premonition of something big impending: gathering and ready to burst. None of that feeling of confidence, offensiveness, 'personal ascendancy', with which the reports so delight our people at home. Mutual helplessness and lassitude, as when two boxers who have battered each other crouch dancing two paces from each other, waiting for the other to hit. Improvised organization, with its red hat, has muddled out romance. It is not the strong god of the Germans that makes their Prussian *Beamter* [officials] so bloody and their fight against fearful odds so successful. Our organization is like a nasty fat old frowsy cook dressed up in her mistress's clothes: fussy, unpopular, and upstart: trailing the scent of the scullery behind her. In periods of rest we are billeted in a town of sewage farms, mean streets, and starving cats: delightful population: but an air of late June weariness. For Spring again! This is not Hell as I hoped, but Limbo Lake with green growths on the water, full of minnows.

So one lives in a year ago – and a year hence. What are your feet doing a year hence? (For that feeling of stoniness, 'too-old-at-fortyness', and late afternoon of which you speak, is only you among strangers, you in Babylon: you were forty when I first saw you: thirty, donnish, and well-mannered when you first asked me to tea: but later, at tennis, you were any age: you will be always forty to strangers perhaps: and you then as you get to know them, be they knowable. And after all, friends are the same age.) All this in a bracket: but where, while riding in your Kentish lanes, are you riding twelve months hence? I am sometimes in Mexico, selling cloth: or in Russia, doing Lord knows what: in Serbia or the Balkans: in England, never. England remains the dream, the background: at once the memory and the ideal. Sorley [*Somhairle*] is the Gaelic for wanderer. I have had a conventional education: Oxford would have corked it. But this has freed the spirit, glory be. Give me *The Odyssey*, and I return the New Testament to store. Physically as well as spiritually, give me the road.

Only sometimes the horrible question of bread and butter shadows the dream: it has shadowed many, I should think. It must be tackled. But I always seek to avoid the awkward, by postponing it . . .

To Professor Sorley, 15 July 1915 [France]

Your letter, dated 11th, has just arrived. We are now at the end
of a few days' rest, a kilometre behind the lines. Except for the
farmyard noises (new style) it might almost be the little village
that first took us to its arms six weeks ago. It has been a fine day,
following on a day's rain, so that the earth smells like spring. I
have just managed to break off a long conversation with the
farmer in charge, a tall thin stooping man with sad eyes, in
trouble about his land: les Anglais stole his peas, trod down his
corn and robbed his young potatoes: he told it as a father telling
of infanticide. There may have been fifteen francs' worth of
damage done; he will never get compensation out of those shifty
Belgian burgomasters; but it was not exactly the fifteen francs
but the invasion of the soil that had been his for forty years, in
which the weather was his only enemy, that gave him a kind of
Niobe's dignity to his complaint.

Meanwhile there is the usual evening sluggishness. Close by,
a quickfirer is pounding away its allowance of a dozen shells a
day. It is like a cow coughing. Eastward there begins a sound (all
sounds begin at sundown and continue intermittently till
midnight, reaching their zenith at about 9 p.m. and then dying
away as sleepiness claims their makers) a sound like a motor-
cycle race thousands of motor-cycles tearing round and round a
track, with cut-outs out: it is really a pair of machine guns firing.
And now one sound awakens another. The old cow coughing
has started the motor-bikes: and now at intervals of a few
minutes come express trains in our direction: you can hear them
rushing toward us; they pass going straight for the town behind
us: and you hear them begin to slow down as they reach the
town : they will soon stop: but no, every time, just before they
reach it, is a tremendous railway accident. At least, it must be a
railway accident, there is so much noise, and you can see the dust
that the wreckage scatters. Sometimes the train behind comes

very close, but it too smashes on the wreckage of its forerunners. A tremendous cloud of dust, and then the groans. So many trains and accidents start the cow coughing again: only another cow this time, somewhere behind us, a tremendous-sized cow, θαυμάσια μεγάλη [wonderfully great] with awful whooping-cough. It must be a buffalo: this cough must burst its sides. And now someone starts sliding down the stairs on a tin tray, to soften the heart of the cow, make it laugh and cure its cough. The din he makes is appalling. He is beating the tray with a broom now, every two minutes a stroke: he has certainly stopped the cow by this time, probably killed it. He will leave off soon (thanks to the 'shell tragedy'): we know he can't last.

It is now almost dark: come out and see the fireworks. While waiting for them to begin you can notice how pale and white the corn is in the summer twilight: no wonder with all this whooping-cough about. And the motor-cycles: notice how all these races have at least a hundred entries: there is never a single cycle going. And why are there no birds coming back to roost? Where is the lark? I haven't heard him all today. He must have got whooping cough as well, or be staying at home through fear of the cow. I think it will rain tomorrow, but there have been no swallows circling low, stroking their breasts on the full ears of corn. Anyhow, it is night now, but the circus does not close till twelve. Look! there is the first of them! The fireworks are beginning. Red flares shooting up high into the night, or skimming low over the ground, like the swallows that are not: and rockets bursting into stars. See how they illumine that patch of ground a mile in front. See it, it is deadly pale in their searching light: ghastly, I think, and featureless except for two big lines of eyebrows ashy white, parallel along it, raised a little from its surface. Eyebrows. Where are the eyes? Hush, there are no eyes. What those shooting flares illumine is a mole. A long thin mole. Burrowing by day, and shoving a timorous enquiring snout above the ground by night. Look, did you see it? No, you cannot see it from here. But were you a good deal nearer, you would see behind that snout a long and endless row of sharp shining teeth. The rockets catch the light from these teeth and the teeth glitter: they are silently removed from the poison-spitting gums of the mole. For the mole's gums spit fire and, they say, send something more concrete than fire darting into the night. Even when its teeth are off. But you cannot see all this from here: you can only see the rockets and then for a moment the pale ground beneath. But it is quite dark now.

And now for the fun of the fair! You will hear soon the riding-master crack his whip why, there it is. Listen, a thousand whips are cracking, whipping the horses round the ring. At last! The fun of the circus is begun. For the motor-cycle team race has started off again: and the whips are cracking all: and the wares-man starts again, beating his loud tin tray to attract the customers: and the cows in the cattle-show start coughing, coughing: and the firework display is at its best: and the circus specials come one after another bearing the merry-makers back to town, all to the inevitable crash, the inevitable accident. It can't last long: these accidents are so frequent, they'll all get soon killed off, I hope. Yes, it is diminishing. The train service is cancelled (and time too): the cows have stopped coughing: and the cycle race is done. Only the kids who have bought new whips at the fair continue to crack them: and unused rockets that lie about the ground are still sent up occasionally. But now the children are being driven off to bed: only an occasional whip-crack now (perhaps the child is now the sufferer): and the tired showmen going over the ground pick up the rocket-sticks and dead flares. At least I suppose this is what must be happening: for occasionally they still find one that has not yet gone off and send it up out of mere perversity. Else what silence!

———

To Arthur Watts, 26 August 1915 [France]

Your letter arrived and awoke the now drifting ME to consciousness. I had understood and acquiesced in your silence. The re-creation of that self which one is to a friend is an effort: repaying if it succeeds, but not to be forced. Wherefore, were it not for the dangers dancing attendance on the adjourning type of mind which a year's military training has not been able to efface from me I should not be writing to you now. For it is just after breakfast and you know what breakfast is: putter to sleep of all mental energy and discontent: charmer, sedative, leveller: maker of Britons. I should wait till after tea when the undiscriminating sun has shown his back a fine back on the world, and one's self by the aid of tea has thrown off the mental sleep of heat. But after tea I am on duty. So with bacon in my throat and my brain like a poached egg I will try to do you justice.

On the whole except for the subtle distinction that I am at the front, you not (merely a nominal distinction for the present) I am disposed to envy you. I am moving smally [sic] to and fro over an unblessed stretch of plain a fly on a bald man's head. You are at least among rich surroundings, like the head of hair of your half-Slav. I wonder how long it takes the King's Pawn, who so proudly initiates the game of chess, to realise that he is a pawn. Same with us. We are finding out that we play the unimportant if necessary part At present a dam, untested, whose presence not whose action stops the stream from approaching: and then a mere handle to steel: dealers of death which we are not allowed to plan. But I have complained enough before of the minion state of the 'damned foot.' It is something to have no responsibility, an inglorious ease of mind.

So half-lit nights with the foam and flotsam of the world here we have only the little ordered breakers that lap pleasantly merry on the English shores has its charm to the imagination. Possibly its romance fades by experience and leaves a taste of

damp blotting-paper in the mouth as of one who has slept with
his mouth open. But yet these men and women whom you meet
must by their very needs and isolations be more distinct and
living than the very pleasant officers with whom I live. Very
pleasant they are: humorous, vivacious and good comrades: but
some have never entered, most perhaps have entered and now
keep locked and barred:

The heart's heart whose immured plot
hath keys yourself keep not!
[from 'A Fallen Yew' by Francis Thompson]

They have stifled their loneliness of spirit till they scarcely
know it, seeking new easy unexacting companionships. They are
surface wells. Not two hundred feet deep, so that you can see
the stars at the bottom.

Health and I don't know what ill-health is invites you so
much to smooth and shallow ways: where a happiness may only
be found by renouncing the other happiness of which one set out
in search. Yet here there is enough to stay the bubbling surface
stream. Looking into the future one sees a holocaust somewhere:
and at present there is thank God enough of 'experience' to keep
the wits edged (a callous way of putting it, perhaps). But out in
front at night in that no-man's land and long graveyard there is
a freedom and a spur. Rustling of the grasses and grave tap-
tapping of distant workers: the tension and silence of encounter,
when one struggles in the dark for moral victory over the enemy
patrol: the wail of the exploded bomb and the animal cries of
wounded men. Then death and the horrible thankfulness when
one sees that the next man is dead: 'We won't have to carry him
in under fire, thank God; dragging will do': hauling in of the
great resistless body in the dark, the smashed head rattling: the
relief, the relief that the thing has ceased to groan: that the bullet
or bomb that made the man an animal has now made the animal
a corpse. One is hardened by now: purged of all false pity:
perhaps more selfish than before. The spiritual and the animal

get so much more sharply divided in hours of encounter, taking possession of the body by swift turns. And now I have 200 letters to censor before the post goes . . . You'll write again, won't you, as soon as the mood comes – after tea? And good health to you.

———————

To Professor Sorley, 5 October 1915 [France]

Many thanks for the letters which arrived with the rations this morning. We are now embarked on a very different kind of life; whether one considers it preferable or otherwise to the previous, depending on one's mood. It is going to be a very slow business, but I hope a steady one. There is absolutely no doubt that the Bosch is now on his way home, though it is a long way and he will have many halts by the wayside. That 'the war may end any year now' is the latest joke, which sums up the situation . . .

You will have seen that we have suffered by the loss of our chief: also that our battalion has lost its finest officer otherwise commissioned ranks have been extraordinarily lucky. For the present, rain and dirt and damp cold. O for a bath! Much love to all.

This was Sorley's last letter. He was killed a week later by a German sniper while assuming command of his company during an attack on German trenches south of the Hohenzollern Redoubt. Hastily buried the next day, an undated pencil-written sonnet was found in his kitbag and was published later under the title 'When You See Millions of the Mouthless Dead'.

Rebecca West
The Cordite Makers

As this piece was published in wartime, it was subject to censorship and no mention could be made of the fact that Rebecca West was writing about the massive Dornock Munitions Factory that lay between Gretna and Annan in the western Scottish Borders. Rebecca West and Arthur Conan Doyle were the only journalists permitted to visit this top-secret site.

The world was polished to a brightness by an east wind when I visited the cordite factory, and shone with hard colours like a German toy-landscape. The marshes were very green and the scattered waters very blue, and little white clouds roamed one by one across the sky like grazing sheep on a meadow. On the hills around stood elms, and grey churches and red farms and yellow ricks, painted bright by the sharp sunshine. And very distinct on the marshes there lay the village which is always full of people, and yet is the home of nothing except death.

In the glare it showed that like so many institutions of the war it has the disordered and fantastic quality of a dream. It consists of a number of huts, some like the government-built huts for Irish labourers, and some like the open-air shelters in a sanatorium, scattered over five hundred acres; they are connected by raised wooden gangways and interspersed with green mounds and rush ponds. It is of such vital importance to the State that it is ringed with barbed-wire entanglements and patrolled by sentries, and its products must have sent tens of thousands of our enemies to their death. And it is inhabited chiefly by pretty young girls clad in a Red-Riding-Hood fancy dress of khaki and scarlet.

Every morning at six, when the night mist still hangs over the marshes, 250 of these girls are fetched by a light railway from their barracks on a hill two miles away. When I visited the works they had already been at work for nine hours, and would work for three more. This twelve-hour shift is longer than one would wish, but it is not possible to introduce three shifts, since the girls would find an eight-hour day too light and would complain of being debarred from the opportunity of making more money; and it is not so bad as it sounds, for in these airy and isolated huts there is neither the orchestra of rattling machines nor the sense of a confined area crowded with tired people which make the ordinary factory such a fatiguing place. Indeed, these girls, working in teams of six or seven in those clean and tidy rooms, look as if they were practising a neat domestic craft rather than a deadly domestic process.

When one is made to put on rubber over-shoes before entering a hut it might be the precaution of a pernickety housewife concerned about her floors, although actually it is to prevent the grit on one's outdoor shoes igniting a stray scrap of cordite and sending oneself and the hut up to the skies in a column of flame. And there is something distinctly domestic in the character of almost every process. The girls who stand round the great drums in the hut with walls and floor awash look like millers in their caps and dresses of white waterproof, and the bags containing a white substance that lie in the dry ante-room might be sacks of flour. But, in fact, they are filling the drum with gun-cotton to be dried by hot air. And in the next hut, where girls stand round great vats in which steel hands mix the gun-cotton with mineral jelly, might be part of a steam-bakery. The brown cordite paste itself looks as if it might turn into very pleasant honey-cakes; an inviting appearance that has brought gastritis to more than one unwise worker.

But how deceptive this semblance of normal life is; what

extraordinary work this is for women and how extraordinarily they are doing it, is made manifest in a certain row of huts where the cordite is pressed through wire mesh. This, in all the world, must be the place where war and grace are closest linked. Without, a strip of garden runs beside the huts, gay with shrubs and formal with a sundial. Within there is a group of girls that composes into so beautiful a picture that one remembers that the most glorious painting in the world, Velasquez's *The Weavers*, shows women working just like this.

One girl stands high on a platform against the wall, filling the cordite paste into one of the two great iron presses, and when she has finished with that she swings round the other one on a swivel with a fine, free gesture. The other girls stand round the table laying out the golden cords in graduated sizes from the thickness of rope to the thinness of macaroni, the clear khaki and scarlet of their dresses shining back from the wet floor in a perpetually changing pattern as they move quickly about their work. They look very young in their pretty, childish dresses, and one thinks them good children for working so diligently. And it occurs to one as something incredible that they are now doing the last three hours of a twelve-hour shift.

If one asks the manager whether this zeal can possibly be normal, whether it is not perhaps the result of his presence, one is confronted by the awful phenomenon, beside which a waterspout or a volcano in eruption would be a little thing, of a manager talking about his employees with reverence. It seems that the girls work all day with a fury which mounts to a climax in the last three hours before the other 250 girls step into their places for the twelve-hour night shift. In these hours spies are sent out to walk along the verandah to see how the teams in the other huts are getting on, and their reports set the girls on to an orgy of competitive industry. Here again it was said for attention, enthusiasm and discipline, there could not be better workmen than these girls.

There is matter connected to these huts, too, that showed the khaki and scarlet hoods to be no fancy dress but a military uniform. They are a sign, for they have been dipped in a solution that makes them fireproof, that the girls are ready to face an emergency, which had arisen in those huts only a few days ago. There had been one of those incalculable happenings of which high explosives are so liable, an inflammatory mixture of air with acetone, and the cordite was ignited. Two huts were instantly gutted, and the girls had to walk out through the flame. In spite of the uniform one girl lost a hand. These, of course, are the everyday dangers of the high-explosives factory. There is very little to be feared by our enemies by land, and it is the sentries' grief and despair that their total bag for the eighteen months of their patrol of the marshes consists of one cow.

Surely, never before in modern history can women have lived a life so completely parallel to that of the regular Army. The girls who take up this work sacrifice almost as much as men who enlist; for although they make on average 30s a week they are working much harder than most of them, particularly the large number who were formerly domestic servants, would ever have dreamed of working in peacetime. And, although their colony of wooden huts has been well planned by their employers, and is pleasantly administered by the Young Woman's Christian Association, it is, so far as severance of home-ties goes, barrack life. For although they are allowed to go home for Sunday, travelling is difficult from this remote village, and the girls are so tired that most of them spend the day in bed.

And there are two things about the cordite village which the State ought never to forget, and which ought to be impressed upon the public mind by the bestowal of military rank upon the girls. First of all there is the cold fact that they face more danger every day than any soldier on home defence has seen since the beginning of the war. And secondly, there is the fact – and one wishes it could be expressed in terms of the saving of English and the losing of German life – that it is because of this army of cheerful and disciplined workers that this cordite factory has been able to increase its output since the beginning of the war by something over 1500 per cent. It was all very well for the Army to demand high explosives, and for Mr Lloyd George to transmit the demand to industry; in the last resort the matter lay in the hands of the girls in the khaki and scarlet hoods, and the State owes them a very great debt for the way in which they have handled it.

A.F. Whyte
Sunk

The attempt to force a passage through the Dardanelles, begun on 19 February 1915, was an expensive failure, with the loss of the battleships HMS Irresistible and HMS Ocean to mines. Later the battleships HMS Triumph and HMS Majestic were lost to submarines. By late March it was clear that the Turkish defences could not be breached by ships alone and the following month troops were landed on the Gallipoli peninsula. The naval officer amongst the survivors from the sinking is clearly suffering from some form of post-traumatic stress disorder.

She was an old battleship whose day of power was long past. At the great naval review held to celebrate the sixtieth year of Queen Victoria's reign, you might have seen her in one of the proudest stations of the Fleet; but when the Great War broke out hers was the least of the Battle Squadrons, and she herself a neglected unit at the very tail of British Sea Power, almost ready for the ship-breaker's yard. War brought her to life again and to a glorious end. Being one of the ships concerned in the much-discussed Test Mobilisation of the Third Fleet which took the place of Naval Manoeuvres in 1914, she was unusually ready when war broke out; full complement on board, guns' crews less rusty than usual, and showing a remarkable turn of speed for a lady of her years, though slow as a dray compared with her younger sisters. In company with others of her age and kind she made part of that strange squadron, a motley of ancient and modern, headed by the greatest ship in the world, which won renown at the Dardanelles. Written off by the callous Lords Commissioners of the Admiralty as 'of no military significance', she yet told her tale of shelling sound and fury to the Turkish enemy in such a fashion as to make it signify some considerable damage to him, and to show that even the tail of our Sea Power had a good deal of nasty sting left in it.

One morning in May 1915 she entered the Straits [Dardanelles], the last of five battleships in line ahead told off to support an advance of the troops on shore. With their guns trained on the European side they turned their backs, as it were, upon the Turkish batteries on the Asiatic shore, and when the latter began to bother them our ship was ordered to take station somewhere off Kum Kale and enfilade the Turkish position with her twelve-inch guns. Steadily all day the booming of the guns sounded across the water and went echoing up the Hellespont: and, as if to prove that this was something more than Battle Practice at last, a spout of water would rise now and then not a cable's-length ahead and others of the same round about. Barely, and even then without great effect, did enemy shells fall aboard; but they came near enough to keep the ship's company awake and lively all day. In the soft evening light the guns of this enfilading ship looked like long grey pencils, but where the lead should have been there came ever and anon a red tongue that flashed and vanished: and after the red tongue a great cloud: and after the cloud a voice of thunder: and far up the Asiatic shore the shell found its mark. Then sunset came and put an end to the noisy day's work; and the ship took her night station under the lee of the European shore, put out her torpedo-netting anew like a great steel skirt, and lay awaiting the return of day. Darkness gathered about her with that sudden descent which surprises men from the north used to the long twilight of summer, and long before midnight land and sea were lost to view under the heavy cloak of a black starless sky.

The officer of the watch, a Royal Naval Reserve lieutenant from the Orkneys, peered into the night and listened to the low

gurgle and murmur of the tide running strongly through the
torpedo-netting and making the ship swing slowly to her anchor.
And as he listened an old Orcadian rhyme came into his head:

> Eynhallow frank, Eynhallow free,
> Eynhallow stands in the middle of the sea;
> With a roarin' roost on every side,
> Eynhallow stands in the middle of the tide.

So he stood: in the middle of another tide with a roarin' roost on
every side, and a ship under his feet which seemed as firm as the
Eynhallow rock itself. Little did he think that before dawn she
would prove but a frail refuge. As little did he realise that the
campaign on which he was engaged was but the latest link in a
long chain of stirring events that had made the Hellespont famous
from the most distant times. Had he been of a reflective turn of
mind he might have conjured up before him the whole matchless
pageant of history that lies folded in those narrow waters: the
Trojan scene: the oft-repeated passage of that great sea river by
conquerors from East and West: the glory of Byzantium and its
decay: the prowess and cruelty of the Ottoman Turks: and all the
lore of those waters of ancient memory. But he was a simple
seaman from the merchant service, drawn into the service of the
King at war, and no such high historic thoughts came to distract
him from the duties of his watch.

Presently he was joined by another officer who came up from
below for a breath of night air. They talked together for a while,
recalling the incidents of the day's work, speculating upon the old
theme of Ships v. Forts, pitying the 'poor devils ashore' who were
never out of fire, and wondering when Aohi Baba would fall.
They talked 'shop' because there was nothing else to talk about;
and though the subjects never varied, they never seemed to lose
their zest. In every ward-room of the motley fleet assembled
round the snout of the Gallipoli Peninsula, the same kind of talk

might be heard, varied a little in each ship, and always flavoured with the expressive service slang so beloved and so little understood by the Gentlemen of the Press who accompanied them. The officer of the watch and his companion continued their conversation in low tones for a while, and then stood for a moment silent. With a 'Good night: I'm going to turn in,' the latter had set his foot on the topmost rail of the steel ladder and was about to descend when a sudden exclamation arrested him. He turned.

'What's that?' said the officer of the watch in a sharp whisper. 'Where?'

'Over there,' he pointed to the shore on the port side.

'I can't see a thing.'

They strained their eyes, peering out into the night. They listened intently, but heard nothing except the murmuring tide now sounding its eerie accompaniment to the inaudible movement out of sight. They strained their ears; but neither sight nor hearing but some other uncanny sense was awake in them hinting of something about to happen.

The officer of the watch spoke again.

'I can't see a thing, and I can't hear anything; but I swear there's something moving out there.' He pointed again to the European shore.

'Troops, perhaps?'

'Can't be; we'd have been warned.'

They waited again in silence. How long they stood tense, neither could afterwards say: each second was a long agony of suspense. The eddying tide whispered and bubbled beneath them. A faint stirring of the night air caressed their faces. But to their anxious questions no answer came. In the deep shadow under the land there was a secret, holding life or death perhaps, a moving threat hidden in the night. But what it was? or whence? or why? they could not tell.

Suddenly the officer of the watch clutched his companion's arm.

'A destroyer. Look!'

Just where a gully dipped to the sea there was a patch where land and water met that was faintly luminous. It was not light: merely less black than the rest: but the contrast was enough to give the eye an impression of light. With bursting pulses the watchkeeper saw a long, low, black shape pass stealthily across the patch.

'Shall I challenge? It may be one of our "Beagles" coming back from the Narrows. They went up towards Chanak, two of them, after dinner. I saw them.'

'No; it can't be. They'd never come like that. You've had no signal from the Flagship?'

'No.'

'Then it's *der Tag* for us, old man! Keep your eye on him, and I'll tell the skipper. You'd better pass the word for "Action Stations" to the port battery. We must be quick about it, and quiet; otherwise our number's up.'

He went to rouse the captain. The officer of the watch made his preparations, watched his orders being swiftly and almost noiselessly carried out, and turned again to peer through the darkness. Two minutes passed. He inflated his 'Gieve' [lifebelt], and as he tucked away the tube, a faint splash was heard in the darkness away on the port-beam.

'God! A torpedo,' he exclaimed

He waited for the torpedo to strike – another long suspense: but within thirty seconds the splash was answered by a roar from the 4-in. port battery of his own ship. Tongues of flame leapt from the muzzles, lighting up the night, and the shells whistled to their all but invisible mark. But before they could fire another round, the torpedo struck. The ship quivered, a tremor running through every plate and rivet: her stern shivered like the hindquarters of a dog coming out of water. Then she was heaved upwards by some monstrous power beneath. A great spout of water rose, and a great flame leapt out of the ship's belly with a

deafening roar, sending its licking tongues high in the midnight
sky. And all this was simultaneous: the quiver, the heave, the
spout, and the flame were all blended in one vast, hot, terrifying
chaos. A second explosion followed, rending the ship to her very
vitals. Guns, boats, men, all were flung into the air like leaves in
a whirlwind: one of the steamboats was seen spinning like a
blazing top a hundred feet up in the air. The great ship herself
reeled over to port, hung awhile with her decks steep aslant, and
then plunged with a terrible hiss and roar to the bottom. The
spot where she had been was thick with men and debris, the
awful flotsam of a torpedoed battleship now lit up by a searchlight's occasional gleam. The risk to other ships was too great at
first to permit anything more than a momentary and fitful use
of their welcome beams by the destroyers and auxiliary craft
hastening to the rescue. Death might still lurk in the dark corners
of the land on either side. And so, until the screening patrols had
swept the strait, a wholesome caution shrouded the life-saving
operations in gloom. Even without the pall of darkness the night
was eerie enough. The cries of the injured men suffering agonies
in the ice-cold water rang hideously through the still air; and
though the work of rescue was well and quickly done as the
picket-boats and trawlers nosed their way about, death was too
often too quick for them; and of those that lived, even with all
the despatch and skill of the rescuers, many a survivor suffered
the tortures of the damned in a desperate struggle with the
freezing cold and the still more freezing fear that in the confusion
and darkness he would not be picked up.

Two hours later the last searchlight had swept the eddying
surface, the last picket-boat had returned. The sudden danger
had passed, leaving a wreck in its track: and the

> Waters of Asia, westward-beating waves
> Of estuaries, and mountain-warded straits,
> Whose solitary beaches long had lost

The ashen glimmer of the dying day,
Listened in darkness to their own lone sound
Moving about the shores of sleep . . .

The following evening four officers sat at a bridge table in the deck smoking-room of an auxiliary lying in Mudros harbour. A burly merchant captain, wearing the woven stripes of a lieutenant-commander in the RNR [Royal Naval Reserve], the 'tea-cosy' decoration, as a facetious merchant skipper once called it; his chief engineer, a good Scot, in great demand all over the harbour for his inexhaustible stock of yarns; a lieutenant-commander, RN, rescued ten days before from a torpedoed battleship, and now awaiting 'disposal'; and a King's messenger in the uniform of the Volunteer Reserve, as well-mixed a foursome as ever played a hand. The call of war had brought them together from their vocations of peace and had dumped them temporarily in the good ship *Fauvette*, which was wont in happier times to ply a busy trade between London and Bordeaux. They had hardly dealt the cards for a second game when a movement on deck disturbed them, and before they could rise to ascertain the cause a troupe of strangely clad youngsters appeared at the door.

'May we come in, sir?' said one of them, who was, in sober truth, a 'thing of shreds and patches'.

'Make yourselves at home, boys,' said the skipper, waving a chubby hand round the room.

A signalman entered with his pad, and handed it to the skipper.

'Gad! Of course,' he cried, 'you're the stowaways we've been expecting all day. Well, what's it like being torpedoed?'

There was silence. None of these midshipmen was adept at public speech in the presence of unknown superiors. So for the moment the skipper's question remained unanswered. As they settled in a group in the corner of the smoking-room they

presented a fine study in motley. Every stitch on their backs had
been borrowed from willing lenders. One waddled in the blue
overalls of a benevolent but too burly friend; another looked like
an example of record promotion, for there were three gold
stripes half-concealed under the folded cuff of a sleeve that was
a hand's length too long for the wearer; a third wore the tweeds
of a war correspondent, who had doubtless exacted 'copy' as
interest on the loan of his clothes; and the rest of them, in various
ways, completed the picture of incongruity. But for all that they
had passed through one of the greatest ordeals of war, they
showed but little sign of strain or fatigue, and only asked
whether they might have something to smoke and whether they
could write home. Their needs were supplied; and the skipper
repeated his question:

'Come on and tell us what it's like being torpedoed.'

'It's always the same,' broke in the lieutenant-commander at
the card-table. 'A frightful din: and a bit of a shake an' a heave,
and then you're in the water. Your "Gieve" does the rest. That's
all there is to it.'

'I wish to God it was,' said a new hollow voice at the door.
'I was on watch when the damned thing struck us, and I was in
the water among the bodies for a hell of a time; and if that's all
you knew when your packet sank, you're lucky. Damned lucky!'
he repeated slowly in a dull voice.

The figure in the doorway was at once familiar and strange,
like that of a strong man grown suddenly wizened. He was
visibly shrunken: and as he walked unsteadily across the room
and sat down on a swivel-seat, he talked continuously but almost
incoherently, half to himself and half to the watching group. The
contrast between him and the unscathed midshipmen was very
strong and unexpected. He and they had come from the same
ship, passed through the same night of alarm, and been hauled
out of the same cold waters by the same rescuing hands. The
experience had set no mark upon the boys: yet in the grown man

it had wrought such a sea-change as made one almost fear to look at him. His tanned cheeks were still brown, but it was a bloodless tint; and the lines that seamed his face gave him a sepulchral look. His eyes alone were bright, too bright. The softer quality that makes the human eye so expressive was gone, and there remained a vivid stare as of eyes straining to see the invisible. There he was, in our company, but certainly not of it: for his brain was working and wandering whither we could not follow, and the words that came from his lips were the half-automatic expression of an absent mind.

'Gimme a cig'ret,' he said with the husky slurred articulation of a drunk man: and he sat puffing and biting the end of it into pulp. Then he would grip the short arms of his seat, start up and look downwards between his knees, and then sit down again with a look of shamed annoyance. He was clearly struggling to get away from something, and we were powerless to help.

We tried to distract him. The steward brought a tray loaded with sandwiches and drinks, which he refused. We were getting a little uneasy about our strange guest; the doctor whom the skipper had sent for was long in coming, and each renewal of our efforts to divert the patient failed. We gave him the 'Bystander' and 'Punch', but he was beyond the reach of Bairns-father and George Morrow: we tried to draw him into a game at the table-poker, bridge, patience, anything – but he remained immovable.

At last the doctor, a thicket-bearded Fleet Surgeon, came and took charge, and reversed our procedure. Where we had been gentle, almost timid, he was rough. Where we had coaxed, he ordered. Where we had fumbled and faltered with the unknown, he acted with the confidence of experience. After a rapid examination and cross-examination, in the course of which he drew more from his victim in five minutes than we had extracted in an hour and more, he hustled him below and packed him into a bunk with various aids to sleep which he did not specify. Then the Fleet Surgeon returned to the smoking-room.

'You're a bright lot,' he said; 'why didn't you put him to bed at once? He's absolutely done: but if he can sleep, he'll be all right soon. Never seen a man quite so worn out.'

'Do you mean to say that he's only tired? He looked like going off his chump.'

'So would you if your nerves had been living on shocks without any solid support. What he went through has got such a hold on him that until he's had a good twenty-four hours' sleep as a preliminary and a course of feeding up and regular sleep without any work to do after that, he won't quite know where he is. But I bet he's sitting up and taking nourishment this time tomorrow. He was on the verge of being a bad case, but we've caught him just in time.'

The doctor was right. Our patient slept till midday next day, took a light meal and slept again till sunset. Then he awoke and dined; but in an hour he was asleep again. Clearly he had been put to bed at the psychological moment. By the following afternoon he was taking the air in a deckchair, and ready, perhaps a little too ready, for his health to talk about the sinking of his ship.

When the explosion occurred he was thrown clear of the ship on the starboard side. He was half-stunned, but his swimming waistcoat kept him afloat. The rest must be told in his own words.

'I don't know how long it was before I realised where I was: but it was long enough to let me get pretty cold. You know what the water's like. I picked up two men close by me, still swimming, but pretty nearly done. Neither of them had belts on. One, I knew by his voice, was a wardroom steward. They hung on to me for a while, the "Gieve" keeping us all afloat so long as we made a bit of an effort ourselves. We could hear the picket-boats going about, and sometimes a searchlight picked us up; but nothing came near enough to rescue us. And before long one of the fellows hanging on to me began to groan and his teeth chattered. I told him to keep moving: but it was no good. He slipped off, and I never saw him again. That was bad enough: but when the other fellow's teeth began the same game, I got the creeps; but I couldn't save him, and after a few moments he went too. It was a ghastly feeling. The sudden silence, and the cold creeping right into me made me want to give up too: when suddenly I thought I had touched bottom. I tried to walk, but the thing I touched slipped away: and I realised with a shudder what it was. And after that I swear I must have touched a dozen of them before I was picked up. That's what knocked me out. But, I say, let's chuck it. I must get away from it.'

He passed his hand over his face. The old troubled look came back: and for the moment I could see that, like Orestes pursued by the Furies, his spirit was haunted by the ghosts of the men whose bodies his feet had touched in the dark waters of the Hellespont. He had indeed suffered a sea-change: and the war was over for him.

Biographical Notes

J.J. Bell 1871–1934

The novelist and journalist John Joy Bell was born in Glasgow and was educated at Kelvinside Academy and in Perthshire at Morrison's Academy. He studied chemistry at Glasgow University but left without taking a degree. While a student, he started writing poetry and his first collection, *The New Noah's Ark*, was published in 1899. Most of his writing was in journalism and it was from a series of sketches published in the Glasgow *Evening Times* in 1901 and 1902 that he came to publish at his own expense *Wee MacGreegor*, a sentimental novel about a little boy and his adventures in Glasgow, which was an instant success, selling over a quarter of a million copies. Bell followed the formula in his sequels, *Wee MacGreegor Again* (1904) and *Wee MacGreegor Enlists* (1915). Although less assured than the original novel, the story of Wee MacGreegor's service in a Scottish infantry regiment captures the early enthusiasm for the war.

Text: J.J. Bell, *Wee MacGreegor Enlist*s (London: Hodder & Stoughton, 1915)

James Bridie 1888–1951

James Bridie was the pen name of playwright and author Osborne Henry Mavor, who was born in Glasgow, the son of an engineer. Trained as a doctor at Glasgow University, where he was a member of the Officer Training Corps (OTC), Mavor joined the Royal Army Medical Corps (RAMC) at the outbreak of war and served with the 42nd Field Ambulance in France in 1915 and 1916, mainly on the Ypres sector. In 1917, he served in Mesopotamia, Persia and Trans-Caucasia, where the front had come into being to stymie the construction of a rail-way from Berlin to Baghdad. In the latter stages, Mavor served in a force led by Major-General L.C. Dunsterville, who led a mission to Tiflis to forestall a Turkish advance to the Baku oilfields. After the war Mavor emerged as a highly successful dramatist and a leading enabler in Scottish cultural life.

Text: James Bridie, One Way of Living (London: Constable, 1939)

John Buchan 1875–1940

Born in Perth the son of a minister of the Free Church of Scotland, John Buchan was educated in Glasgow at Hutcheson's Grammar School and at Glasgow University and Brasenose College, Oxford. After a short career as a barrister and journalist, he served with Lord Milner in South Africa and on returning to London pursued a career as publisher and author. At the outbreak of war he was a director of Thomas Nelson and Sons. Unfit for service in the armed forces, Buchan served his country in other important capacities. In 1915 he visited the Western Front as a special correspondent for The Times; he was attached to General Sir Douglas Haig's Headquarters as an observer; and in 1917 was appointed Director of Information under Lord Beaverbrook. During this period, he also found time to write a number of novels, which are set against the background of the war, including The Thirty-Nine Steps, Mr Standfast and Greenmantle. Buchan also wrote, almost single-handedly, the twenty-four volumes of Nelson's *History of the First World War.*

Texts: John Buchan, *The Watcher by the Threshold*, London, Hodder & Stoughton, 1918; *Mr Standfast*, London, Hodder & Stoughton, 1919; *History of the First World War*, vol. VIII (Edinburgh and London: Thomas Nelson, 1915–19)

Donald Walter Cameron of Lochiel 1876–1951

As a soldier and 25th head of Clan Cameron, at the beginning of the war Lochiel threw his weight behind the call for volunteers to serve in the Special Service Battalions of the Queen's Own Cameron High-landers. He believed that men who joined up together should serve together in the same battalion and offered his personal guarantee that 'at the end of the war the battalion would be brought back to Inverness where it will be disbanded with all possible dispatch'. He returned at once to Scotland, and at meetings in Glasgow and Inverness stirring appeals for recruits for the new Battalions were made. These met with so enthusiastic a response that within a fortnight the 5th and 6th Battalions were raised, and recruiting for the 7th Battalion was in full swing. Lochiel himself commanded the 5th Battalion and led them into their first action on 25 September, the first day of the Battle of Loos. During the attack on the German lines, his brother Allan was killed.

Text: *The Cameron Highlanders at the Battles at Loos, Hill 70, Fosse 8 and the Quarries* (Inverness: Inverness Courier, 1924)

R.W. Campbell *b.* 1876

A novelist and soldier, Robert Walter Campbell served with 2nd Royal Scots Fusiliers during the Boer War (1899–1902) and then retired to the Special Reserve. At the outbreak of war in 1914, he rejoined his regiment and served with the 5th Battalion, Territorial Force, which was recruited from Ayrshire. With them, he served in Gallipoli, an experience which gave him the background for his first war novel, *The Kangaroo Marines* (1915), but at the end of the campaign he returned to the reserve and served for the rest of the war in an administrative capacity. Campbell's next novel, *Private Spud Tamson*, was published in 1916 and quickly went through several editions. Its successor *Spud Sergeant Tamson VC* repeated the formula, although less successfully, and his hero reappeared in 1926 to save a mining village in *Spud Tamson's Pit*. After the war Campbell lived in Lochmaben and then in Edinburgh, but little is known about his subsequent life and career. During the war Campbell had also been well known for his jaunty war poems, which were published in *The Making of Micky McGhee* (1916). Campbell described the men of Spud Tamson's 'Glesca Mileeshy' as 'a noble force, recruited from the Weary Willies and Never-works of the famous town of Glasgow'.

Text: *Private Spud Tamson* (Edinburgh and London: William Black-wood, 1916)

J. Storer Clouston 1870–1944

Novelist Joseph Storer Clouston was born in Carlisle and educated at Merchiston Castle School in Edinburgh and Magdalen College Oxford, but through his father's family he enjoyed a strong affinity with Orkney, where he settled in 1903 following his marriage to Winifred Bertha Clouston, a distant cousin. Although he had been called to the English Bar, he never practised as a barrister and devoted himself to writing a range of light novels and short stories, becoming a prolific and highly successful writer. During the First World War, he served as Sub-Commissioner for Orkney and Shetland in the National Service Department. He also wrote *The Spy in Black*, a spy thriller set on Orkney that was later made into an equally successful film of the same title, directed by Michael Powell, from a screenplay by Emeric Pressburger and starring Conrad Veidt. It was premiered in the UK in August 1939, on the eve of the Second World War.

Text: J. Storer Clouston, *The Spy in Black* (Edinburgh and London: William Blackwood, 1917)

Vera Christine Chute Collum 1883–1957

Archaeologist, anthropologist and feminist, V.C.C. Collum (as she always styled herself) was best known for her 1931 excavation of the megalithic tomb at Tresse in Brittany, which she claimed was constructed during the Roman period and was associated with the cult of the mother goddess. At the beginning of the war, she was working in the London office of the National Union of Women's Suffrage Societies but soon joined Dr Elsie Inglis's Scottish Women's Hospital and served with them in France at Royaumont, where she later became a radiographer. Early in 1916 she was badly injured when the ship bringing her back from leave was torpedoed in the English Channel. After the war she wrote a number of challenging accounts, attempting to harmonise the world's philosophies, the best known being *The Music of Growth* (1933). Her work for *Blackwood's Magazine* was published under the pseudonym 'Ski'.

Text: Ski (V.C.C. Collum), 'Torpedoed!', *Blackwood's Magazine*, May 1916, pp. 690–8

William Fraser 1890–1964

Soldier and diarist The Hon. William Fraser was a younger son of the 18th Lord Saltoun of Philorth in Aberdeenshire. After school he attended Sandhurst and was commissioned into 2nd Gordon Highlanders while they were serving in India. In 1912, the battalion moved to Cairo, returning to England when war was declared, before crossing over to France at the end of September. During the First Battle of Ypres, Fraser was badly wounded and his brother Simon in the same battalion was killed. He returned to the front in March 1915 and was posted to 1st Gordons. In April 1917, he was given command of 6th Gordons, a Territorial battalion in the 51st (Highland) Division, which was commanded by Major-General G.H. Harper, popularly known as 'Uncle'. Towards the end of the war Fraser took over command of 1st Gordons. Throughout the war he kept a diary that was initially written in pencil in a notebook – 'Army Book 136'. Following the Armistice, he remained in the Army and in 1927 transferred to the Grenadier Guards.

Text: David Fraser, ed., *In Good Company: The First World War Letters and Diaries of the Hon. William Fraser, Gordon Highlanders* (Salisbury: Michael Russell, 1990)

Lewis Grassic Gibbon 1901–35

Lewis Grassic Gibbon was the pen name that James Leslie Mitchell used for his fiction trilogy *A Scots Quair*. He was born at Auchterless in Aberdeenshire, where his father was a farmer, but when he was eight the family moved to the Howe of the Mearns and Mitchell was educated at Arbuthnott Village School and Mackie Academy, Stonehaven. Having left school early, he worked as a journalist in Aberdeen and Glasgow before joining the Army in August 1919 and serving in the Middle East. He was discharged in 1923, but, unable to find work, he enlisted in the Royal Air Force and served with them until 1929. The background to his novel *Sunset Song*, the first part of the *Scots Quair* trilogy, is the First World War and the break-up of the already declining small farming communities in the Howe of the Mearns. The unifying figure in each novel is Chris Guthrie, a farmer's daughter who marries Ewan Tavendale.

Text: Lewis Grassic Gibbon, *Sunset Song* (London: Jarrolds, 1932)

Douglas Haig 1861–1928

British Field Marshal and the Commander-in-Chief of the British Expeditionary Force on the Western Front from late 1915 to the end of the war, Haig was born in Edinburgh and, after education at Sandhurst, was commissioned in 7th (Queen's Own) Hussars. Although a traditionalist who believed in the primacy of the cavalry, he was also a reformer who rose steadily in prominence fighting in Victorian colonial wars. At the outbreak of war, he was commander of I Corps and succeeded General Sir John French as commander-in-chief in December 1915. Serenely self-assured, he was also intensely religious and was bolstered by his Protestant faith to believe that he was 'a tool in the hands of the Divine Power'. His diaries give a telling insight into his management of the war and the problems facing the high command. Historians still argue over his direction of the war and while he has been censured for the costly offensives on the Somme in 1916 and at Third Ypres the following year, the consensus view is that he was the architect of eventual victory in 1918, even though there were deep flaws in his design.

Text: National Library of Scotland. NLS, Acc3155, 96–140. Papers of Field Marshall Sir Douglas Haig OM, KT, GCB, GCVO, 1st Earl Haig.

Cicely Hamilton 1872–1952

Playwright, actress and suffragette, Cicely Hamilton worked as clerk to the Scottish Women's Hospital at Royaumont in France. Although she was not born in Scotland, she was proud of her ancestry and of the fact that her father, Denzil Hammill, had served in the Gordon Highlanders. Aged 42 at the outbreak of war, she did not hesitate to volunteer to work in the voluntary hospital that had been founded by the remarkable Dr Elsie Inglis. Described by a colleague as 'a thorough Bohemian', Hamilton felt deeply about the tragedy of ordinary people caught up in the war and admitted that she never hardened herself to their suffering. A committed feminist, she later became secretary of the International Suffrage Conference in Geneva and advocated free birth control and the legalisation of abortion.

Text: Cicely Hamilton, *Life Errant* (London: J.M. Dent, 1935)

Sir Ian Hamilton 1853–1947

Soldier and poet, Ian Standish Monteith Hamilton was born in Corfu and spent his childhood with his paternal grandparents in Argyll. He was educated at Wellington and Sandhurst, and in 1872 was commissioned into the 12th (East Suffolk) Foot before transferring to the 92nd (Gordon) Highlanders. He served in Afghanistan and fought in the Boer War of 1899–1902 as Chief of Staff to Lord Kitchener, and in 1904 was head of the British Military Mission during the Russo-Japanese War. The publication of *A Staff Officer's Scrap Book* (1912) confirmed his reputation as an astute military theorist and in the rank of full general he was given command of the Central Force, which was responsible for the defence of the United Kingdom. His supreme moment came in March 1915 when he was appointed commander of the Allied ground forces in Gallipoli, the operation to capture Constantinople and to knock the Ottoman Empire out of the war. Lack of a workable plan, inadequate forces and untried field commanders led to a costly Allied failure and in October Hamilton was replaced in some disgrace. Although charming and highly personable, Hamilton lacked the dominating personality and iron will demanded of the successful commander-in-chief. In his 'Contemporary Scottish Studies' column in the *Scottish Educational Journal* of 25 August 1925 the poet Hugh MacDiarmid wrote: 'The war may have been for the British War Office a war to save civilisation – Sir Ian was one of the very few of our military leaders who had that civilisation in a degree worth saving.'

Text: General Sir Ian Hamilton, *Gallipoli Diaries*, vol. I (London: Edward Arnold, 1920)

Ian Hay 1876–1952

Novelist and dramatist Ian Hay was the pen name of John Hay Beith, a schoolmaster at Fettes College in Edinburgh. Following the success of his first light romantic novels, he became a full-time author and a regular contributor to *Blackwood's Magazine*. An officer in the Territorial Force, he enlisted for regular service on the outbreak of war and served with 10th Argyll and Sutherland Highlanders. In January 1915, Neil Munro reported to George Blackwood a sighting of Ian Hay with his battalion on Loch Lomondside 'trudging in front of his platoon, his shoulders covered by an old waterproof sheet which spouted rain down his kilt and legs. He was carrying the rifle of a dejected Tommy who limped behind him in the first section of fours.' By then Hay had started contributing to *Blackwood's Magazine* the scenes of life in the volunteer army that were published later that year as *The First Hundred Thousand*. For this and its successor, *Carrying On* (1917), he adopted the pseudonym 'The Junior Sub' in order to preserve his identity as a serving officer. Brilliantly conceived, and narrated in the first person and present tense, Hay's creation was akin to a homely correspondence and the sketches became an immediate bestseller. The two novels also provided a keen insight into the military mind, so much so that many brigade and divisional commanders recommended them as reading matter for their newly joined officers.

Text: Ian Hay, *The First Hundred Thousand* (Edinburgh & London: William Blackwood, 1915)

James Jack 1880–1962

Brigadier-General James Lochhead Jack was born in 1880 the son of a Paisley carpet manufacturer and he was educated in Edinburgh at Merchiston Castle School. He began his military career fighting in the Boer War (1899–1902), in which he served with the Argyll and Sutherland Highlanders, first as a private soldier and then as a commissioned officer. Following the war in South Africa, he remained in the army and became an excellent polo player. When war broke out, he was Adjutant of 1st Cameronians (Scottish Rifles) and he took part in the early battles at Mons and Le Cateau, where he was awarded the Croix de Chevalier of the French Legion of Honour. In August 1916, he was promoted to command 2nd West Yorkshire Regiment, but returned to command 1st Cameronians in the summer of 1918. Almost every day of the war he made a jotting in a tiny notebook and wrote this up later in a regular and hugely illuminating diary that was published after his death.

Text: John Terraine, ed., *General Jack's Diary 1914–18: The Trench Diary of Brigadier-General J.L. Jack* (London: Eyre & Spottiswoode, 1964)

John Jackson *fl.* 1910–30

When the war broke out, John Jackson was working with the Cale-donian Railway Company in Glasgow and joined up almost immediately in the Queen's Own Cameron Highlanders. Sent north for attestation, he volunteered for service in the 5th Battalion based in Aldershot. Following a 21-hour journey south, he arrived to find that the battalion was up to strength and that he and the other recruits would form the 6th Battalion at nearby Rushmoor Camp. Wounded in 1916, he returned to the Western Front and ended his war with 1st Queen's Own Cameron Highlanders and was awarded the Military Medal for his bravery during the Third Battle of Ypres in 1917. Throughout the conflict, Jackson kept a diary and wrote this up in 1926. It was finally published in 2004, with a foreword by Professor Sir Hew Strachan. After the war, he returned to his employment with the Caledonian Railway.

Text: John Jackson, *Private 12768: Memoir of a Tommy* (Stroud, Tempus, 2004)

Sir Harry Lauder 1870–1950

Music-hall artiste, singer and philanthropist, Harry MacLennan Lauder was born in Portobello, Edinburgh, and his childhood years were spent in Arbroath and Hamilton. He started his stage career singing at miners' concerts and turned professional in 1894. The success of songs such as 'I Love a Lassie' and 'Roamin' in the Gloamin'' helped to make him one of the most successful music-hall performers of his day and a very wealthy man. At the outbreak of war, Lauder had just finished a world tour, but he threw himself into a fresh round of concerts to boost recruiting and, in the USA, to promote the British war effort. For his war work, Lauder was knighted in 1919. His only son, John, was killed in 1916, while serving on the Western Front.

Text: Harry Lauder, *A Minstrel in France* (London: Andrew Melrose, 1918)

Eric Linklater 1899–1974

Novelist and historian Eric Linklater was born in Penarth, South Wales, the son of a shipmaster, but his family had their roots in Orkney, where he spent much of his childhood and much of his later life. He was educated at Aberdeen Grammar School and Aberdeen University, where he set out to read medicine before war interrupted his studies. In 1917, he enlisted in the Fife and Forfar Yeomanry, but transferred to 4th/5th Black Watch in order to serve in France. Having been badly wounded in 1918, Linklater returned to Aberdeen to study English and after graduating took up journalism as a career before enjoying immense success as a writer. He made some use of his military memories in his novel *Magnus Merriman* (1934) whose eponymous hero has adventures that clearly resemble those experienced by his creator.

Text: Eric Linklater, *The Man on My Back* (London: Macmillan, 1941)

Hugh MacDiarmid 1892–1978

The greatest Scottish poet of the twentieth century and the founder of the Scottish literary renaissance of the 1920s, Hugh MacDiarmid was the pen name of Christopher Murray Grieve, who was born in the Borders town of Langholm. In 1908, he became a pupil-teacher at Broughton Junior Student Centre in Edinburgh (later Broughton High School), where he came under the influence of his English teacher, George Ogilvie. Between 1911 and the outbreak of the First World War, he worked as a journalist in Scotland and South Wales. A reservist in the Territorial Force, he was called up in July 1915 to serve in the Royal Army Medical Corps and in the following year he was posted to Salonika with the 42nd Field Hospital RAMC. Although this was one of the quieter fronts, British casualties were heavy – 481,000 from malaria and 18,000 from combat. After the Armistice, Grieve was detached to the Indian Medical Services to serve with Section Lahore Indian General Hospital and was not demobilised until July 1919. By then he had started writing seriously. Throughout his war service Grieve maintained a lively correspondence with his former teacher in which he discussed political matters and his own literary aspirations.

Texts: Alan Bold, ed., *The Thistle Rises: An Anthology of Poetry and Prose by Hugh MacDiarmid* (London: Hamish Hamilton, 1984); Catherine Kerrigan, ed., *The Hugh MacDiarmid–George Ogilvie Letters* (Aberdeen: Aberdeen University Press, 1988)

Compton Mackenzie 1883–1972

Edward Montague Compton Mackenzie was born in West Hartlepool, the son of a theatrical impresario. He was educated at St Paul's School in London, and Magdalen College, Oxford. By the time of the outbreak of war, he had written a clutch of bestselling novels, including *The Passionate Elopement* (1911), *Carnival* (1912) and *Sinister Street* (1913–14). He applied for a commission in the Seaforth Highlanders, but was rebuffed by a War Office official who told him, 'Your job is to keep us amused.' Through the influence of General Sir Ian Marsh, who admired his literary work, Mackenzie was commissioned in the Royal Marines and served with them in the Gallipoli campaign of 1915. During the Cape Helles landings, he acted as an official war correspondent and his reports showed a clear understanding of the tactical problems that confined the Allied forces to their landing beaches. In 1916, he became military control officer in Athens, and the following year moved to a role in military intelligence as director of the Aegean intelligence service, an experience that gave him the material for his novel *Extremes Meet* (1928). Although the overall tone of his war memoirs is regret for the passing of the Edwardian world, he was critical of the faulty planning and bad leadership that brought about the Allied failure in Gallipoli.

Text: Compton Mackenzie, *Gallipoli Memories* (London: Cassell, 1929)

John Maclean 1879–1923

Pacifist and Marxist, John Maclean was born in Pollokshaws, near Glasgow, where he was educated at Pollock Academy and as a student-teacher at Glasgow University. After graduating in 1904 he immersed himself in the work of the Marxist Social

Democratic Foundation and in 1916 was partly responsible for
the creation of the Scottish Labour College. During the First
World War, Maclean advocated a termination of hostilities,
opposed the introduction of conscription and supported the
Glasgow rent strikes in 1915. As a result of his activities, he was
arrested in 1916 under the terms of the Defence of the Realm Act
and was sentenced to three years in prison. Released in 1917, he
was re-arrested the following year on charges of sedition and
spent three further periods in prison before finally being released
in October 1922. Maclean's position as a revolutionary socialist
is unrivalled in Scottish political history, but his health was
weakened during the latter periods of imprisonment when he was
force-fed after going on hunger strike. In January 1918, he was
elected to the chair of the Third All-Russian Congress of Soviets
and a month later was appointed Bolshevik consul in Scotland, a
post he was unable to set up due to government opposition.

Texts: Nan Milton, ed., *John Maclean: In the Rapids of
Revolution*: *Essays, Articles and Letters* (London: Allison and
Busby, 1978); Index to the Issues of *The Vanguard* in the
National Library of Scotland.

Naomi Mitchison 1897–1999

Novelist and social reformer, Naomi Haldane was born in Edinburgh, a daughter of the eminent physiologist John Scott Haldane
and a niece of the Secretary of State for War, Richard Haldane,
who was responsible for the creation of the Territorial Force. She
was educated at the Dragon School in Oxford and shortly after
war broke out she became engaged to Gilbert Richard 'Dick'
Mitchison, a barrister serving with 2nd Dragoon Guards
(Queen's Bays), which had crossed over to France with the British
Expeditionary Force in 1914. While he was on the Western Front,

she worked as a VAD (Voluntary Aid Detach-ment) nurse at St Thomas's Hospital in London. After their marriage in 1916, Mitchison was injured in a motorbike accident and his wife crossed over to France to help nurse him. She kept a diary of the experience, which was published in the second volume of her autobiography. After the war Mitchison began a prolific writing career, producing over seventy novels and works of non-fiction.

Text: Naomi Mitchison, *All Change Here: Girlhood and Marriage* (London: The Bodley Head, 1975)

Neil Munro 1863–1930

Novelist and journalist Neil Munro was born in Inverary, Argyll. The family came from a Gaelic-speaking farming background and much of Munro's work reflects his love for the history, both real and imagined, of his native county. After a five-year period working in a law office in Inverary, he turned to journalism in Glasgow and to writing fiction under the pseudonym Hugh Foulis. Two of his earliest works, *The Lost Pibroch* (1896) and *Gillian the Dreamer* (1899), were Celtic romances and he gained huge popularity following the success of a series of historical adventures including *John Splendid* (1898), *Doom Castle* (1901) and *The New Road* (1914). Too old to enlist, Munro returned to journalism full-time during the First World War; his son Hugh was killed in action in France in September 1915 while serving with 8th Argyll and Sutherland Highlanders. After the war Munro's reputation declined – unjustly so – and he is perhaps best remembered for his humorous stories involving Para Handy and the crew of a Clyde puffer called the *Vital Spark*.

Text: Neil Munro, *The Brave Days* (Edinburgh: The Porpoise Press, 1931)

John Reith 1889–1971

John Charles Walsham Reith, the founding father of the British Broadcasting Corporation, was born in Stonehaven, and educated at Glasgow Academy and Gresham's School in Norfolk. While serving with 1/2nd Highland Field Company RE, he was badly wounded in the face and jaw. After convalescing, Reith was put in charge of a new rifle factory near Philadelphia in the USA and between May 1918 and April 1919 he worked on an Admiralty project establishing a hydroelectric submarines barrage in the English Channel. Reith wrote his war memoir during a three-week spell in 1937, but his friends advised against immediate publication, fearing that his outspoken view would damage his reputation.

Text: John Reith, *Wearing Spurs* (London: Hutchinson, 1966)

David Rorie 1867–1946

Medical practitioner, folklorist and soldier, David Rorie was born of Aberdeenshire parents in Edinburgh. He studied medicine there and in Aberdeen, and after graduating worked as medical officer at the Bowhill Colliery in Fife, where he developed a lifelong interest in folk culture. In 1905, he returned to the north-east to work as a general practitioner in Cults on Lower Deeside, which was to be his home for the rest of his life. Although he was aged 47 at the outbreak of war, he enlisted in the Royal Army Medical Corps (RAMC), in which he held a reserve commission and served in France with a Field Ambulance in the 51st (Highland) Division. Rorie ended the war as a brevet-colonel, was awarded the Distinguished Service Order and was made a member of the Légion d'honneur. As a poet, his best-known creation was 'The Lum Hat wantin' the Croon'.

Text: David Rorie: *A Medico's Luck in the War* (Aberdeen: Milne and Hutchinson, 1929)

Saki (Hector Hugh Munro) 1870–1916

Novelist and short-story writer, Saki was the pen name of Hector Hugh Munro, the son of Charles Augustus Munro, a Scottish-born officer in the Burma Police. The early death of his mother in a bizarre accident involving a cow had a baleful influence on his childhood – he was sent back to England to be cared for by unsympathetic aunts in a puritanical household. After school he followed his father into the Burma Police but was invalided out in 1895 and returned to England to live in London, where he made a living as a journalist. He wrote political satire for the *Westminster Gazette*, and between 1902 and 1908 he worked as a foreign correspondent for the *Morning Post*, covering events in Poland, Russia and Paris. His first short stories feature the elegant and effete young men-about-town Reginald and Clovis, who take mischievous delight in the discomfort of their conventional, pretentious elders. Although aged 43 at the outbreak of the war, Munro enlisted in a yeomanry regiment, the King Edward's Horse (The King's Overseas Dominions Regiment), but transferred to the 22nd Royal Fusiliers in order to see action as a private soldier in France. He was killed by a sniper in November 1916 at Beaumont-Hamel in the dying days of the Battle of the Somme. To the end of his days, he was intensely proud of the fact that he could call himself a member of Clan Munro.

Text: Saki, *The Square Egg, and Other Sketches* (London: John Lane, 1924)

Charles Hamilton Sorley 1895–1915

Poet and soldier, Charles Hamilton Sorley was born in Aberdeen, where his father was Professor of Moral Philosophy. In 1900, his family moved to Cambridge, where his father had been appointed Knightsbridge Professor, and young Sorley was educated at King's College Choir School and at Marlborough. Although brought up and educated in England, Sorley remained aware of his family's Scottish background, telling Arthur Watts in a letter dated 16 June 1915 that 'Sorley is the Gaelic for wanderer.' At the end of 1913, having won a place at University College Oxford, he spent some time in Germany and was attending the University of Jena when war broke out. After returning to England, he enlisted and was commissioned in 7th Suffolk Regiment, moving across to France with his battalion in March 1915. He was killed by a sniper in October that year during the Battle of Loos. Sorley was an avid correspondent and his letters written both before the war and during it were collected for publication by his father.

Text: Charles Hamilton Sorley, *The Letters of Charles Sorley* (Cambridge: Cambridge University Press, 1919)

Rebecca West 1892–1983

Cicely Isabel Fairfield was born in London to a Scottish mother and was educated at George Watson's Ladies College in Edinburgh. She left school when she was sixteen, but her sister Letitia proceeded to medical school and became one of the first fully qualified female doctors in the country. After returning to London, Cicely trained as an actress and adopted the stage name 'Rebecca West' from the rebellious young heroine in *Rosmersholm* by Henrik Ibsen. Before the war she had an affair with the author H.G. Wells; the relationship lasted ten years and they had one son. By then she had emerged as an influential and combative journalist and her account of the huge government ammunition complex in the western Scottish Borders was published in the *Daily Chronicle* on 6 November 1916. 'The Cordite Makers' produced a stunning picture of the surrounding area, with its low scattered marshes where 'there lay the village which is always full of people, and yet is the home of nothing but death'. Gretna had been chosen as the site because it was safe from German attack and because it enjoyed good communications north and south, but what attracted West was the sense of otherness she discovered in the whole area. In the 1920s, she emerged as one of the country's leading writers and her novel *The Return of the Soldier* (1918) contains one of the first accurate descriptions of the effect of 'shell shock' or post-traumatic stress disorder.

Text: Jane Marcus, ed., *The Young Rebecca: Writings of Rebecca West 1911–1917* (London: Macmillan, 1982)

A.F. Whyte *fl.* 1915

Nothing is known about this author, who contributed his story to *Blackwood's Magazine* under the pseudonym R.N.V. The magazine's archive reveals this to have been A.F. Whyte, a Glasgow-trained surgeon who served in the Royal Naval Volunteer Reserve. A medical post-graduate of that name is listed on the Roll of Honour at Glasgow University.

Text: 'Sunk', *Blackwood's Magazine*, October 1916, pp. 470–7

Further Reading

Bold, Alan, *Modern Scottish Literature* (London, 1983)
——, *MacDiarmid* (London, 1988)
Brown, Ian, Susan Manning, Thomas Owen Clancy and
   Murray Pittock, *The Edinburgh History of Scottish
   Literature, vol. II, Enlightenment, Britain and Empire
   (1707–1918)* (Edinburgh, 2007)
Brown, Ian and Alan Riach, *The Edinburgh Companion to
   Twentieth Century Scottish Literature* (Edinburgh, 2009)
Burgess, Moira, *The Glasgow Novel: A Complete Guide*, 3rd
   edn (Hamilton, 1999)
Craig, Cairns, *The History of Scottish Literature*, vol. IV
   (Aberdeen, 1987)
Crawford, Robert, *Scotland's Books: The Penguin History of
   Scottish Literature* (London, 2007)
Devine, T.M., *The Scottish Nation 1700–2000* (London,
   2001)
Donaldson, William, *Popular Literature in Victorian Scotland*
   (Aberdeen, 1986)
Finlay, Richard, *Modern Scotland 1914–2000* (London, 2004)
Goldie, David, 'Scotland, Britishness, and the First World
   War', in Gerard Carruthers, David Goldie, and Alastair
   Renfrew (eds), *Beyond Scotland: New Contexts for
   Twentieth-Century Scottish Literature* (Amsterdam & New
   York, 2004)
——, 'Scotland For Ever? British Literature, Scotland, and the
   First World War', in Edna Longley, Eamonn Hughes and
   Des O'Rawe (eds), *Ireland (Ulster) Scotland: Concepts,
   Contexts, Comparisons* (Belfast, 2003)

Hart, Francis Russell, *The Scottish Novel: A Critical Survey* (London, 1978)

Harvie, Christopher, *Scotland and Nationalism: Scottish Society and Politics 1707–1977* (London, 1977)

——, *No Gods and Precious Few Heroes: Twentieth Century Scotland* (Edinburgh, 1998)

Hay, Ian, *Their Name Liveth: The Book of the Scottish National War Memorial* (rev. ed., Edinburgh, 1985)

MacDonald, C.M.M., and E.W. McFarland, eds, *Scotland and the Great War* (East Linton, 1999)

Royle, Trevor, ed., *In Flanders Fields: Scottish Poetry and Prose of the First World War* (Edinburgh, 1988)

——, *Flowers of the Forest: Scotland and the First World War* (Edinburgh, 2006)